Critical Acclaim for
In Search of Duncan Ferguson

'Pattullo teases out the complexities of his subject meticulously in what amounts to one of the most impressive football books of recent times. The writing is sharp, his handling of a complex character sympathetic without being sycophantic and the level of research is impressive. The section on Barlinnie testifies that Pattullo is an excellent journalist, not just an excellent sports journalist'
Alasdair McKillop, *Scottish Review of Books*

'People continue to take an interest in the adventures and misadventures of Duncan Ferguson. Alan Pattullo's new book, *In Search of Duncan Ferguson*, gives a well-informed and fresh account of the former player'
Kevin McCarra, *The Times*

'This meticulous book is a must-read for every Everton fan – and anyone who wondered what made "Big Dunc" tick'
Sunday Mirror

'Scotland loves success, but the maverick underachiever also has a place in our heart . . . It is [the] attention to merest detail that marks the search for Duncan Disorderly. Pattullo, who writes beautifully, has a strong-willed adherence to discovering the truth rather than adding to the enigma . . . Sympathetic but rigorous, Pattullo never lectures but slowly, inexorably one is aware that he is uncovering a truth about Scottish football and its devotees'
Hugh MacDonald, *Herald*

'Alan Pattullo seeks to tease out exactly what kind of character inhabits the imposing frame of the man who once spent three months in Glasgow's Barlinnie Prison for butting an opponent on the field of play at Ibrox'
Roddy Forsyth, *Telegraph*

'Duncan Ferguson's life brought to book at last . . . gripping'
Aidan Smith, *Scotsman*

'Thoughtful and even-handed'
When Saturday Comes

www.**transworldbooks**.co.uk

In Search of
Duncan Ferguson

The Life and Crimes of
a Footballing Enigma

Alan Pattullo

MAINSTREAM
PUBLISHING

EDINBURGH AND LONDON

TRANSWORLD PUBLISHERS
61–63 Uxbridge Road, London W5 5SA
www.transworldbooks.co.uk

Transworld is part of the Penguin Random House group of companies
whose addresses can be found at global.penguinrandomhouse.com

First published in Great Britain in 2014 by Mainstream Publishing
an imprint of Transworld Publishers
Mainstream paperback edition published 2015

The italicized text in part one of the prologue is fictional. These words have been
chosen by the author and aim to reflect what Duncan Ferguson might have been
thinking as he left prison after 44 days to resume his football career and life.

The author wishes to thank John Burnside for his kind permission to use an
extract from the poem 'Dundee' as the epigraph. Also Mike Scott, for his
permission to use the song title 'Fisherman's Blues' as one of the chapter headings.

A CIP catalogue record for this book
is available from the British Library.

ISBN
9781780576800

Typeset in Adobe Caslon Pro
Printed and bound by CPI Group (UK) Ltd, Croydon, CR0 4YY.

Penguin Random House is committed to a sustainable
future for our business, our readers and our planet. This book is
made from Forest Stewardship Council® certified paper.

1 3 5 7 9 10 8 6 4 2

To my mum and dad, for unstinting support and belief,
and, above all else, their love.

And to Nathalie, who arrived to save the day.

Acknowledgements

The entry in my notebook confirms that work on this book began as long ago as 12 June 2008, when the search for Duncan Ferguson led me first to Jim McLean's house in Broughty Ferry, a suburb in Dundee. It hardly requires saying that in what has been a lengthy process there are a lot of people I need to thank for their help, guidance and support. Many, I suspect, might well have forgotten in what way they contributed, while in some cases these thanks have come too late.

It is very poignant to listen back to some old interview tapes and hear voices from beyond the grave. Without George Skelton and Dick Taylor's recollections, the chapters on Duncan Ferguson's early years would have been greatly diminished, while Jim Farry, the former chief executive of the Scottish Football Association, also passed away shortly after I spoke with him, at a much-too-young age of 56.

With regards to the many others who have helped, it is perhaps easier to break them down into phases of Duncan's life, but even then the list is by no means exhaustive.

Stirling/early years: Iain McMenemy, Stan Collins, Gary Stewart, Alex Smith, David Halcrow, Willie McIlvaney.

Dundee United: Michael O'Neill, Ray McKinnon, Paul Sturrock, Dave Bowman, Grant Johnson, Jim McLean, Graeme Liveston, Spence Anderson, Christian Dailly, Maurice Malpas, Jim McInally, Alex Cleland, Tam McMillan, Paul Hegarty, Fionan Lynch.

Scotland: Craig Brown, Pat Nevin, Craig Levein, Nicky Walker,

Scott Booth, Andy Roxburgh, Berti Vogts, David Findlay, Brian Irvine, Jock Brown, Tom Boyd, Alan McLaren, John Robertson, Alex McLeish, Darryl Broadfoot.

Anstruther hotel-bar incident: Frank Downie.

Rangers: Ally McCoist, Walter Smith, Ian Durrant, Fraser Wishart, Sir David Murray, Mark Hateley, John Brown.

Headbutt/court case: Jock McStay, Jimmy Nicholl, Sandy Eccles, Kenny Clark, Donald Findlay, Eric McCowat, Richard Elias.

Newcastle: Steven Caldwell, Stephen Glass, Ruud Gullit, Paul Robinson, Paul Ferris.

Prison: David McCue, Roger Houchin, Bill McKinlay, Willie McGurk, Willie McBride, Willie Hendry, Dr Andrew McLellan, David Graham Scott.

Pigeons: Michael Lakin

Media and press: Fraser Mackie, Gordon Waddell, Keith Jackson, Ronnie Cully, Stephen Halliday, David Leslie, Stephen McGowan, Brian Marjoribanks, Hugh MacDonald, Michael Grant, Dave Prentice, Phil McNulty, Patrick Barclay, Peter Rundo, Dave Cottrell, Paul Joyce, Alan Oliver, Justin Slee, Bill Borrows, Andy Hunter, Alan Myers, Gary Ralston, Jonathan Northcroft, Douglas Alexander, Stewart Weir, Paul Forsyth, Andrew Smith, Stuart Cosgrove, Colin Duncan, Aidan Smith, Jim Black, Simon Pia, Archie MacGregor, Paul Burns.

Everton: Darren Griffiths, Becky Tallentire, Ian Ross, Alan Myers, David Harrison, Howard Kendall, Joe Royle, Graeme Sharp, Alan Irvine, Mike Walker, Mark Ward, Mick Rathbone, Steve Jones, David Weir, Kevin Kilbane, Steve Simonsen, Bill Kenwright, Peter Johnson, Neville Southall.

A.L. Kennedy has described the process of writing a book as being 'a tiny bit like having a long-term illness: people enquire after it and your relation to it for the first few months, and then they don't – not unless they're rather peculiar and/or enjoy the discomfort of others'. Thank you to those who stopped enquiring about my progress, probably out of sympathy.

Special appreciation:

Without Jim McLean's cooperation, the book would have been a non-starter. He was a colossus in football management with Dundee United, something, as a Dundee fan, I know to my cost. His input runs throughout the book.

Osmo Tapio Everton Raihala and Maria Puusaari made significant contributions to the text and provided kind hospitality in Helsinki.

Kenny MacDonald and Gordon Parks should be included in the press/media mentions above, but they went above and beyond. Again, there might not be a book without them.

Graham Bean and Colin Leslie, sports editors at *Scotland on Sunday* and *The Scotsman* respectively, for patience – and for granting a sabbatical request.

Donald Walker, my former sports editor at *The Scotsman*, who was there to witness Duncan Ferguson's first senior goal, as well as his first Everton red card, was a constant source of inspiration, and guidance, and has helped me from day one, reading and re-reading, having the graciousness to pretend his patience was not being completely exhausted. He also sent me on my first Duncan Ferguson assignment in November 1998, to cover his sudden transfer from Everton to Newcastle United. That trip set in motion this book.

David McCue, whose hospitality at his lovely home in Fife was so appreciated, particularly since he also proved such a credible source of information about Barlinnie prison, a place I knew little about before researching this book.

Mark Stanton, my agent, for guidance and reassurance, and Colin McLear, for feedback and constructive criticism. Neil Forsyth, for advice and encouragement back in the beginning. To Emma Vinnie, my sisters Katie and Rosanne, and my extended family, and all others who got burned by the project, thank you, too, for patience and support.

Martin Greig and Neil White, who sought to give me the benefit of their wisdom when it comes to writing sports books. I only hope I have been able to offer something of worth and interest in return.

Ian Preece, Karyn Millar and Debs Warner for sterling editing work and patience beyond what could be expected.

Richard Moore, who encouraged me to begin searching and then kept my spirits up on innumerable occasions when it felt like the journey had reached a dead end, who read and re-read chapters and was there right to the very end.

And of course Duncan Ferguson, an often misunderstood footballer who I felt deserved another hearing.

Contents

'The one who stands here proven after all.'
                     – From the poem *Dundee* by John Burnside

PROLOGUE

Liberated at Dawn

Glasgow, 24 November 1995
The corrugated steel gate slides open; a city is beginning to stir. It is just before 6.40 on a brisk winter's morning. People are already milling around below street lamps, telltale notebooks peeking out from the top of jacket pockets. In the near distance, a sinister stone-brick building looms: one that, in the half-light, looks especially grim and unyielding.

Barlinnie.

Joining the reporters are fans, four of whom have travelled from Liverpool just to get a glimpse of their hero. And a glimpse is all they get. As the Daimler draws away, the driver negotiates the speed bumps and tries to ignore the camera flashes. There is a 6 ft 4 in. frame folded into the back seat. Those peering through the tinted glass can just about make out the figure of a £4 million footballer.

At least that is what Duncan Ferguson had been when he was confronted by the sight of Barlinnie's imposing, time-blackened edifice from the back of a blue prison van 44 days earlier.

Willie McGurk, the long-serving physical-education supervisor at the prison, sounded a warning to his staff: 'Listen, this is a £4 million footballer coming in – if he goes out anything less than a £4 million footballer, we could be in bloody trouble.'

The comment cuts to the truth of the matter. Ferguson wasn't going to be treated like any other prisoner. How could he have been? He was a professional footballer with Everton Football Club, one who could lay claim at the time to a record British transfer fee, having previously played for Dundee United and Rangers.

McGurk was alert to the danger. The most recently published Scottish Office report on Barlinnie had spelled it out: 41 assaults on prisoners by prisoners in the previous 12 months; 34 suicide attempts.

As well as Ferguson being one of the highest-profile footballers in the country, something else marked him out: his sister, Audrey, was on the Scottish Prison Service staff at Glenochil, in central Scotland.

Ferguson wasn't inside for only a night or two. He served exactly half of a three-month sentence. There is a saying in Scotland, sometimes used to describe lower league players wheezing up the wing: 'slow as a week in Barlinnie'. Ferguson endured six of these.

Just a few months earlier, ahead of the FA Cup final between Everton and Manchester United at Wembley Stadium, Ferguson had shaken the hand of Prince Charles. Now he was being detained at his mother's pleasure. And, to think: he used to get changed beneath the portrait of the Queen that hangs in the home dressing-room at Ibrox.

McGurk, a Celtic supporter, was one of the good guys during Ferguson's stay in Barlinnie. In the gym – 'McGurk's Gymnasium' is what McGurk barked down the phone when calls were put through – Ferguson had been able to briefly forget about the cell in D Hall that he had had to clean out himself. McGurk had devised a game called skittle-ball, where Ferguson and five others would split into two teams of three and aim to score a goal by flattening one of two skittles at each end of the hall. Unsurprisingly, Ferguson impressed with his shooting. 'Like "Hot Shot Hamish",' according to one of the wardens.

They were all right, the wardens.

David McCue, his gallery officer, looked out for him a bit, too; McCue's wife's family are fierce Evertonians. Strangely, McCue is another Celtic fan, a rarity at the time among prison officers in Barlinnie, where the majority favoured Rangers. He asked Ferguson to sign his copy of *Fever Pitch*, which he did, dedicating it to Cameron, McCue's newborn son, in black ink and capital letters. Ferguson would later name his own son Cameron. Published three years earlier, *Fever Pitch* had proved an eloquent account of one man's obsession with football – or, more specifically, Arsenal Football Club. It is associated with the gentrification of the game. An irony, then, that a copy had made its way inside the less-than-gentrified Barlinnie, where it was clutched by a footballer who, in many people's eyes, was an unreconstructed thug, an embodiment of all that was holding back progress in the game.

And yet, conversely, Ferguson was also a symbol of football's new era of wealth and prosperity. During his stay in Barlinnie, it is estimated that he was paid £60,000 in total by Everton, who ignored the public clamour to suspend his wages.

Was this yet another snapshot of football's skewed morals?

Of the other 34 prisoners who had, in prison parlance, been 'libbed' along with Ferguson that same morning, a few – if they had jobs at all – might have found their bosses relishing the excuse to get rid of them. And yet here was a convicted criminal preparing to be whisked away in a limousine, back to England, where adoration awaited.

Prisoner No. 12718 completed his final chores in the hospital wing. He searched out McGurk, shook his hand and promised to send up some Everton strips for the prison football team. 'That's kind, son, but we cannae accept gifts from prisoners,' McGurk explained. He then handed back his red-and-white striped prison shirt. Next, it was his regulation blue jeans – a different pair to the ones he had originally been given, which had proved so humiliatingly short in the leg. It was time to go home.

Just a few years earlier, home would have meant Stirling, the ancient capital of Scotland. It is where he had gone to school. Bannockburn High School is a building shaped like a jack-knifed juggernaut, where the windows are so small and so numerous people often said it looked just like a prison. It made Ferguson shudder. Perhaps this is why he became so fond of pigeons and the sensation of letting them go from cupped hands. And here he now was, about to be set free. Liberated at dawn, like pigeons are on race day.

So this is what it feels like: freedom.

Home was now Liverpool, a town he'd grown to love – the blue half, at least. He could even admit to a sneaky fondness for the other lot, the red half.

The red shite. They bring out the best in me.

Just before he left, one of the wardens made a joke about the colour of the limousine waiting outside. 'Burgundy? I thought you played for Everton?' It reminded Ferguson of the time, just over a year earlier, when, oblivious to the connotations, he had worn a scarlet jacket for the press conference when he signed for Everton on loan from Rangers. He hadn't thought too deeply about it. He remembered getting a bit of a ribbing from the press boys. 'Like turning up in a green suit to sign for Rangers,' one sneered.

Fucking idiots. No wonder I don't talk to them.

Scrawling his signature on a three-month contract, he thought he wasn't going to be at Everton long. Just enough time to find his scoring touch again, then back to Rangers, back to the club who had made him what he once was: the most expensive football player in the land.

At least that had been his plan. Goodison Park, the Grand Old Lady, was meant to have been a temporary shelter from the storm, the means to an end. Instead, Everton became his everything.

Dundee United, Rangers, Newcastle United?

You forget the rest.

Everton got under his skin. He would never ever forget how it felt to soar into the air, to head that first goal against Liverpool, before sinking to his knees with joy and relief in front of the Gwladys Street End; the legend before the player, the rise before the fall. On the same date 12 months later, he was languishing in jail.

He had stressed how he wanted no one but members of his own family to visit him in prison. However, Joe Royle, his Everton manager, and the chairman, Peter Johnson, had been insistent, even coming up to Glasgow to sit in the public gallery for the trial in the bleak-looking, stone-built Sheriff Court, alternatively known as 'the Kremlin on the Clyde'. 'Best bacon sandwiches I ever tasted,' according to the colourful Johnson.

And now they have sent a car for me.

This was his new family. He hadn't even been playing for the club at the time of the incident. 'The first professional footballer to be jailed for an on-field offence': that was his new tag, now clipped to him like the leg band on a pigeon. The only thing that had kept him going were the letters, hundreds of them, day after day. There had been nothing, though, from Jim Farry, chief executive at the Scottish Football Association.

And even now, knowing Ferguson had faced the degradation of having to slop out his own shite every morning, Farry was still seeking to impose an additional 12-match ban on the footballer. No word of support, either, from Rangers, or from Jim McLean, Ferguson's manager at Dundee United. McLean had been his first prison warden, patrolling the corridors at Tannadice Park, ruling with an iron fist, phoning up his digs to make sure he had not absconded to the pub the night before a match.

My own personal fucking night-watchman.

And then there was McLean's accusation – the main one, anyway – flung at him again and again and again: 'The game means far too much to me, I know that. But it means fuck all to you.' It was roared at him, over and over, accusingly, spittle forming in the corners of McLean's mouth, strands of hair from an artful comb-over – something that the players used to dare each other to laugh at – hanging free in front of his red face. 'You just don't love it enough!' he would scream. 'You can't prove to me that you want it, can you?'

Well, try fucking loving a game that puts you where I've just been.

*

WAITING FOR DUNCAN
Liverpool, March 2009

'Here for the big interview, then?' smiles David Prentice of the *Liverpool Echo*. He is one of the few people I know in the French-themed restaurant-turned-VIP suite of Liverpool's iconic Adelphi Hotel, although many other faces are familiar.

There's Howard Kendall, who enjoyed three stints as Everton manager and, between 1985 and 1987, led the side to two English league titles. Over in the corner is David Unsworth, the broad-chested former Everton defender known in these parts as 'Rhino'. Another recognisable face is Graham Stuart, a Londoner still loved by the Goodison Park fans after scoring twice on the afternoon in 1994 when Everton managed to stage a last-day recovery from two goals down against Wimbledon to preserve their long-standing top-flight status.

Yet everyone, even the other VIPs present, those who have played hundreds of games for Everton and other clubs between them, await the entrance of one man. Duncan Ferguson is the figure that has dominated the countdown to this Hall of Fame dinner. He has made the occasion an essential one to be seen at for any self-respecting Evertonian. Attendance, too, is obligatory for any serious-minded biographer of the man known to everyone here as 'Big Dunc'.

Prentice, a friendly bear of a man, is one of those with tales from the Ferguson frontline. Ferguson had asked Prentice about the possibility of obtaining tickets for a title fight at Liverpool's St George's Hall featuring the Scottish flyweight boxer Paul Weir. Prentice spoke with the promoter. 'He was buzzing. He was like: "Duncan Ferguson? Of course you can have two tickets." I gave them to Duncan. "How much do you want for them?" he asked, and took out a big wad of cash. I said: "No, he doesn't want paid, Duncan." He took them, seemed thrilled about it, and then never turned up.'

This, of course, is the fear tonight. Ferguson has made a habit of being conspicuous by his absence – from the Everton first team, from Newcastle United, from Scotland and, lately, from Merseyside. While waiting, I take the opportunity to speak with another trusty eyewitness source.

Alan Myers flitted in and out of Ferguson's life, initially as communications officer for Everton and then as a reporter on the Merseyside beat for Sky Sports – or, as his business card described him: 'North West Bureau Chief'. However, not even such an impressive title, combined with the fact that he and Ferguson were once colleagues at the same football club, was enough to convince Big Dunc to grant the journalist what he most wanted: the Big Interview.

Myers tells me about once being offered money by Ferguson *not* to interview him. The tale reflects well on Ferguson. It offers a glimpse of the softer side of his character, something about which I was hoping to find out more during the course of my research. But the episode also illustrates the lengths to which he is prepared to go to remain unknowable.

Myers explains: 'When I started working for Sky as a freelancer, I asked Ferguson for an interview. While he was more than happy to make sure I didn't lose out, he didn't want to do it. We were on a plane. Everton were going on tour and I went with them. "Listen, I'll give you the day's pay," he said. "How much would you earn for it?" I think I said about £150. And he said: "I'll give you the money, I just won't do the interview.'"

Welcome, then, to the 11th Gwladys Street Hall of Fame dinner. Ferguson is the 100th, and also the last, inductee – or so it was claimed at the time. It is an honour that has drawn him back to Merseyside for a rare visit. Although four others, including Unsworth and Stuart, will also be inducted on the same night, it is abundantly clear that Ferguson is the star of the show. More than 700 tickets have been sold on the back of the promise that Ferguson will be present. However, even now, an hour or so before kick-off, there is still the worry that the nearest we will get to his presence is the huge banner that is hanging in the banquet hall bearing the inscription: 'Duncan Ferguson – Braveheart'.

The tension is palpable. Much of it emanates from me. I haven't even got my own ticket yet, having been invited down by one of the organisers, former amateur boxing champion Brian Snagg, who, on the phone before I made the journey south from Edinburgh, told me: 'Come along an hour or so before the do is supposed to begin and I'll make sure you get to sit down with Duncan. You can ask him whatever you want. That'll be no problem. I'll set it up.'

Snagg is helping to maintain the Liverpudlian reputation for kindness and hospitality. He is also upholding that endearing Scouser trait for hopeless optimism. I politely inform him how grateful I am for such an opportunity, all the time realising he has more chance of persuading either of the two stone birds perched on top of the city's Liver Building to speak to me than he does Ferguson.

Bouncers guard the door of the VIP lounge and won't budge for anyone lacking the required accreditation. Snagg, who is running the event on behalf of Bluenose Promotions, is still in a room upstairs, no doubt frantically trying to figure out how 720 people are going to fit into a banqueting suite designed to hold around 200 fewer diners. Snagg knows his reputation in the city hinges on Ferguson showing up.

He has assured me that the footballer is already in town. Yet he probably won't believe it until he sees Ferguson for himself.

None of us will.

CHAPTER 1

Sky Born

Duncan Ferguson clocked off from life as a professional footballer in appropriately dramatic fashion, scoring a last-minute equaliser for Everton in a 2–2 draw with West Bromwich Albion on the last day of the 2005–06 season. His 68th Premier League goal – no Scottish player has scored more to date – came with the last kick of a career that saw him become arguably the most controversial British footballer of the modern era.

He then turned his back on the game, to the surprise of no one. Having been sold between clubs for combined transfer fees of over £18 million, he could afford to. Thousands of footballers have left the game behind without provoking the slightest curiosity. But this was not the fate of Duncan Ferguson.

One of the highest-profile players of the 'Premiership era', he is also among the least known. Unusually for someone with a story to sell, he has consistently refused to tell it. He shelved plans for an autobiography at the moment when his life appeared to have reached its most interesting point.

His problem was that the publishers of the tome, provisionally titled *A Blue by Blue Account*, had some firm ideas about what they wanted the main thrust of the book to be. They expected him to revisit places he was desperate to forget. He would have to acknowledge his status as the first professional British footballer to be jailed for an offence committed while on the field of play.

He would have to go back to Barlinnie.

Ferguson, unsurprisingly, had no intention of doing that.

Almost from the day he'd walked out of the prison gates, others had been trying to put him back in there, wanting to hear how it felt to be a £4 million footballer reduced to slopping out. To this day, *A Blue by Blue Account* has an online presence, a ghost book haunting the cyber shelves.

For a year – before Chris Sutton moved from Norwich City to Blackburn Rovers for £5 million in July 1994 – Ferguson struggled to live up to the billing of 'Britain's most expensive native footballer'. His £4 million move from Dundee United to Rangers in July 1993 broke the then record transfer fee between two British clubs, which had been set when Blackburn Rovers paid £3.3 million to Southampton for England striker Alan Shearer at the start of the previous season.

When Roy Keane moved from Nottingham Forest to Manchester United just five days after Ferguson's arrival at Ibrox, he cost £3.75 million. That deal exceeded the then English record, but not quite the British one. Ferguson was the story. ITV's News at Ten programme even sent a camera crew to Ibrox to film the 21-year-old footballer climbing a flight of stairs to meet his destiny – and his fate.

The Ferguson I had become intrigued by pre-dates even this headline-stealing episode. I watched him score the third goal of his career in a Dundee derby in the Scottish Cup in 1991. It was a trademark header – or at least of the sort that would later become his trademark.

On the night I saw him play for the first time, many others did too. Sky had chosen to show the Scottish Cup quarter-final meeting between Dundee United and city rivals Dundee on what was then called the Sports Channel. 'It's England's turn to enjoy some Scottish hospitality,' announced the presenter Richard Keys, as the fledgling station thrilled at this novel advance north of the border. The fixture was among the first games Sky televised in Scotland, as they prepared to change football in Britain forever.

Ferguson himself would become one of many beneficiaries, as the money poured into the game by television stations found its way into the pockets of players. Then there was Bosman: Jean-Marc Bosman, who won the landmark case that ruled clubs could no longer hold on to a player's registration after their contract had expired, a development that would further enrich the sport.

This was news that several of those who had lined up for Dundee United against Dundee on 4 March 1991 were waiting to hear. Many of the younger players in the team felt that the club had control of their lives to an extreme extent, though this feeling also owed rather a lot to Dundee United's autocratic manager, Jim McLean.

For the Tannadice club, the early 1990s were a period of transition and evolution – though this did not appear to extend to the treatment of players. The likes of David Narey, Dave Bowman and Jim McInally remained following the club's run to the UEFA Cup final in 1987, while an exceptionally talented group had graduated from the youth ranks and were creating some elbow room for themselves in the first team. Ferguson was among them, alongside the likes of Ray McKinnon, an elegant midfielder bursting with potential, and Christian Dailly, a fast-as-lightning striker.

An old guard, who had helped establish the club as a force in Europe, were approaching the end of their careers. Stalwarts such as Narey and Paul Sturrock were conscious of the new wave of talent in the youth and reserve teams – and these teenagers often had the attitude to go with the skill.

While Ferguson was foremost among them, few would have picked him out as the one who would go on to become the club's most saleable asset, as he persistently failed to yield to McLean's strong will.

The manager would argue that his methods got results. McLean had managed to take a club with average crowds of around 10,000 to the brink of European success in both the European and UEFA cups, after all; an unthinkable achievement today.

One of the reasons for this success was that players were rewarded for a good performance and nearly always for a good result – although there was one instance when McLean held back what he described as 'an entertainment bonus': this followed a 6–1 *win* over Motherwell in the Scottish Cup, when the team were deemed by McLean to have played inexusably poorly at the start of the game. While a player's basic salary was low in comparison to that of the likes of Rangers and Celtic, the United way was to ensure that the players gave their best when performing in front of the paying fan. The trouble was, football was changing and so was society; the young guns were not prepared to put up with what their elders had endured under McLean. His methods had become unsound. They belonged to a different era. Younger players glimpsed what was happening elsewhere; they were restless.

Ferguson was one of two teenagers picked to line up that evening in March 1991 against Dundee – midfielder John O'Neil was the other. McKinnon, meanwhile, had just turned 20. Others, such as the 17-year-old Christian Dailly, had already done their bit that season and were being rested.

It was an intriguing fixture, if not an uncommon one. The clubs had been drawn together in the same competition in the previous four seasons, but it was still an attractive meeting for the fans. Over 16,000 made their way to Tannadice. It was Ferguson's first taste of the Dundee derby; his biggest match to date.

Up in the gantry was Andy Gray, making his way as a pundit and clearly excited at this opportunity to return to Tannadice in his new role. Gray had begun his career at United, where the fans would croon, to the tune of 'Camptown Races', 'Who's the boy with the golden hair? Andy, Andy!'

Gray had scored 47 goals in 95 appearances for United and, when he was just 18 years old, had led the line in a Scottish Cup final against Celtic. In *The Tannadice Encyclopedia*, Mike Watson notes the 'tremendous sense of loss' felt among fans in 1975 when Gray left to join Aston Villa. Jim McLean later said that the first result he looked for after finishing his commitments with United in the afternoon was the Aston Villa one. If they had won and – better still – Gray had managed to score, then 'everyone at Dundee United is a little happier', MacLean said.

If Ferguson represented the absolute nadir in McLean–player relations, then Gray was the pinnacle. He and McLean still exchange Christmas cards to this day. 'The start is most important in a young guy's career,' Gray tells me. 'And at Dundee United, under Jim, I had the perfect start.'

'I have very vivid memories of being told to stay behind after training, and it's Jim and me, just the two of us. He's banging balls at me to control, showing me how to make runs and how to turn defenders. And then he's going out onto the wing and banging over crosses, and I was coming in and heading them into an empty net.'

McLean has since spoken about his regret at devoting so much time to United at the expense of his family, but Gray, whose own father had walked out of the family home in Drumchapel, Glasgow, when he was just two years old, clearly benefited from the arrangement. In 1977, he was voted the PFA Player of the Year and the PFA Young Player of the Year, a then unique double.

And then, in 1979, at the age of just 23, he became Britain's most expensive footballer when he moved from Aston Villa to Wolves in a £1.5 million deal. It is not overstating it to say that, in McLean, the teenage Gray had found the father he'd never had. 'We still talk when we need to talk,' Gray says.

This clearly marks a huge contrast in how Ferguson regards McLean. The similarities between Gray and Ferguson are obvious – not least because Ferguson would later inherit Gray's title of 'most expensive British player'. As well as playing for Everton, both Gray and Ferguson had spells at Rangers, though at different stages in their careers. Neither would claim they showed the Ibrox support the best of themselves. Intriguingly, Gray might have ended up managing Ferguson following Joe Royle's departure as Everton manager in 1997; however, he made an eleventh-hour decision to stay with Sky and it wasn't to be.

Back at Tannadice, near the start of his broadcasting career, Gray catches his first glimpse of Ferguson, emerging from the tunnel wearing bicycle shorts that are just peeking out from under his black Dundee United shorts. To top off the look, Big Dunc has taken to the pitch, in front of the watching nation, chewing a chunk of gum.

United are given a shock when Dundee take the lead, but they recover to score three times. Sitting up in the gantry, Gray would have recognised something of himself in Ferguson – a fearless striker with a prodigious heading ability, who was partial to a night out – and surely he liked what he saw.

The goal that settled the tie came from Ferguson, who proved an unsettling presence for the Dundee defence throughout. 'He has an excellent temperament for the game,' noted commentator Jock Brown at one point.

Ferguson's strike came in the second half, a header at the far post after a cross from John O'Neil. Ferguson wheeled away at the end of the ground, then known as the Arklay Street End – where a stand funded by his sale would, in time, block out the view of garden allotments and tenement flats – before kissing the United badge on his jersey. Teammate Dave Bowman hoisted him aloft before

Ferguson strolled back to the halfway line, floppy hair and still-furiously-chomping jaws forming what might be described as a perfect picture of teenage nonchalance. He had recently turned 19.

The game has all the hallmarks of a coming-of-age occasion for Ferguson, who emerged the victor in a rugged battle with Dundee defender Willie Jamieson.

The performance didn't overly impress McLean, however. It wasn't the best showcase of Scottish football, he fumed. A long way from it, in fact.

'It's not my type of football,' McLean complained in a post-match interview. 'If there had been aeroplanes around, they would have needed to ground them.' It was typical McLean: a pithy comment on the frequency of the long, hopeful airborne pass. The Scots word 'dour' might have been invented for the United manager. Even though his side had won, he appeared miserable.

After McLean's interview, the camera switches back to the pitch, where the players are going through their warm-down exercises. This is deemed novel enough for a discussion to ensue between Gray and Keys on the merits of such 'newfangled' techniques. All the while the camera remains fixed on the gaggle of United players, their breath still visible in the chill of a Tayside night. There, standing lanky and lofty, like a lighthouse, is Ferguson, his long legs stretched out, his hands resting on his hips. He is gazing into the distance, bored already of such chores.

And, as Gray points out, he is still chewing gum.

CHAPTER 2

Duncan Disorderly

When I was asked who I would most like to write a book about, I didn't have to think twice: Duncan Ferguson. My firmness surprised me. But this was something that I had few doubts about. A publishing contact wanted to know more. What was it about Ferguson that fascinated me?

I told him my story and it intrigued him further, because my background isn't Dundee United and Everton, as he had presumed. Indeed, it is the precise opposite: Liverpool and Dundee FC – United's great rivals. While Ferguson was a hero to Everton fans, Liverpool were my team growing up, as was the case with many Scottish youngsters in the late 1970s and '80s, when the Anfield club's success was built upon a backbone of Scots – the holy triumvirate of Kenny Dalglish, Graeme Souness and Alan Hansen.

Although I grew up near Dundee, the first professional goal I saw with my own eyes was on Merseyside. It was April 1982. I had just turned nine years old and Dalglish gifted me a late birthday present when he scored the winner in a 1–0 victory over West Bromwich Albion at Anfield.

While it often seemed Dalglish had just stepped out of a comic book story – a match-winning goal to clinch the League Championship in his first season as player-manager being one good example – Ferguson's tale seemed a lot less *Boy's Own*. When Dalglish scored, joy radiated from him; he raised both arms in the air in giddy abandonment. By contrast, when Ferguson scored a goal, the celebration tended to be either comically exaggerated or shot through with aggression. If he wasn't taking his shirt off and swinging it around above his head, he was clenching a fist as though preparing to swing at someone. There was something else going on there – it was as if every goal was a response, a riposte, to someone or something.

Ferguson had started to make his name at Dundee United during a spell when I was following Dundee most fiercely, having concluded that the satisfaction that came from celebrating Liverpool's glories mostly from afar didn't match the thrill of watching live football. With Dundee United just beginning to establish themselves as a force in Europe, opting to support their then down-at-heel neighbours across the single street that divides the two football clubs might have seemed like a perverse choice, but they had the history: a run to the European Cup semi-finals in 1963, as they sought to become British football's first champions of Europe. United were perceived by Dundee fans to be the upstarts, the second team in the city. However, United were bidding to establish themselves in Scottish football's firmament following their own run to the last four of the European Cup in 1984 by bleeding in new stars at the end of the decade and the start of the new one. They had McLean, a man who couldn't rest without knowing he had done as much as possible to make Dundee United as good as they could be. And they had Ferguson.

As a tall, skinny centre-forward for the University of Dundee football team, I was compared to 'that lanky streak' who was just breaking into the first-team up the road at Tannadice, to my outward chagrin and inward delight. For all that I adored Dundee, I was aware that we didn't have anyone remotely like Duncan Ferguson, who I saw around the pubs and nightclubs in the west end of the city, where footballers and students alike did their carousing.

Fortunately, I didn't have to be conscious of the bouncers clocking my whereabouts and relaying the information back to someone once described as a 'master snoop' in Dundee. Fortunately, I did not have to explain myself to Jim McLean – a looming presence in Ferguson's young life, and a bogey man in mine, having inspired United to assume the position of top dogs in the city. Intensifying Dundee fans' discontent was the knowledge that McLean had left his position as coach with Dundee to join United, piqued at having been overlooked for the Dens Park manager's job.

After graduating from Dundee, still unsure about what to do

next, I headed to Newcastle, enrolling on a Masters course at the university there. Duncan wasn't long behind me, signing for Newcastle in what was an unproductive, if lucrative move. He remained there for only a season and a half – but it was still far longer than my own stay on Tyneside.

By the time he joined the St James's Park club, I had joined *The Scotsman* as a sports writer, one of my first assignments being to cover Ferguson's press conference at Newcastle. After it had finished, I went to the only place I knew in the town: an old building housing an English department I had entered only once (to tell my course tutor that I was leaving after barely a fortnight in order to pursue a career in journalism). I sat down and wrote the first paragraph in my first ever story about Duncan Ferguson: 'The Tay, the Clyde, the Mersey and now the Tyne. Duncan Ferguson has spent much of his footballing career on the riverbank, never quite having made the splash he should have.'

It was used on *The Scotsman*'s back page. In a way, I felt like I was up and running. In the piece, I noted that the last time I had been in the same room as Ferguson he had been standing half-naked on top of a table at the Tally Ho bar in Dundee, belting out a karaoke number, clearly drunk but also flushed at the prospect of the journey ahead. By 1998, when he joined Newcastle United, he had held the title of most expensive footballer in British football, albeit for only one year. He had also been in jail, making history again as the first footballer to be given a prison sentence for an on-field offence. Who would not be fascinated?

Finding out more was not straightforward. We live in a society obsessed by celebrity, and footballers are, in many ways, the ultimate modern celebrities, their lives lived out in the tabloids and magazines, their fame amplified by lifestyles that include fast cars, fast living, WAGS and, of course, vast wealth.

Duncan Ferguson is arguably a product of this culture, certainly in terms of the dizzying amounts he was valued at – and earned. And yet, one of the many Ferguson paradoxes is that he managed to resist so many of its trappings. On one of the few occasions that his name was associated with the lavish spending habits of top Premiership footballers, he'd splashed out on a floodlit landing strip so his adored pigeons could return home more easily at night. Ferguson was definitely a bit different.

In particular, he shunned the fame part. Perhaps this is the ultimate irony of these times: to be famous for not wanting to be famous.

It cannot be said, of course, that Ferguson's fame, or infamy, is owed solely to his talent. There is more to it than that. But Ferguson's desire for privacy – whether as a consequence of an experience that made him bitter and distrustful, or something else – makes him more interesting, as it always does.

Because of the sometimes overly physical nature of his game, Ferguson gathered a degree of renown. And yet – another paradox – he was only red-carded once in his Dundee United career. It was off the pitch that he began to develop a 'reputation'. Again, though, this didn't set him too far apart from many of his peers. Scuffles in bars were as popular among young footballers then as tattoos are now.

What changed everything for Ferguson was an incident on 16 April 1994, when he tangled with an opponent during a Scottish Premier Division game between Rangers and Raith Rovers at Ibrox Stadium, watched by 42, 545 people.

And yet, crucially, several of the main protagonists claimed not to have seen anything. Referee Kenny Clark, his two linesmen, and opposing managers Walter Smith and Jimmy Nicholl, were all meant to be watching the action, yet all missed what occurred in the 35th minute of a match that Rangers eventually won 4–0 – with Ferguson scoring the third goal, his first for Rangers after 14 appearances. All five later shook their heads: they hadn't been watching, or it had happened so quickly, so unexpectedly, they were not quite sure what had unfolded.

What they missed was Ferguson head-butting Jock McStay. It wasn't quite the shot heard around the world, but it was a head-butt that reverberated around Scottish football. He and McStay had been jostling for possession of the ball, ten metres infield and twenty to thirty metres from the Raith goal line, in a corner between the main stand and the Broomloan Road stand.

There was some pushing, a tangle of arms, what could loosely be termed a headlock attempt by Ferguson. But then Ferguson propelled his head towards McStay, who had turned to confront him. The Raith player's knees buckled and he collapsed to the turf, holding his face.

Had this act gone well beyond what could be considered normal physical contact in a football match? Conceivably, Ferguson might have been trying to eyeball his opponent and had just got his distances wrong. That might have been the case. Some accused McStay of falling to the ground too easily. That is what a sheriff had to assess. He had the unusual luxury of being able to watch it again and again.

Crucially, the incident was captured by the cameras, both television and long lens varieties. When it was shown the next day on *Scotsport*, the pictures had already helped establish Ferguson's guilt in the eyes of many viewers, as had the photographs in the same day's newspapers.

If the head-butt reverberated around Scottish football, Ferguson's subsequent imprisonment made headlines all around the world. Suddenly, his notoriety was off the scale. His career appeared to be in jeopardy. He was still to reach his mid-20s.

Ferguson's spell in prison left him resentful; it certainly coloured the rest of his career, though deciding to what extent is difficult. Even before 16 April 1994, doubt had been cast about whether Ferguson actually wanted to succeed. Some wondered whether he even liked the game from which he was making a career. Most prominent in this camp was his old manager Jim McLean. A product of the old school, McLean viewed Ferguson's sometimes-questionable attitude with distaste. The player was already bucking against authority. McLean told me that if they had sent his wages to Ferguson's home address each week, then 'he wouldn't have turned up for the game on a Saturday'.

According to McLean, the player's greatest crime is not what he did or didn't do on the pitch that day against Raith Rovers. Rather, it is that he did not make the best of himself. 'Unfortunately, the way he felt about football was completely different to the way I felt about it,' he says.

Football made Ferguson rich. It also appeared to make him angry. He seethed at his treatment from the courts, and from football's governing bodies, specifically the Scottish Football Association, who were so determined to see him serve a 12-match ban after the McStay clash, despite his legal team's protestations that it prejudiced the forthcoming court trial.

He cold-shouldered journalists and roughed up opponents,

racking up a Premier League record, one he shares at the time of writing with Patrick Vieira, formerly of Arsenal, and one-time Everton centre-half Richard Dunne, of eight red cards.

In actual fact, it could be ten, if we count a retrospective red card received after he aimed an elbow at Aston Villa's Thomas Hitzlsperger in 2003, as well as the other red card he would surely have received after throttling Leicester City player Steffen Freund in 2004, were he not already walking from the field – after being sent off.

Or it could even be eleven, considering that, just four months before he retired from the game, Ferguson was involved in another post-red card confrontation, this time with Wigan Athletic player Pascal Chimbonda, which referee Mike Dean later said would have been worthy of another red card on its own had he only seen it. Even everybody's favourite pantomime villain Vinnie Jones only managed seven.

It is easy to form the impression that Ferguson loved no one – except perhaps Everton fans, whose support helped sustain him during his 44-day spell in prison. A ten-year-old Wayne Rooney was among those who wrote to him at Barlinnie and who, to his surprise, got a reply from his hero. So, too, did hundreds of others.

They regard big, swashbuckling No. 9s as a birthright at Goodison Park, and Ferguson fitted the bill. His status as an idol was further helped by just how ordinary those around him often were, in an era when Everton struggled to cope with the new gold dream that was the Premiership. It is notable, however, that when the book *Everton Greats* was first published in 1997, Ferguson's name was not included. While Rooney adorned the cover of the revised and updated version in 2003, Ferguson is dismissed by authors Jon Berman and Malcolm Dome. 'If ever there has been a player at Goodison who has let himself down badly, it is Duncan Ferguson,' they write. He is a player, they conclude, who 'will forever carry the tag "if only".'

There is a striker called Duncan included, but it isn't Ferguson. Rather the skilful, charismatic and outspoken Duncan McKenzie makes the cut, despite having spent only two trophy-less seasons at Goodison Park in the '70s.

Although Ferguson won the FA Cup in his first season at the club, the mid-to-late '90s were not a memorable period for Everton. Until the emergence of Rooney, Ferguson had few rivals for the fans' affections, although when it came to value for money, many

– even some of his most ardent supporters – would have to admit that he fared badly in comparison with other, less celebrated figures.

Graeme Sharp, who wore the No. 9 shirt with such distinction when Everton won two league titles in the '80s, pondered the enigma that is his fellow Scot in his own autobiography, *Sharpy: My Story*, published in 2006. 'When I first saw him play, I thought he had all the attributes you need to be a top-class centre-forward; he had decent pace, great control, raw aggression and power – he had it all,' writes Sharp. 'But we just didn't see enough of it.'

The Everton Encyclopedia describes the ongoing reassessments in the entry for Ferguson. As befitting its title, the book, published in 2012, is set out in alphabetical order, which means Ferguson is listed directly after Marouane Fellaini, a more recent Everton hero, and before Mick Ferguson, another injury-prone striker, who is chiefly remembered for being literally too big for his boots – his size seven feet were out of proportion to his 6 ft 3 in. frame and were reckoned to be the cause of long-running ankle ailments.

To describe Ferguson, terms such as 'less than triumphant return' and 'costly burden' are employed by writer James Corbett. While he acknowledges Ferguson's Everton career was marked by 'occasional brilliance', the conclusion is fairly damning: 'Plenty of men with less formidable talent outperformed him during his Goodison years, yet without sharing the same affinity with the crowd.'

So what was it about Ferguson? The deal that saw Everton spend £3.75 million when bringing him back from Newcastle United, to whom they had sold the player for £8 million less than two years earlier, sounds on the face of it like a masterstroke. In *Everton Greats*, however, it is described as one of the club's 'greatest follies'. In an article in *The Observer* in 2003, sports writer Jamie Jackson quotes an Everton insider who rates it as 'the worst deal in the club's history'.

While most would concede that both Ferguson's spells at the club were interrupted by too many injuries and suspensions, there was a lot about Ferguson the fans adored and which made them gloss over the obvious failings and frustrations.

'If we didn't have Big Dunc, then we would have had to create him,' one supporter, Steve Jones, tells me, with reference to the otherwise dire '90s.

Ferguson was the antidote to Michael Owen, the seemingly

squeaky-clean Liverpool striker who wrote his name across the football landscape in the late '90s and who, woundingly for Evertonians, had once been one of them. Indeed, Owen was the latest in a long line of Everton fans – including such illustrious names as Ian Rush, Robbie Fowler and Steve McManaman – who went on to make an impact on the other side of Stanley Park, at Anfield.

But while Owen was counted out, someone else was counted in. Ferguson perhaps better reflected the Evertonian character at the time: attritional, combative, embittered.

Everton, along with neighbours Liverpool, were the dominant English team of the '80s and yet, through no fault of their own, were fated not to enjoy the fruits of their first league title win for 15 years, in the 1984–85 season. The victory coincided with the riot involving Liverpool and Juventus fans at the Heysel Stadium in Brussels before the European Cup final in May 1985. It led to the deaths of 39 supporters and the UEFA-imposed ban on English clubs competing in Europe, which lasted until season 1990–91.

During 1984–85, Everton also lifted the European Cup-Winners' Cup; it is as good as it has been for the Goodison Park club. They did win the Championship – and again were denied entry to the European Cup – in 1986–87, but after losing the FA Cup final against Liverpool in 1989, the club went into gradual decline. They sank lower and lower in the league table – sixth, ninth, twelfth and thirteenth. The next campaign, 1993–94, which was the season before Ferguson arrived, saw Everton cling on to their Premiership status, narrowly missing their first demotion from the top flight since the early 1950s. They were crying out for a hero.

Where once the club's commitment to skill saw them labelled 'the School of Science', the Everton of this latest era had earned themselves a new name – 'the Dogs of War'. It was not the kind of football many had grown up expecting at Goodison Park, but then times were hard.

When Ferguson signed, initially on a temporary loan deal from Rangers, Everton were sitting near the bottom of the Premiership table. Even so, it's fair to say that news of Ferguson's arrival from Scotland, where he had scored just two league goals in fifteen months at Rangers, failed to enthuse Evertonians.

They had, perhaps, more reason to be excited about the identity of Ferguson's companion in the two-player loan package from Ibrox. Ian Durrant had battled back from a career-threatening knee injury to score in what, to all intents and purposes, had been a Champions League semi-final tie with Olympique de Marseille in the Stade Vélodrome, two seasons earlier. He was a player with proven pedigree, one who had spent his entire career at Ibrox.

As for Ferguson, he was starting to reek of trouble, while also failing to live up to his price tag. However, few players while still in their early 20s could have coped with his particular burden. He had, at the very least, been expected to challenge an ageing Mark Hateley for a place in the Rangers side and yet had patently failed to do so. Further marking him out as an undesirable, as far as Everton fans were concerned, was his impending court appearance after being charged for the assault on McStay.

Ferguson won them over, if not immediately. Durrant had already left by the time the striker's love affair with the fans truly began, in the 56th minute of a derby match with Liverpool and in his seventh appearance for his new club. Everton, with just one win in their opening sixteen matches, were struggling again, while Liverpool were in fourth place. Everton had also just dispensed with manager Mike Walker and brought in Joe Royle, an old Goodison favourite from his playing days and someone who knew as well as anyone what it took to be a centre-forward at the club. But nobody gave the home side a prayer against their city rivals.

Enter, Duncan Ferguson.

Crashing into the six-yard box, rising above both goalkeeper David James and defender Neil Ruddock, Ferguson headed Andy Hinchcliffe's corner into the net, then set up strike partner Paul Rideout for the second goal in a stirring 2–0 win.

Further helping seal Ferguson's place in local legend was his chosen method of preparation. In the early hours of the morning of the previous day, he had failed a breathalyser test after driving through a bus station on Paradise Street, in Liverpool's city centre, having 'misinterpreted' a 'No Entry' sign.

Duncan Disorderly had arrived on Merseyside.

CHAPTER 3

Legoland

Of all the places Duncan Ferguson could have been born, he had to be born in Bannockburn. Nowhere in Scotland is there a place more associated with Scottish pride and independence, literally: the Battle of Bannockburn saw a famous victory in the fourteenth-century Wars of Scottish Independence, with Robert the Bruce defeating King Edward II's army to secure an independent monarch for Scotland.

Bannockburn itself sits on the south-east fringe of the ancient Scottish capital, Stirling, one of Scotland's seven cities. There is abundant evidence of both status and neglect. For a site of such national significance, writes James Robertson in his epic novel *And the Land Lay Still*, Bannockburn 'is unspectacular', hemmed in by housing schemes and roads. You can imagine coachloads of tourists being slightly underwhelmed on arrival, electing to push on to Stirling Castle, four miles away, or else to clamber up to the Wallace Monument, a tower dating back to the 1860s. The structure commemorates William Wallace, who led the Scottish rebellion against Edward I in the late 1200s, and overlooks the surrounding carse, the Scottish term for the low, fertile flatland that wheels around the area.

One can only hope that the opening of the new heritage centre to commemorate the battle's 700th anniversary will help to change the landscape. For some time now, the area has been in need of regeneration. The original heritage centre, a rather drab, inconspicuous concrete slab, is not actually situated in Bannockburn. Instead, it is based in what is known as Whins of Milton, another in a series of villages on Stirling's hem. It is bisected by a road out to Glasgow and it is on the street where Ferguson's parents now live.

Even though it is a site of cultural significance, the area is studded with the charmless features of Everytown – discount stores, bookies and pubs. According to the Scottish poet Kathleen Jamie, Bannockburn 'is not so much a place, as an idea'. One plain brick building, the King Robert Hotel, almost pleads to be knocked down. It can seem depressing and yet, when looking away from Stirling, away from the castle perched on a lump of volcanic rock and out across the open fields, it's possible to imagine the clanking of claymores. Freedom was won on these fields, though such indomitable spirit has almost been crushed by decades of degeneration, which can be dated back to the early 1950s and the end of the textile era. Decline had taken a firm hold by the time Duncan Ferguson was born in 1971, on 27 December, a Monday.

Ferguson's family – mother Iris, father Duncan senior, and sisters Iris and Audrey – lived in an area of Bannockburn known locally as 'Legoland', close to Bannockburn High School, which itself is a huge, imposing building set in green playing fields. On the Legoland estate, the houses are rather strange-looking structures, painted chocolate brown. As with Lego, they are square-shaped, with flat roofs. The entire scheme has a higgledy-piggledy arrangement, with roofs that slope in different directions and cut-throughs that run between each house and the small front garden. To get to Ferguson's old house in this tightly packed cul-de-sac, you have to go down a small, narrow road: McLean Court.

The Fergusons were typical of the area: working-class. But Duncan would not be the first member of the family to play senior football, nor the first to sign for one of the Dundee clubs. Willie Cunningham, the brother of his mother, Iris, has that distinction.

In the early '60s, Cunningham played for Dundee, then a club at the height of its powers. A goalkeeper, he did not play a first-team game for the side that reached the semi-finals of the European Cup in 1963, however he distinguished himself in another way at Dens Park, and would continue to do so at Raith Rovers and Stenhousemuir, where he moved after Dundee. Remarkably, for someone whose position is heavily reliant on communication, Cunningham had a significant hearing defect.

Overcoming his disability, he signed for Dundee in 1960, joining a club who were then managed by Bob Shankly, the brother of Liverpool's Bill. This was an achievement for Cunningham in itself, as was overcoming the inevitable cruelty of a banter-heavy environment. Craig Brown, the former Scotland manager, was a player at Dens Park at the time. He believes the good relationship he would go on to forge with Ferguson hinged on his treatment of Cunningham in a dressing-room where others were not quite so sympathetic.

When Brown managed the Scotland Under-21 team, he selected Ferguson. Brown recalls: 'The first time I picked Duncan, he said: "My uncle Willie was asking after you."' According to the former Scotland manager, some of the boys 'used to take the piss out of' Ferguson's uncle. 'I didn't,' says Brown. 'I faced him when I spoke to him. I wasn't trying to be soft; I was just trying to be kind to the guy. I also learned some sign language when I was a student, so I could also make an effort to use that with him.'

There is no doubt that Cunningham had ability. 'It's just that, for a goalkeeper, good hearing and being able to listen to tactical calls is essential,' says Alex Smith, who played with Cunningham at Gowanhill, the well-known Stirling amateur side. 'It stopped Willie being a really top-class goalkeeper.'

Were it not for his disability, the perpetrators of such dressing-room banter might have thought twice about taking liberties with a 6 ft 3 in. goalkeeper. In the Gowanhill amateurs team group photograph, it isn't hard to spot Ferguson's uncle. He towers over the other players. 'The Gentle Giant' they called him, remembers teammate Jim Lennon.

'His deafness was not a problem – only if you had to shout at him,' Lennon adds. 'We used to have a laugh. I remember on one occasion he was looking the other way and the ball went into the back of the net. I asked after the game: "What were you doing, Willie?" He said, "I was watching a birdie, pal."'

Ferguson inherited his uncle's love of pigeons, as well as his talent for football, although his father had, by all accounts, been a decent centre-half in his day at amateur level.

Bannockburn remained a resolutely working-class village, even when, as Ferguson grew up, the traditional industries were closed down or struggled to survive. The sense of belonging to that class, of being working-class, with all it implied, was deeply ingrained. 'It was always a very working-class area,' says Ferguson's old friend from Bannockburn High, Iain McMenemy. 'In those days, perhaps more so.

'There were very few houses that were not council housing,' continues McMenemy. 'Legoland wasn't rough. It was newer, three-bedroom housing. But there was a working-class outlook. You had to have a bit of bottle about you growing up. Bannockburn High was not the greatest school. Seats would get thrown out of the school bus on the way home; the police would have to come. Unless you stood up for yourself, life could be an absolute misery.'

Another childhood friend, Gary Stewart, says Bannockburn pupils 'were considered the poor relation' of their better-dressed peers in Stirling. And perhaps there is still something in this. While all the other secondary schools in Stirling have been rebuilt since the late '90s, Bannockburn High was only refurbished.

Although Bannockburn High was non-denominational, it was considered to be the Protestant school in the area. Bannockburn, like many settlements in central and west Scotland, suffered from the blight of sectarianism. As is so often the case in Scotland, life was viewed through the prism of either religion or football, although both are often really an excuse to create division. The Empire Bar was seen as the 'Rangers pub' and the Newmarket Inn as the one frequented by Celtic fans.

'Everyone supported either Celtic or Rangers,' points out Stewart. 'And it didn't help that the Albion were shite,' he adds, with reference to the local club, Stirling Albion.

For McMenemy, who returned to Bannockburn after a spell away in the United States with his family, it was like landing in another world, one ruled by closed-mindedness. 'I came back from the States in 1984. I looked at it with a fresher eye than most people and I just didn't get it,' he says. 'Why is religion attached to what football team you support? It was very stark, and quite depressing.'

He remembers pupils from Bannockburn and St Modan's, a nearby Roman Catholic school that attracted children from a wide catchment area, meeting up to fight. According to McMenemy, Ferguson stood apart from all that. At that stage, anyway, he wasn't interested in looking for trouble.

Although he came from a Rangers-supporting family, and his

boyhood hero was the talented Rangers left-winger Davie Cooper, he was not as passionate about the club as was later reported. McMenemy has a vivid memory of Ferguson turning up at school in a tangerine-and-black Dundee United scarf, one he preferred to tie tightly round his neck, as was the fashion at the time. United, it must be remembered, were then enjoying a rather more successful time of it on the field than Rangers.

'He didn't seem to get into the Rangers and Celtic thing,' recalls McMenemy, who portrays a more sensitive Ferguson than might be expected. At football practice, Ferguson tried to let McMenemy, who lacked his friend's expertise with the ball, down gently: 'You know what you want to do, but it is just not quite there,' he would tell him.

'Duncan was never aggressive, he never looked for trouble,' adds McMenemy. 'He had a natural instinct to stand up for himself, which you later saw on the pitch. But he was never hanging around at night. There were gangs, things going on, between the schools, between St Modan's and Bannockburn. Duncan wasn't interested in that.'

Visiting a modernised Bannockburn High today, it is immediately obvious that it has retained the peculiar angled shape of old, while it has also been given a lick of orange paint – or 'terracotta', as it might be described in the more bijou areas of Stirling. There are three storeys, small windows criss-crossed with white panels. It is clear to see why it has been compared to a prison.

The school helped create a sense of alienation. 'Bannockburn High was geographically and demographically out of it,' says Stewart. 'And the siege mentality was fostered not only by the pupils but the teachers, too. Whereas St Modan's had the history and drew from all over Stirling, and Stirling High had kids from "well-to-do" areas such as King's Park, all the pupils at Bannockburn High came from the immediate surroundings and the old mining towns of Cowie and Plean.

'You have to bear in mind there was no mining any more,' Stewart continues. 'Times were particularly tough out there. The whole school was very blue collar.' He recalls the school's Under-13 team, featuring himself and Ferguson, beating St Modan's on their own turf. 'Back then it was the equivalent of Partick Thistle turning Rangers over at Ibrox,' he contends.

McMenemy remembers Ferguson 'liked to be the class clown – like I did, I suppose. He had no real malice. He just liked people to laugh at him. He liked to be the centre of attention.'

These days, McMenemy runs his own PR firm in Edinburgh and is on the board of directors at Stenhousemuir Football Club. He has lost contact with Ferguson, having last seen him shortly after leaving school. He does, though, have fond memories of his old pal from chemistry class.

'We often partnered up for projects and once had to distil alcohol as an experiment,' he recalls. 'At the end you had to "prove" it had worked by lighting the Petri dish with the alcohol in it. Duncan and I were partners, so we lit the alcohol. The teacher says, "Great, now put it out." Rather than cupping it, Duncan thought: "I'll just blow it out." Nothing happened, so he blew harder, and of course the alcohol was blown across the counter, quickly followed by the flame. He set fire to the whole bench.'

'Duncan wasn't a bad lad at all, but neither was he the kind of guy you push around. I had a lot of time for him; he was a good friend. We seem to forget footballers are not rocket scientists, just boys out on the lash with a higher profile and more cash to spread around. I went to university because I wasn't good enough to play football. Duncan played football because he was good at it.'

Football wasn't Ferguson's chief obsession at the time, however. David Halcrow, his physical education teacher, recalls him forgetting his football boots on purpose. Why? 'He wanted to go home at lunchtime and feed his pigeons,' Halcrow smiles.

A statue of Robert the Bruce riding his war horse, gazing, it has been said, 'with a hint of dismay', is set in what is thought to be the old Bannockburn battleground. However, the exact spot where freedom was earned by the heavily outnumbered army of Scottish warriors is the subject of heavy debate. One popular theory contends that the ground on which Bannockburn High School stands is where the fighting took place. It is a battle that certainly continues to exert a significant hold on the Scottish psyche. It would probably have seemed too good to be true had the Scotland international football team finally found its saviour in a corner of such sacred turf.

And so it proved.

Ferguson's relationship with his country is a complicated one, beginning when he spotted a Saltire flag lying on the trackside while warming up prior to making his competitive debut for Scotland against the Netherlands at Euro '92. He picked it up, clenched his fist in the direction of the Scottish supporters and got one of the biggest cheers of the day. Years later, his presence on a football pitch in Scotland was more likely to inspire a volley of jeers.

Stirling had already produced a footballing icon in Billy Bremner, born nearly 30 years before Ferguson. The two have much in common. For one thing, they share the ability to start a fight on a football pitch – and other places besides. 'Combative' would be one description. And yet it could never be claimed that Ferguson occupies a place in the heart of the Scottish football supporter the way Bremner does.

The parallels are irresistible, however. Bremner's Scottish international career came to a premature end in 1975 following a late night fracas in Copenhagen, for which he was given a *sine die* ban by the Scottish Football Association. 'That hurt Billy,' says Alex Smith, Bremner's best friend and former best man. Bremner had already won 54 caps and had led his country at the World Cup finals in Germany in 1974.

When he died, in 1997 at the age of just 54, nowhere was he more deeply mourned than on the streets of Raploch, the once notorious housing estate where he grew up in north-west Stirling, and close to where Ferguson would spend his formative years two decades hence. An engraved pathstone has been laid in honour of Bremner, with the inscription: 'Born in Raploch 1942, Billy Bremner spent his childhood swimming in the River Forth and pestering for a game with the bigger lads at Shell Park.'

While Bremner was a much-loved son of Scotland, who carried Raploch with him and left a bit of himself there, Ferguson, on the other hand, is an absence in the streets around his home in Bannockburn. He is certainly not exulted. Equally, what did Bannockburn give him? Return to Bannockburn, to the streets where he grew up, and you will find little to indicate its part in his design. Visit the Anchor, the nearest bar to where the footballer and his parents moved after Legoland, and there are no pictures on the wall of the footballer. In the Borestone and Falcon bars, a little farther down the road, you are met with suspicion when you enquire after

Ferguson, rather than any evident pride. True, some of the bar staff were not born when this was Ferguson's stomping ground. But it is not as though he has disappeared. Rather, it is as though he never existed.

Certainly that is my initial impression, only confirmed when I make the effort to visit Ferguson's parents – an undertaking carried out with some trepidation. I crunch up the gravel path, past daffodils and flowerpots, leading to a small, grey, pebbledashed, detached home on the outskirts of what was once the village of St Ninians but which has long since become subsumed by Stirling itself.

Echoing in my head are the words of the young reporter who, just three months into his journalistic career with *The Herald*, was handed the assignment of obtaining some form of reaction from Ferguson's family following the news of his imprisonment. The reporter was Jonathan Northcroft, now chief football correspondent for the *Sunday Times*, but back then he was barely out of journalism school.

'Death-knocks', where reporters are forced to turn up on doorsteps to elicit comments from a recently bereaved family, have been described as the closest thing journalism has to an initiation ceremony. But Northcroft would gladly have opted for such uncomfortable circumstances if it meant avoiding a trip to one particular doorstep in Stirling. With each crunch of gravel as he approached the front door of the Ferguson family home – along the same path I was now walking – his anticipation of the inevitable rebuff grew stronger. Northcroft later reflected on the spasms of terror that shuddered through his body in a piece in the *Sunday Times*, published in 2003.

'Glasgow Road, St Ninians, Stirling,' he wrote, setting the scene for an article that sought to highlight the latest crossroads at which the then 31-year-old Ferguson's career had arrived. 'A drab street on a tough estate in Scotland. I am there as a nervous – terrified, if truth be told – young news reporter, straight out of a journalism course.'

Northcroft is alert to the 'short-straw nature' of the assignment, handed to him after Ferguson's appeal against his prison sentence had been rejected. He has been sent to 'doorstep' Ferguson's parents and obtain a hopefully quotable reaction from either one of them, as well as to gauge the feeling in the surrounding area.

Northcroft started out at the local pub, 'where the only splash of colour amid its sepulchral interior comes from the ripple of fruit machine lights'. There is some hostility. 'Duncan's all right, it's you in the press that's the trouble,' Northcroft was told. Later there were fewer words, but slightly more menace: 'At the house in Glasgow Road, Duncan senior, Ferguson's father, a tower block of a man, sends me scampering away with a glare.'

From the rear of the house, there had come an incongruous sound. Northcroft eventually discovers the source: 'the gentle cooing of pigeons' he writes.

Northcroft was also conscious of another noise – the guffawing of the less-than-sympathetic photographer who had joined him on this thankless expedition to Ferguson's backyard. As is often the case in episodes of heightened tension, laughter becomes an almost involuntary reaction. It was, of course, a grave situation – it had to be, given the circumstances of a young man's incarceration – but the seriousness only made the nerves worse, the giggles more likely. Northcroft's companion succumbed.

'Stories of Ferguson's father being a bare-knuckle fighter contributed to my fear,' says Northcroft now. 'I recall him being a huge figure. I said, "Hello, I am sorry to bother you, I am from the *Glasgow Herald*." The words were hardly out of my mouth before the door closed again. It was not slammed shut, just closed slowly. Because of that, it seemed more menacing. The photographer was pissing himself laughing.'

In a way, I wish I had a companion with me now, however unhelpful, as I make my way down the same front path.

A story that emerged early in my research provides me with a shard of optimism. In my notes, it is labelled 'the Graceland story' because this is how Ian Macdonald, a spokesman for the Everton Independent Supporters Club, termed the occasion when he described how a busload of Everton fans had turned up outside the family home of their then idol.

En route home from a testimonial match in Aberdeen, the Everton fans found themselves drinking in a bar in Stirling, one of numerous appointed refreshment stops. They knew they were in Ferguson's hometown, just not that it was his neighbourhood.

Macdonald explains: 'One of the barmen looked up and, seeing our Everton tops, said: "I suppose you've come to see Duncan's house?" All our ears pricked up.' The helpful barman informed them that the house was about 150 yards up the road. According to Macdonald, 'It was like someone had told them where Santa Claus lived. And these were grown men.'

An advance party headed up. 'I spoke to one of the sensible ones and told him: "Listen, if you knock on the door, Duncan's mum and dad live there, so give them maximum respect." Eventually, he too wandered along the road to be confronted by the sight of about 50 Everton fans in a semi-circle around the doorway, in which stood Mr and Mrs Ferguson.

'I could see the party shaking hands with Duncan's parents and taking mementoes from the garden. "Mad Alex" still has a stone from the driveway in his wallet, to mark how he was once at Graceland – i.e. Duncan's mum and dad's house. For Elvis, read Big Dunc.'

There was an extra surprise in store for Macdonald. He was invited into Graceland. He was permitted entry to his hero's old lair. 'I got to see his FA Cup medal, his caps,' he says.

He was offered a whisky or a cup of tea and, because of the over-indulgence of the previous days, he chose the latter. 'I said: "I would love a cup of tea, Mrs Ferguson." They are both tall, like Duncan. I was sitting there, talking away. His mother said: "Duncan's been in a lot of trouble lately, and in the papers." And then she said something I found quite poignant. She said: "You know, he doesn't really like football. He just loves his pigeons."'

Their pilgrimage to the parental home of Duncan Ferguson had yielded more, much more, than Macdonald and his fellow Everton supporters could ever have hoped. But then, they were not journalists. They were not writing a book about Duncan Ferguson. The prospect of my being offered a cup of tea seemed remote, though I was hopeful of an opportunity to state my case, at least.

And so, at the end of the path, I knock on a brown front door with frosted glass, at first gently, then more firmly. Nothing. Not a sound inside. I walk to the back door and try that. Nobody answers, so I return to the front door and try the bell, which I probably should have tried first. Still nothing. Not even the cooing of pigeons. The car is there – a BMW, with registration plate: FERG 1E – but no one seems to be in, though the lights are on. I return to the car and take a few deep breaths, unsure whether to feel disappointed or slightly relieved.

Curiously, after I have set off towards Stirling, I wheel round the roundabout at the bottom of the road and go back past the house, no more than three or four minutes later; when I look to the left, I see a tall male figure at the window, hands pressed to the glass, peering out into the late afternoon gloom.

Ferguson and Bremner are perhaps the two best footballers to emerge from the area, but they are not the only ones. Indeed, don't let the curious lack of a top-flight club in Stirling fool you. Since 1970, Stirling has produced more Scotland internationalists per head of population than anywhere else. There have been ten to date, including Ferguson and Bremner, from a population of just over 82,000.

'Aye, it is a football place,' agrees Alex Smith, who comes from Cowie, a mining village in the Stirling area, and who would later enjoy a career as a player and a manager, a job that took him to many of Scotland's top clubs, including Aberdeen and Dundee United. 'There were quite a lot of senior pros around and anyone who does well in football gets recognised in the street.'

Perhaps this explains Ferguson's awkwardness as he began to make a name for himself. 'It was quite a difficult time for him,' says Smith, who remembers first becoming aware of Ferguson when he scored 'four or five goals' in a reserve game for Dundee United at Aberdeen, where Smith was manager at the time. Ferguson was becoming a marked man on the streets as well. 'I think it was hard for him to find a neutral zone,' says Smith, who agrees that both Bremner and Ferguson 'came out of the same environment, really'. Smith describes Stirling as 'a close community', but he might also mean closed. Like in many small towns or cities – Stirling was granted city status in 2002, to mark the Queen's Golden Jubilee – when a native begins to gain some prominence, the suspicion and envy in others tends to grow quickly.

'When you start making a name, you attract attention,' Smith goes on to explain. 'Billy went away to Leeds when he was 15. That probably helped him. He got out of the area, away from the idiots.'

Ferguson stuck around a bit longer but came to resent some of the attention that came his way as football was transformed from the old 'working-man's pursuit' to a game played by millionaires – yet it was still being watched by those who didn't have much more than before. According to Gary Stewart, and despite what politicians claimed, the economic boom was not felt by the man in the street: while the construction of soul-less shopping centres meant the landscape changed, the lives of the locals carried on as normal.

'In essence,' says Stewart, 'Stirling was a small town with small people trying to understand why everyone was talking the place up when it seemed, well, the same. That meant when a relatively minor celeb like Big Dunc came on the scene, the best thing for him to do would have been to bail out of Stirling because he suddenly became the most famous face in town.'

Ferguson himself was alert to the dangers. 'It bothers me that I can't go to certain places or do certain things just to avoid trouble from bampots in the street,' he told *Scottish Football Today* in 1992. 'But then I want to be a footballer and that is what drives me on.'

Ferguson did have drive, did have ambition. He wanted to succeed, to be the best. But he realised that people's perception of him was changing, although he also seemed to understand it was a price he had to pay. 'It's other people – they see you as the big man who thinks he's worth £2.5 million,' he said in the same interview. 'That just isn't true. Some Saturdays my dad doesn't think I'm worth 30 bob. I just want to be able to get out the house for a few beers and a laugh. But I know that isn't on.'

Smith owned an eponymously named restaurant in Stirling and, because he understood the pressures on high-profile young footballers, he knew how to look after them if they visited. 'Stirling was not so big a place that Duncan could avoid people confronting him,' says Smith. 'In fact, I remember saying to him: "Son, you have a girlfriend?" "Aye," he said. So I told him: "Listen, why don't you bring her down to my place on Saturday night, after you have played your game. Have a beer, have a few laughs, and then get yourself home. You'll get some peace."

'I said to him: "Bigger names than you have come down here, Bremner and the like." I used to kid him on: "You are one of the big names now, but you are not the best from Stirling. You have a long way to go until you are the best."'

Meanwhile, Bremner, says Smith, 'took an interest' in Ferguson. 'Billy was great for that, helping those who were trying to make their way. When Alex Ferguson was having a hard time down there [at Manchester United], he would do a piece in the newspapers saying this young manager from Aberdeen is going to be outstanding.

Just give him a chance. He was good for giving people a boost, particularly those from his own area. He would champion people.

'He championed Duncan.'

Yet despite such a strong recommendation, Ferguson's absence from the area now appears total. Even his first international Schoolboys cap, gifted by him to his school in what might be considered a surprisingly thoughtful gesture, has gone.

According to David Halcrow, Ferguson's old PE teacher at the school, it disappeared during the recent refurbishment, along with another gift from a Scottish international rugby centre. 'We had Ian Jardine's Scotland rugby international jersey. He was a pupil here, too, and then we had Duncan's cap – they are both gone. We don't know where they went.'

Halcrow continues: 'We don't even have any pictures. The only one we had, the *News of the World* nicked off us and never gave it back. They did a piece on him and I said to the journalist: "You are not getting dirt off me because there is no dirt." They took the photo away with them of Duncan in the Under-16 Scotland international side.'

In Halcrow, Ferguson found somebody who was supportive. Halcrow himself had played senior football and made a clutch of first-team appearances for Brechin City, in the Scottish lower divisions. A bad ankle break, sustained while playing rugby at Jordanhill College of Education in Glasgow, dashed his hopes of a football career at just 18, though he went on to play for Camelon and then Bannockburn Juniors. Halcrow was desperate to see Ferguson do well and make the most of the chance that he himself had been denied because of injury.

When Ferguson was selected to represent his country at Under-16 level, the school even covered the cost of his Scotland team blazer. Ferguson repaid Halcrow in goals. 'I always remember us going to play Larbert High – he went out there and beat them himself, which gave me no end of satisfaction because it's my old school, where I captained the football team,' Halcrow recalls. 'I remember thinking: that guy is a bit special.'

Sitting in a staff room at Bannockburn High, where he still teaches, Halcrow smiles warmly as he recalls Ferguson. 'He was my little left winger,' he recalls. His affection is evident as he stretches to pull out the bottom drawer of a desk. After some rummaging, he pulls out a photograph. So there is one that has survived, taken before a teachers versus pupils challenge match. There, two from the right in the front row, is that unmistakable broad grin. The 14-year-old Duncan Ferguson has still to begin the growth spurt that would see him terrorise centre-halves, hence his then deployment as a nippy and skilful operator out on the left flank.

Later, the strapping Ferguson would be manoeuvred to the back row of team photographs. However, Big Dunc was 'Little Dunc' back then. Despite this, he remains instantly recognisable in his striped shirt of light-and-dark blue, the colours of Bannockburn High School.

Not that Ferguson was able to wear this shirt and represent his school as often as he wished. His early teenage years collided with the teachers' strike in the mid-1980s, which ended the tradition of free vocational sports training that teachers had given to pupils. This industrial action, following a dispute over pay and working conditions, and aimed principally at Margaret Thatcher's Conservative government, had a devastating effect on the development of Scotland's young sportsmen and women; its unwelcome legacy is perhaps illustrated by the alarming decline in the national football team's fortunes on the world stage in successive decades.

Perversely, despite Bannockburn's reputation as a socially challenged area once reliant on the mills and mines, it happened to fall in a Conservative-governed region on account of the more opulent areas in the north of Stirling, such as Bridge of Allan and King's Park. It meant Bannockburn was a target school, as the teachers' union sought to inflict maximum damage on the local Conservative Member of Parliament, Michael Forsyth.

'Some schools kept the sport going, but here we had to stop all the extracurricular stuff,' says Halcrow. Bannockburn High were sitting top of the league at the time and had their eyes on the Scottish Schools' Cup. 'But we got hit and that was it,' he laments. 'It has really never recovered from 1985.'

Before this, Bannockburn High School were regularly turning out four teams. 'Not bad for what is quite a small school,' says Halcrow. One pupil stood out, even before he began the growth spurt that might well have contributed to his injury problems in later years. 'When Duncan got taller and bigger,' reflects Halcrow, 'he moved into the middle of the park and in his fourth year at the school he got into the Scotland Under-16 team.

'He was the first-ever Under-16 international schoolboy that we had,' he adds. 'And the last'.

An unintended consequence of the teachers' strike, and the diminishing opportunities at Bannockburn High, was that the local boys' clubs grew stronger. It was this scene that set Ferguson on the path to his professional career – a path that led to Dundee, a city an hour away from Stirling, with not one but two leading professional clubs.

CHAPTER 4

Get that Lad Signed

It is possible to pinpoint the moment Duncan Ferguson's football career began in earnest. Or at least this is the contention of George Skelton, a likeable teacher and part-time scout – although some might have disputed the term part-time, given his enthusiasm for the role. The location was Stirling University, where Dundee United ran a satellite academy at the time. Ferguson was still seeking to impress his would-be suitors. For those looking to enter the more stable world of accountancy, for example, there is a rigid, non-negotiable path that has to be taken, one involving exams, traineeships and long, often mundane hours of book work. Footballers, however, tend to have to rely on inspiration, on fortune, on a collision of circumstances that result in someone being convinced enough of the subject's talent to take a chance.

As Skelton, accompanied by a senior member of the United coaching staff, looked on, Ferguson seized his opportunity on the red-ash pitch, set within the scenic university grounds in the village of Bridge of Allan, three miles from Stirling itself.

'I remember Duncan was out by a corner flag, with a guy trying to jockey him,' Skelton recalls. 'Duncan flicked the ball up with his right foot behind his left leg, and then hit it with his left foot into the far corner of the goal. That was when Walter Smith turned to me and said: "Get that lad signed."'

As assistant manager to Jim McLean at the time, this would not be the last time Smith would utter this command in reference to Ferguson. He 'got that lad signed' on a further two occasions, at rather greater expense. But it was here, on the campus of Stirling University, that Ferguson set off on his career.

Given the significant role Skelton played, it's gratifying to learn that he benefited from the first of Ferguson's big-money moves. The former history teacher – many of United's scouts tended to have schoolmaster backgrounds – and passionate mountaineer pocketed the not inconsiderable sum of £10,000 when Smith later made Ferguson the most expensive footballer to move between two British clubs.

As one of United's Central Belt scouts, the arrangement Skelton had with United meant he was guaranteed to receive a quarter of 1 per cent of any transfer fee commanded by one of his discoveries. It might sound meagre; however, when it is a percentage of £4 million, the amount becomes a worthwhile one, indeed – enough, certainly, for the substantial home improvements that were funded, Skelton recalls, by his finder's fee.

'I remember Kenny Cameron, one of the United coaches, saying to me: "You will be asked on when Dunc is on *This Is Your Life* now."'

Although Skelton was grateful for the unexpectedly large windfall and was proud of the part he played in the striker's development, he did not consider Ferguson to be the best player he unearthed for the Tannadice club. According to Skelton, Tom McMillan was the player who should have made it big in the game. Signed by United from Grahamston Boys' Club, McMillan represented Scotland at both Under-15 and Under-16 levels, playing in the side who made it all the way to the World Cup final when Scotland hosted the event in 1989, before losing to a suspiciously mature-looking Saudi Arabian side.

Misfortune struck McMillan, however, when he ruptured his cruciate at the age of only 17, months after being in the Scotland team beaten at Hampden Park on penalties. 'He was captain of the reserves at just 17 years old,' recalls Skelton, between sips of coffee in the cafe of a Sainsbury's supermarket in Stirling. He remembers McMillan, who has gone on to become a successful businessman, with fondness, as he continues to ponder those other gems plucked from boys' football. 'Yes, Tom was my number-one player.'

And Ferguson? He must have been number two? 'No,' responds Skelton, enjoying this bit of mischief at my expense. 'At two is David

Stoddart. The guy was exceptional; he had speed and fitness. The ability he had with his left foot was incredible.' Then the all-too-familiar distractions of booze and girls got in the way.

'I knew a year after I signed him that he was not going to make it,' Skelton continues. 'He kept wanting to take the easy option. He talked about wanting a pair of Predator boots to make it easier to score goals.'

Finally, Skelton concedes. 'Ferguson, aye, he was my number three.'

According to the scout, he had something Stoddart didn't possess. 'He was passionate about his football – he would go from here to hell for a game.'

Over the following years, as Ferguson's relationship with Jim McLean deteriorated at United and he was handed such cheerless tasks as whitewashing the walls of the gym, he might have wryly observed that he did in fact go to hell for a game, with the result that this passion for football, in time, simply ebbed away.

Skelton first spotted Ferguson playing for a boys' side then called ICI Juniors, whose colours of tangerine and black anticipated the beginnings of Ferguson's senior football career. Both ICI's and Dundee United's club badges are also similar, depicting a lion rampant on a shield. The junior side's story is a complicated one, since it has involved a number of name changes on account of its association with the ICI factory in Grangemouth, on whose recreation ground they have played since the 1960s. The team may now be known as Syngenta but some things have remained unaltered. 'C'mon, the Dyes!' the parents shout from the sidelines, a nickname that has its origins in the dye manufacturing that began in Grangemouth back in the early 1920s.

Skelton, who taught history and modern studies at Falkirk High for more than 20 years, was well versed in all these details. But on those days when he turned up the collar of his jacket and made his way to the parks in the shadow of the vast chemical works, all that concerned him was spotting those who were exhibiting signs that they might make it in football. Given the identity of the man that he worked for, it was fortunate that he clearly had a discerning eye for a player. Just as you could trust his encyclopaedic knowledge of passable trails on the mountains that were his other enduring passion in life, you could trust Skelton's judgement on young footballers. He watched them on Saturdays and Sundays, as well as three nights during the working week. It was a full-time job, effectively.

'He was always down here, watching Ferguson,' recalls Willie McIlvaney, another hero of the local boys' football circuit. Not that Skelton needed to have been too astute to pick out Ferguson. 'One game he was here, Duncan scored five goals – that's what really caught his eye,' continues McIlvaney. 'Of course, when he went to Carse Thistle, George followed him there; he never let him out of his sight.'

McIlvaney felt bereft, as well as more than a little let down at Ferguson's departure to Carse Thistle, with whom, he says, ICI always had a 'bit of a thing'. What McIlvaney considers a flagrant piece of poaching on Carse Thistle's part did not help relations between the clubs.

But then some serendipity had led to Ferguson joining ICI in the first place. McIlvaney first met Ferguson's father while working at the Mossmorran gas plant in Fife. 'Duncan's dad was a rigger at the time; I was a crane driver,' recalls McIlvaney. 'He asked if he could bring Duncan along and we signed him.' The association did not last, however, partly because of the worsening relationship between McIlvaney and Duncan senior, and also because of the desire on Ferguson's father's part for his son to play his football nearer to home in Stirling rather than in Grangemouth, which, while hardly the other side of the moon, was still a 20-minute drive away, along the M9.

McIlvaney is unequivocal on the matter. 'Carse nicked him,' he says. And yet, McIlvaney concedes, the switch of clubs made sense for Ferguson in terms of logistics. 'I fell out with his father when he left here,' he recalls. 'I used to run young Duncan all over the place. I'd pick him up at Stirling and take him to wherever we were playing, and on training nights too. When he left to go to Carse, I was annoyed. I was disappointed, but I accepted it after a while. I could see the reasons.'

Why did he and Duncan senior fall out? One reason was McIlvaney's discovery that Ferguson was giving financial inducements to his son – a pound for every goal he scored. 'I told him: "You have to stop that, there are other players in the team,"' says McIlvaney. This episode anticipated the investigation carried out by the *Observer* newspaper into the high wages being paid to players in the Premiership for very little return; at the time, in 2003, they calculated that each of Ferguson's twelve league goals since returning to Everton from Newcastle three years earlier worked out at £400,000 each.

'Aye, but it was only a pound back then,' smiles McIlvaney. 'And it was still too much.'

Another tense moment came at a tournament called the Thistle Cup, held at the BP Club in Grangemouth in the summer of 1984. 'The Olympics were on; it was the time of Ovett and Coe,' recalls McIlvaney. 'It was a scorching summer's day. I went into the club to watch the race and had a pint of shandy, just to quench my thirst. Ferguson's dad came in and said: "If I knew this was going on, I wouldn't have let the laddie join." I protested: "But it's only a shandy!"'

'He was fiercely teetotal by the time his son played here. To be fair, Duncan was not a bit of trouble,' McIlvaney continues. 'He was great at training, a real athlete. I remember we had a sponsored run one night to raise funds. He just kept going. He wouldn't stop. He must have gone on for miles that night.' Once again, the image contrasts with the one of Ferguson as a reluctant trainer at Dundee United, and sometimes elsewhere.

McIlvaney says that Ferguson was good for the club, even if he didn't respond to a letter he wrote requesting a signed strip in order to help raise funds. 'He's the only one that really made it,' he tells me. 'You could see he had it in him, even then.'

But then, as Dick Taylor chuckled to me, in a joke he told against himself, you could be half-blind and still see Ferguson's potential. Despite having sight in only one eye, Taylor – or 'Auld Dick', as he became known – was the inspiration behind Carse Thistle, the club he founded in 1973.

Carse Thistle were Ferguson's springboard and the name lives on, even if the club does not. An entry on the club website now notes that everything the club achieved has now been dedicated to Richard 'Dick' Taylor, who died in November 2011, at the age of 83. The club itself had folded just months earlier. 'It was fun, wasn't it?' the message ends.

Two years before Taylor died, I rang him at home and we arranged to meet at his suggested rendezvous point of the cafe at Stirling train station. Although slightly physically infirm, Taylor proved himself to be fine company. He had the same guttural laugh as Pogues lead singer Shane MacGowan, which was once described as a cross between 'a rattlesnake's hiss and a portable toilet being flushed'.

He explained why they opted for the name Carse Thistle. 'Well, me and the chap who started the team with me were in a cafe someplace and there was a copy of the *Falkirk Herald* sitting there, and in it was an advert looking for teams for the Central Boys' League, and we applied to join. We were looking out of the window and there was the Carse of Stirling, sweeping all the way out from the bottom of the castle. We added the Thistle bit because I support Partick Thistle.'

And then that laugh.

Remarkably, when we met, Taylor still held the role of club general secretary. 'Everything goes through me,' he said. 'I still pay the bills.' Two years earlier Taylor had been named the 'Best Volunteer in Youth Football' at a Hampden Park awards dinner, where Kenny Dalglish presented him with a glass souvenir.

Meeting Dalglish apart, he didn't much enjoy the occasion: 'I had just got out of hospital, and the first thing I see is a menu which was take it or leave it – and I didn't much fancy anything on it. Then there were the speeches and all that sort of thing.' They wanted a group photo of all the winners at the end, but Auld Dick wasn't there. He was out in the car sleeping. 'I was knackered!'

'I didn't enjoy it,' he added. 'I am not one of those people who like to pat themselves on the back, or have anyone else pat me on the back.'

While this might be a warning not to describe Dick Taylor as 'the Man Who Discovered Duncan Ferguson', it's difficult to avoid. Journalists making even the most rudimentary investigation into Ferguson's career tended to land on his doorstep, he told me. And Taylor's success at rearing young footballers didn't start and end with Ferguson. In all, it's said that he was responsible for more than 160 players turning professional. Most recently, he'd garnered publicity for his part in the emergence of Blackburn Rovers striker David Goodwillie, another player to reach the English Premier League via the Carse Thistle–Dundee United route trodden by Ferguson.

Taylor was hugely influential in Ferguson's career, and he was selected, along with Jim McLean and Walter Smith, to provide input on a DVD produced by Everton celebrating the striker's career following his retirement in 2006. Taylor's performance is as unpretentious and to-the-point as you would expect from a former army man. Ferguson has certainly helped raise Carse United's profile, even if he failed to show at a Player of the Year dinner shortly after he made the breakthrough with United, having promised Taylor he would attend to help hand out the awards.

'He was due to arrive at 7.30 p.m. and I got a phone call at ten past seven to say he had gone out with his girlfriend and wouldn't make it,' remembered Taylor, who quickly got on the phone to Alex Smith, another famous footballing son of Stirling. 'He was down in 20 minutes – he's a great man,' added Taylor.

Yet Ferguson also helped give Taylor one the greatest thrills of his 40-year association with youth football when he helped Carse Thistle win the Scottish Cup at Under-14 level, with a 5–0 win over Comrie Colts in 1986, after what the *Stirling Observer* described as a 'dazzling display'.

Goals from Ferguson, Stuart Corner, Alex Bone – who went on to play professional football with St Mirren and Stirling Albion, and whose uncle was the Scotland international Jimmy Bone – and two from Gordon Halley meant Carse were able to take home the Willie Bauld Memorial Cup for the only time in their history.

'Carse Thistle are the best in the land,' trilled the local newspaper. 'It was just reward for a great cup campaign.' On their way to the final, Thistle had scored thirty-five goals in six ties. 'We got to the final five times, but only won it once – when Dunc scored at Tynecastle,' said Taylor.

Ferguson caused a scare by almost not making it to the game in time. 'He gave us all a heart attack,' Taylor recalled. 'He normally came to all the games in his uncle's car. We had put on a bus for Tynecastle, with the parents and kids. As we were going along the road, someone shouted: "Look, there's Duncan's uncle's car – and nae Dunc!" Apparently someone else was taking him. They were caught speeding at about 105 mph to get him to Tynecastle in time for kick-off.'

Taylor recalled the young Ferguson as being a 'bit of a loner – he was never a mixer'. This is a recollection corroborated by George Skelton, who clearly felt protective towards someone they both describe as shy and possibly insecure. Skelton would often drive his Central Belt brood up to games in Dundee. 'In the car, Duncan was always quiet,' he recalls. 'If there was a bright boy in the car, and they suspected Duncan was not very bright, then they would try and take the piss out of him. I had to tell them to shut it.'

Skelton is clearly fond of Ferguson and monitored his progress – or lack of it. He recalls conversations with other scouts, who would invariably ask him about Ferguson. Does he have what it takes to make it, they would ask. 'I really don't know, I don't know if he has a chance or not,' Skelton would reply, having already pinpointed one area where some improvement was possible. 'His stride was too long,' he tells me. 'I tried to get at that very early, when he was only 13. I tried to get him to shorten his stride. What I asked him to do was go to the first stair in his house and keep on going up and down, up and down on the first step. And I told him to keep a logbook of how many he could do in a minute.'

It seemed a straightforward enough exercise. 'I asked to see his logbook a couple of weeks later and, of course, it was blank,' recalls Skelton. 'He told me he couldn't be bothered doing it.'

Kenny Cameron, who had played for both of Dundee's senior clubs, was in charge of the scouting system at United at the time. Skelton was handed responsibility for identifying talent in the Falkirk and Stirling area, a zone that also stretched as far as Dunblane, Moodiesburn and Kincardine. As a grade-one scout, he was paid a flat rate of £50 a week, plus travelling expenses.

'Kenny's system was fantastic,' recalls Skelton. 'He had scouts graded one to three. The threes didn't get paid. The twos got a certain amount, but not much.'

The number-one scouts also got a one-off sum of £1,000 if one of their discoveries passed the ten-game mark for the first team. There was a significant incentive culture in place at United at the time, from the first team – where moderate wages were supplemented by generous win bonuses – all the way down to those occupying more casual staff positions, such as Skelton. United, to their credit and future benefit, were taking youth development seriously at the time. Scouts such as Skelton were their eyes on the world of potential talent and, in time, potential profit. It made sense to keep them motivated – not that money was the reason Skelton spent so much of his time standing on the sidelines, inserting observations into a little notebook.

Dundee United's scouting tentacles stretched far and wide. Even the west of Scotland, as well as the Central Belt, was regarded as fair game when it came to recruiting youngsters. Jim McLean often said that there would be no choice when presented with two players of equal quality, one from the west and one from the east coast. He would always go with the player born on the west coast. This was due, he explained, to the grit and desire almost guaranteed to be imbued in a player who had survived what McLean believed was a tougher, more unforgiving environment.

According to McLean, those from the east coast just don't have it so hard. It is one reason why United commandeered a team in the west called Hamilton Thistle to use as a vehicle for their S [Schoolboy] form signings. This nursery team arrangement started in the early '80s and continued until the mid-'90s, under the guidance of youth director Graeme Liveston, another former teacher who was employed by United and whose stock remains high in the game in Scotland.

'There was no youth development league at that time and we were keen to bring all our S-forms together,' Liveston explains. 'We played under the "Hamilton Thistle" banner because the best youth league to play in at that time was called the Scottish Amateur Youth League, which was centred in the west of Scotland – in Glasgow, Lanarkshire, Ayrshire and Renfrewshire.' Liveston concurs with McLean's view that there was a more combative edge to those who grew up on the west coast of Scotland, whether that be down to economic reasons or because boys' football in Glasgow and its environs tended to be a more competitive environment.

'Duncan came down to play with that particular team,' continues Liveston, who remembers McLean telling him, 'This boy is exceptional,' and to keep an eye on him. 'He was Under-14 at the time,' continues Liveston. 'To me, he lacked a bit of coordination. But it just shows how much insight Jim McLean had – he was spot on.'

Ferguson played up front with Stuart Gallacher – who was an S-form signing at Dundee, United's rivals and near neighbours, and who then had a brief spell with Manchester United. It would be cheering to report that Gallacher and Ferguson struck up a profitable partnership, but this seems not to have been the case. 'Duncan hardly ever spoke at that age,' recalls Liveston. 'He didn't say much about anything. But I remember it was May, because the season was finishing off. He came up to me at a game down in Ayr. It was the first time he had really spoken to me about anything very much and he said, "See that Stuart Gallacher, he has not passed the ball to me once this season!" That's all he ever talked to me about – his pigeons and Stuart Gallacher!'

Their careers took different paths in the end, but, like Ferguson, Gallacher graduated to the Premier Division. However, having signed with Dunfermline, he suffered dreadful misfortune on his debut against Celtic. Mere minutes into the game, Gallacher snapped his cruciate ligament; his professional career all but ended there and then, at the age of 19. It was a cruel reminder that even when someone appears to have made the breakthrough, the dream of earning a living from football can be destroyed in an instant. Later, Gallacher collapsed with a previously undetected heart problem while training with Bathgate, having dropped into the ranks of the junior game. He never played again.

At Dundee United, talented youngsters had a better chance of flourishing than at most other clubs. If a teenager showed any kind of promise as a footballer in Scotland at the time, then it was almost inevitable that he would be invited to attend trials with United. And it was equally likely that, given the choice, he would decide to sign for United, since they were garnering a reputation for giving young talent a platform. They were also regarded as one of the top teams in Europe at the time, having given Manchester United a run for their money in 1985 in the UEFA Cup and then reaching the final of the same tournament two years later.

Tannadice was an attractive place to be, no question. However, there was some reason for disquiet, and it came in the shape of the notorious 'four-by-four-year' – in other words, eight-year – contracts they specialised in. For investing in talent, United felt they deserved security in return, although this was not a deal many of the talented, precocious youngsters, Ferguson among them, were willing to comply with – not once they had established themselves, at any rate. 'All the other clubs said it was terrible at the time, but they all want to do it now,' points out Skelton.

Given that Ferguson's career involved so many eyebrow-raising transfer fees, it is little wonder that those involved with his development in his early years felt they – or at least their clubs – deserved to benefit from some sort of trickle-down effect, particularly when these redoubtable figures involved in Ferguson's early football life observed just how conscious United were of safeguarding their own assets.

Although Skelton earned a generous reward from the sale of Ferguson, there are other starlets he claims to have found, and yet for whom, as he puts it, he 'didn't get a slice of the action'.

'That annoyed me,' he says, before trotting off a list of admittedly impressive talents to which United were alerted but for which Skelton received no 'finder's fee', for whatever reason. The list includes Christian Dailly, who joined Derby County from United and earned 67 caps for Scotland; and Alex Cleland, who left United for Rangers and then joined Everton. These players were also first found by Skelton, although he didn't cash in the way he did for Ferguson.

'I should have got a quarter of 1 per cent of £500,000 for Dailly,' says Skelton. 'They said I didn't sign him. But it was me who found him, I can tell you that for free.'

ICI felt particularly sore as they watched Ferguson continue to rise through the ranks after being, in their view, torn from their clutches in the first place. 'He was scouted here and yet we got nothing,' complains McIlvaney, whose club could have done with the financial help. In 2001, they made enormous efforts to raise £75,000 to purchase the well-appointed Earlsgate social and recreation clubhouse, set in surprisingly picturesque grounds, and which, as is the way of things, has since been demolished to make way for an Asda depot. At grassroots level, such battles are commonplace.

'Jim McLean came down here once; he was a dour man,' recalls McIlvaney. 'It was for a trial game. He asked if he could have the place on a Saturday morning. What he did was get a team from Dundee and a team made up of trialists from other parts of Scotland to play against each other.'

McIlvaney arranged the referee, the linesmen and even put up the goals and nets himself. 'And he never even gave us so much as a ball in return,' he says. 'I even paid the referees, and I never even got so much as a thank you.'

Taylor was slightly more forceful with his demands. He wasn't prepared to take no for an answer, as a row threatened to break out following confirmation that Ferguson had agreed to become an S-form signing at United. Carse were furious that there appeared to be nothing in it for them, although suspicions were raised when the doggedly non-flamboyant Taylor suddenly began flying abroad on holiday, to the amusement of many. Whether or not Auld Dick was weighed in personally we will never know, but, when we met, he stressed how determined he was to make sure the club were looked after.

Indeed, Taylor made his own way to Tannadice, telling the receptionist that he was there to speak with Jim McLean and he wasn't prepared to budge until the manager had emerged from his office to see him.

'Oh, Mr McLean can't see you, I am afraid,' he was told, to which Taylor replied, 'Now, wait a minute. I am in my 60s and have come all the way up from Stirling, and you are telling me I can't see the manager?'

Taylor recalled: 'I just planted my backside down on the sofa in reception and said I won't be leaving until he comes and sees me, it's as simple as that. Eventually, he came out.' Before long, McLean was 'muttering an apology' and handing his dogged visitor a cheque for £5,000, written out to Carse Thistle.

Taylor was grateful. He had assumed McLean would just fling a ball at him, 'Then tell me to get lost.'

And what did Carse Thistle do with the money that they eventually extracted from Dundee United for Ferguson? 'We bought a minibus,' Taylor revealed. 'Seen it just the other day. It's in a scrapyard in Alloa.'

CHAPTER 5

The New Breed

After three hours of football, the Scottish Cup replay had gone into extra time at Tannadice. East Fife were still lamenting their inability to see out a 1–0 lead in their third-round tie against United, from two divisions above them. Duncan Ferguson, who was just a matter of weeks into his 20s, hadn't played more than a handful of first-team games for Dundee United, but the East Fife supporters all knew who he was – he had the swagger of a fearless teenager, yet in this case such uninhibited confidence wasn't misplaced.

Each time he got the ball he was one step ahead of everyone else on the pitch. For such a tall player, he was surprisingly unpredictable and had excellent close control, not to mention being a menace in the air. It wasn't hard to see what all the fuss had been about since his debut three months earlier, when he had come on as a substitute against Rangers.

When United's chance came in extra time, it fell to Ferguson. 'I'd like to say he mesmerised ten opponents and then struck an unstoppable shot past East Fife goalkeeper Ray Charles, but it wasn't quite like that,' says Donald Walker, an East Fife fan who witnessed Ferguson's first senior goal on a wintry night at Tannadice. 'In fact, the goal of the game was the one from Stuart Wilson that had put East Fife ahead – it was later voted BBC *Sportscene*'s goal of the month.'

Still, Ferguson showed perfect composure after a through ball had spliced open the East Fife defence. His first goal in senior football was scored at the end known as the Shed. It was not struck with his head, as might have been expected. Rather, it was a neatly finished effort steered under the advancing keeper with his favoured left foot. He didn't even take a touch; he just assessed the situation and then stroked the ball home. Other players of his age and inexperience would have had just enough time to see their name in lights and make a hash of the opportunity.

Ferguson was up and running. It was the first time United had been ahead in the tie, and the strike gave Jim McLean's side a 2–1 win. As the East Fife supporters left the ground that night, there was a certain amount of pride at having taken the tie so far, but there was also regret that they had not finished off United three days earlier in the first match, when a goal in the seventh minute of injury time had saved the Tannadice club from a shock exit at Bayview Park. Ferguson hadn't played that night, so the East Fife supporters were seeing Ferguson for the first time. Indeed, it was only his third appearance in front of the home fans.

Walker recalls: 'On our way to the Tannadice exits, I saw one of my old school friends, who was clearly struggling to come to terms with mixed emotions. "That skinny laddie Ferguson," he said. "He'll never make it."'

*

Only a matter of weeks before scoring his first goal for the club against East Fife, and in what were his last days as a teenager, Duncan Ferguson stormed out of Dundee United for the first time. He had earned manager Jim McLean's displeasure by returning home to Stirling without permission in midweek. This act of ill-discipline was compounded when he arrived late at training the following day. After being fined yet again, Ferguson resolved never to return to Dundee United.

It looked like his career with United was already over. Ferguson had only recently made his breakthrough in the first team when he was sent on as a substitute at Ibrox for another teenager, Christian Dailly, in their 2–1 victory over Rangers on 10 November 1990. He started his first senior match a fortnight later, in a 3–2 defeat against Aberdeen, this time partnering Dailly, in a strike force with a combined age of 36; on this occasion he was described in *The Courier*, the local Dundee newspaper, as showing 'a lot of promise'.

And yet, despite this, and having only just tasted first-team football, Ferguson was prepared to put his career in jeopardy by returning home, burning, it seemed at the time, every bridge between Dundee and Stirling in the process.

He very nearly didn't make it, as the East Fife supporter had predicted, though rather than being thwarted by a lack of talent, as this critical fan seemed to think would be the case, Ferguson's career was knocked off course by what seemed like an act of wanton self-sabotage. However, during ten days spent at home he decided to try to mend those bridges. Presumably, having had time to think, he realised that playing football for Dundee United – even if the strict climate at the club at the time gave rise to fear and no little loathing among many of the players – was preferable to the alternative.

At the time, the Tannadice club was one of the best breeding grounds for young talent in the country – if not the best – with an enviable crop of players coming through the ranks, a wave many thought would help United's status as one of Scotland leading clubs, and perhaps even inspire them to greater heights. And even if Ferguson had wanted to play elsewhere, it simply was not possible: United were in the practice of ensuring their players signed an eight-year contract and he was barely four months into his first professional deal.

Indeed, you cannot embark on any discussion about Dundee United in this era without addressing the notorious four-by-four contracts, the issuing of which was common practice at the time. On closer inspection, Ferguson's first contract, signed in August 1990 and due to expire in July 1994, includes the line that was the source of so much of the strife. 'On expiry of this contract, the four-year option offered can be exercised,' it states, matter-of-factly. In other words, if United wished it, then the player in question was effectively signing up for a length of eight years. When compared to the temporary deals favoured today, and in the post-Bosman era the dramatic way in which power has swung from clubs to players and their agents, it seems almost Victorian. Even at the time the policy, one that all clubs were within their rights to pursue, appeared dangerously close to a form of serfdom.

'United, I accept, used it to their full advantage,' says current club secretary Spence Anderson, who was then on the club's administration staff. 'It does rather seem a bit one-sided, however,' he concedes. 'United had the option to continue the contract or not.'

Of course now, when clubs fear such long-term financial commitment, players actively *seek* such security. Back then, however, United's contractual arrangements felt restrictive; the younger players complained that their careers were being hindered. 'It was a constant source of frustration, and it encouraged the first signs of rebellion from the younger ones,' says Grant Johnson, who, like many of Ferguson's peers at United, is an erudite witness in a time of great change at the club. Now a partner with the Dundee-based law firm Thorntons, after a football career that saw him turn out for Huddersfield Town, as well as Montrose and Brechin City back in Scotland, Johnson was particularly alert to the growing sense of frustration then felt by the younger players – indeed, he too had quit United for a spell in order to continue his studies at university in Birmingham. Because he stayed on until fifth year at school, Johnston arrived at Tannadice a year later than Ferguson, but he had the same chores to apply himself to; teamed up in twos, the apprentices would be given tasks such as cleaning boots, setting up the pitch for training and even cleaning the manager's car.

'I was one of the lucky ones,' says Johnson. 'Because I was already 19, I only signed a three-by-three [six year] contract – and I actually saw out the contract, one of the few who did.' He describes money – or, more accurately, the lack of it – as being a 'constant source of irritation' among the younger players. Ray McKinnon, another of the young talents coming through, actually signed an *extension* to his four-by-four deal. 'At one point he was on an 11-year contract, would you believe,' recalls Johnson. 'What the players were offered by the club was a lump sum in exchange for a three-year contract, so there were some who were effectively signing their lives away.'

As an apprentice, Ferguson was guaranteed £45 per week, while he would earn another £30 each time he made the first-team pool. On 2 August 1990, Ferguson signed his first professional contract. This secured him the princely sum of £160 per week. An extra payment of £72 was included if he made the first-team pool, while another £100 extra was earned if the team then won, and £50 for a draw. Of course, all of this hinged on Ferguson adhering to club rules, something which was not, by any means, a given.

McLean had already shown that he was more than willing to freeze players out of football altogether if they challenged the seemingly never-ending nature of these deals. However, he was also open to accepting an about-turn, providing it included an apology. John Clark – with whom Ferguson would become especially friendly during their days together at United – had felt compelled to repent a few years earlier, having also tired of the strict regime at the club. The versatile Clark, who could play in defence, midfield or attack, returned to Tannadice after a brief spell spent working on his father's fishing boat in the Firth of Forth.

Ferguson, too, quickly relented after his own decision to walk out. Having weighed everything up, Ferguson phoned McLean and asked for the opportunity to 'review' – as he described it, or at least how McLean said he described it – his career at United.

McLean and his coaches had already been closely monitoring his progress amid growing doubt about his worth. His discipline was poor and he had not been the outstanding youth player that they thought he would be. Although Ferguson was only 18 years old when he made his debut at Ibrox, he turned 19 the following month. While he had been a valued member of the United side that won the BP Youth Cup against Hibs on penalties in May 1990 – he is described as a 'six-foot-plus target man' in the programme – Ferguson was a comparatively late developer in first-team terms.

United were not a club who held players back if they thought they were good enough. Dailly, for example, made his competitive debut aged just 16, while John O'Neil, another of Ferguson's peers, did so at 17. In an article in *The Courier* from February 1990, the author – 'the sports editor' – conducts a detailed look at the talent coming through at the time. Surprisingly, and though he broke through later that same year, Ferguson doesn't rate a mention. In addition, he isn't included in the squad photograph for the 1990–91 season. In all, there are 27 players staring back at the camera. But there is no Ferguson.

'There was uncertainty about Duncan – we were not quite sure what to do with him,' recalls Paul Sturrock. Although only in his early 30s, Sturrock was then a coach at the club. The former winger was a loyal servant who played with United all of his career – he was one of the old guard. As well as his dashing wing play, his habit of wearing his socks rolled down while his untucked shirt flapped outside his shorts also ensured that he stood out during his playing days.

Despite this slovenly look, something else also distinguished Sturrock – he had inherited Andy Gray's mantle as being the undoubted favourite of manager Jim McLean. When he was offered a job on McLean's coaching staff, Sturrock accepted it, something he regrets now. Although his effectiveness was being hampered by injury, he was only 32 when he stopped playing to become a member of McLean's backroom team. 'Jim McLean was a hard man to say no to,' he says.

Sturrock was involved in the discussions about whether Ferguson was worth keeping on. They eventually decided that he was. 'His height was the key factor,' recalls Sturrock. One idea that had been mooted was to send Ferguson on loan to Forfar Athletic, where Paul Hegarty, the former United skipper, was now manager. Significantly, United wanted to try Ferguson out as a centre-half at Forfar. It is a switch that Hegarty had himself made on joining United from Hamilton Accies, where he had played as a striker.

'They were obviously swithering about him at centre-forward – they were wondering, "Can he do it?"' recalls Johnson, who played with Ferguson at youth, reserve and first-team level. 'Duncan was unusual,' he adds. 'What you would normally do is go into the reserve team, which was still quite hard to get into because of the depth of squad at the time. Obviously from there, if you did well, then you would get into the first team.'

To Johnson, it almost seemed as if Duncan bypassed the reserves. 'He had those games at centre-half and you were thinking, "Do they not rate him at centre-forward?"' he says. 'And then he seemed to miss out the reserves and went into the first team at centre-forward.' It isn't true that Ferguson was allowed to skip the reserves completely; he had scored 12 times in 19 appearances for the second string prior to his first-team call-up.

The good form he had shown in front of goal for the reserves led to him being called up for his first-team debut at Ibrox, when he came on as a second-half substitute and helped earn his side victory. He was involved in the build-up to his side's first goal, as United recovered from going a goal down to win 2–1, thanks to a Darren Jackson double. John Brown, who played at centre-half that day for Rangers, can still remember being taken aback by Ferguson's prowess with the ball at his feet, as well as his physicality.

'He came on and turned the game, that tells you what a good

player he was,' remembers Brown. 'Goughie [Richard Gough] and myself thought we could handle the majority of opponents, but that afternoon he destroyed us.

'Darren Jackson and Duncan were a great partnership – Darren was a hungry player and Duncan was there to be physical and knock centre-halves on their backside, but he was also so comfortable with the ball at his feet – I could tell that even then,' adds Brown. A fortnight later, and just two days after Margaret Thatcher's resignation as prime minister, Ferguson was picked to play from the start for the first time against Aberdeen, whose 3–2 victory displaced United at the top of the Premier Division table. Even though his side had lost, McLean described the game as the 'best I have ever been involved in'. Much of his enthusiasm stemmed from the fact that seven of United's first team that day were products of the United scouting system. Ferguson's own progress was almost immediately interrupted when, prior to the next game against St Mirren, he endured the first injury setback of his first-team career. He missed the trip to Paisley because of an ankle knock, but a more potentially damaging episode as far as his football ambitions were concerned occurred a few days later.

Despite all this tangible evidence that he was beginning to make it in the game, Ferguson was then prepared to place his entire career in jeopardy days afterwards when he decided to quit the club after being fined for persistent breaches of club discipline. Perhaps he was influenced by the recent decision made by Eddie Conville, his best friend at United, to leave Tannadice to continue his studies after being advised to stop playing football due to a chronic pelvic problem, although he did later make a short comeback. It was clear that Ferguson was already beginning to buck against McLean's strict regime, even if, on this occasion, he also returned – and with his tail between his legs.

In a newspaper article that includes quotes from Ferguson (though it reads as though they have been placed in his mouth by McLean), the player conceded that everything that had happened to him in a disciplinary context at Tannadice had been 'all my own fault'. He acknowledged that he was the 'only one who can sort it out'.

He sounded humble, adding: 'I appreciate that Dundee United is a good club for a youngster to be with because of the opportunities the manager is willing to give teenagers like myself.'

McLean accepted Ferguson's mea culpa. However, the reconciliation didn't last long between the pair.

One incident that has since passed into folklore at Tannadice sums up how the players viewed the hard-to-please McLean – the younger ones, at least. 'Andy McLaren, John O'Neil and Duncan were a bit naughty, and I got them to whitewash a wall of the gymnasium,' recalls Sturrock. 'When he came back 20 minutes later to check on their progress, he was confronted by a sight that stopped him in his tracks. 'They had been busy, all right,' he says. 'On the wall was written: "Jim McLean's a cunt".'

Sturrock went off to retrieve McLean, who came down from his office to see for himself. 'He directed some bluster at the players,' Sturrock remembers. 'To be fair, he was trying not to laugh, too. He took it the right way.'

However, he wasn't known for always being so reasonable. Indeed, there was normally only one way – McLean's way. McLean's methods were often criticised. 'Jim's problem, for me, was that while his message was nearly always correct, if it is delivered in the same way every time then it is not always received,' remembers Michael O'Neill, whose experience with McLean helped inform his own progress in management, from Brechin City to the Northern Ireland international team. 'It was rammed down your throat. If you don't do this, if you don't do that, your life will be miserable.'

Sturrock is of the same opinion: 'He didn't understand the "carrot-on-the-end-of-the-stick" approach – with him it was just the stick.' Even Sturrock admits that McLean was too hard on his players: 'He didn't realise that he could turn people's heads by being their friend, or at least getting respect from them – he did not have the character for that.'

Previous first-team players had been more servile and McLean could not understand why these new players were not grateful for the chance to join United, like their predecessors had been. Of course, theirs had been a different era, when staying at the same club for an entire career was common. O'Neill recalls: 'These new players came in. They called themselves the "new breed". I used to say, more like half-breed.'

There was a struggle of wills within the club, waged between McLean and the players, and also between the players themselves, with the more established stars wary of any new arrivals coming in to threaten their position in the team and, just as significantly, their ability to earn both appearance and win bonuses. So it wasn't completely true that McLean did not understand the concept of a carrot-on-the-end-of-a-stick. Indeed, many would contend that United's success in the 1980s was pinned to the system of financial incentives, where on-field success was rewarded in the form of a fuller pay packet at the end of the week.

'You had around thirty players who could potentially play in the first team and only fourteen could be named in the match squad in those days – eleven in the starting line-up and three on the bench,' recalls Johnson. 'It was a really low basic wage, but if you got in that squad of fourteen you got extra money, which could more than double your wages and, if you were in a team that won, your wages might be as much as tripled. The problem was the majority of the younger players were in and out of the team. So on a given week you could be struggling to pay the bills or you would be flush. But we were all in it together. That built a bond.'

The older generation was suspicious of the influx of floppy-haired teenagers, while these Young Turks saw the more senior professionals as being in league with the coaching staff. In some cases, they resented the older players for not having offered more advice on the contractual front. 'The likes of David Narey, Paul Hegarty and Maurice Malpas had been fantastic players, but they had been at United all their careers, and part of that was because they, too, had been locked into contracts,' says O'Neill. 'The younger players looked at them and asked: "Why didn't you come to us and warn us about that?"'

In amongst it all stood McLean, a dominant presence at the club since 1971, when he had crossed the road after a spell coaching Dundee, for whom he had also played. The pop star posturing of the modern-day player was anathema to the dour traditionalist, but in no way should McLean be considered an out-dated dinosaur. In some areas, he was before his time – something else that created friction. According to Dailly, McLean was several steps ahead of other managers. 'We had a psychologist and a nutritionist and fitness coaches and the best football coaches you could get,' he says. 'I was getting stuff in 1990 that people are only now beginning to bring in. That was Jim Mclean. He was surrounding himself with the best in the business. He was miles ahead. Miles ahead.'

For those who wanted to make the best of themselves, such as Dailly, the support system was in place to do so. However, some of the older players were suspicious of these new fangled ideas, while the younger ones mocked the idea of having to eat correctly and warm-down after matches. The thing was, while he was forward-thinking in many areas, McLean could not accept other aspects of modern football, such as the restlessness of the young players and the creeping transfer of power from the club to the players and their agents.

For McLean, it was enough simply to be considered a professional footballer, to be paid for the privilege of playing football. If it is not too much of a stretch to link this teetotal Presbyterian with a dance instructor, McLean's philosophy could be summed up in the challenge issued at the start of *Fame*, the American series initially aired in 1983 – the year United won their first and, to date, only Scottish league title.

'You want fame?' asks the character played by Debbie Allen at the end of each episode's opening credits. 'Well, fame costs. And right here is where you start paying – in sweat.'

Ferguson didn't really see the need for such a painful-sounding transaction. George Skelton, the scout who recommended Ferguson to United, recalls watching a training session just after Christmas one year. 'They were doing 100-yard sprints up the ash,' he recalls. 'They had 16 or 17 seconds to complete it and then 30 seconds to get back to the start and complete it again.'

According to Skelton, even David Narey, United's genuinely world-class centre-half, was hanging over the railings, being sick. 'I said to McLean: "What are you trying to do?"' continues Skelton. McLean replied that he was trying to 'knock the plum duff out of them'. Pointing towards the lanky striker, McLean told Skelton that he was aware what Ferguson was doing; making sure he raced next to the slower, older players. 'See that lazy pig, he is racing with Maurice Malpas because he knows he can beat him without putting the effort in,' McLean complained.

It was clear that, in Ferguson, McLean had been presented with his greatest test. However, rather than stand back and enjoy watching the explosive show, most players had to concentrate on their own battles with the hard-to-please manager. It wasn't just Ferguson versus McLean. It felt like *everybody* versus McLean, including the press and supporters, some of whom got personal visits from the manager at their homes after sending even mildly critical letters about team selection matters. Perhaps one could understand McLean's indignation at being criticised, since what he had already done for United was unprecedented at the club – and, he and many others felt while observing another new wave of talent coming through, that there was more success to come. 'It was a club that I could plainly see, even having just got in through the door, was laden down with talent,' says O'Neill. 'And they had this raft of young players coming through. At the head of that raft of young players was Duncan.'

After a slow start, Ferguson was proving hard to ignore. After getting off the mark against East Fife, his first league goal was the winner in a 1–0 victory over Dunfermline at the start of March and then, 11 days later, came his first headed goal in the 3–1 Scottish Cup victory over Dundee. He was up and running. The fears of those who questioned whether he would make the breakthrough and instead disappear without trace, just another of Scottish football's lost boys, seemed unfounded, and he posted further notice of his intent with the strike from close range against St Johnstone that sent Dundee United into another Scottish Cup final at the end of his first season as a senior player. 'Hopefully scoring as he did shows him the advantage of being in the box,' grumbled McLean afterwards.

Hard though it might have been to discern, McLean was genuinely relishing the prospect of working with the young players that were coming through at the time. While famed for his curmudgeonly ways, football was his lifeblood and the development of players an overriding concern. 'He was desperate to see everyone fulfil their potential, not necessarily for their own benefit, or even his own, but for the club,' says O'Neill. McLean may have made it a harsh environment for others, but then it could prove brutal for him too, partly because of the demands he placed on himself as he worked all the hours to benefit a football club perched on a hill above the city. He later lamented that such commitment came at a cost to his family life, with his two sons rarely seeing him as they grew up. While United consistently punched above their weight in Europe, there were knockbacks – many of them occurring at Hampden Park. United lost their sixth successive Scottish Cup final under McLean against Motherwell, with Ferguson playing a mostly anonymous part for only the first 45 minutes before being substituted at half-time, suffering from double vision after a head knock. United went on to lose 4–3 in extra-time. At least Ferguson was out of harm's way when four United players were red carded after the final whistle, having complained too vociferously about Motherwell's winner being allowed to stand, with a boot reported to have been tossed towards referee David Syme.

Just to add to the emotion of the day, the Fir Park side were managed by McLean's brother, Tommy; their father, Thomas, had passed away only three days before the game. Uncharacteristically, and admirably, given the circumstances, Jim McLean tried hard to be upbeat on the team coach on the way home to Dundee from Glasgow.

'I was the only one sitting beside him,' recalls George Skelton. 'He started speaking about the young boys coming through, like Duncan; he was being really enthusiastic, about Duncan in particular. And then this bus came past ours, full of United fans, and they were all up against the window, shouting and swearing at him. It was terrible. You might not warm to him, but the guy had done so much for the club.'

Although he kept hinting that his time had come, McLean's retirement party – not that anyone could imagine the manager hosting anything that sounded remotely like fun – seemed a long way off. Indeed, despite the challenges they presented, McLean glimpsed the new wave of talent coming through at the club and found an excuse to remain *in situ*. Why let someone else gain the benefit from such potential? He felt the club could go places again.

At the start of the 1991–92 season, hopes were again high at Tannadice, despite the Scottish Cup final defeat and the absence of European football for the first time in 13 seasons. With Darren Jackson suspended – he was among those shown red cards after the Scottish Cup final – Ferguson was told he would be starting against Celtic in the opening game of the campaign, and the prospect certainly didn't seem to faze the 20 year old.

Sharing both lodgings and a bedroom at the time with the striker, Gordon Parks recalls waking up in the middle of the night on the eve of the season, roused from his slumbers by the smell of cigarette smoke. Desperately seeking a chance to impress at Tannadice, Parks had turned in early prior to the next day's trip to Celtic Park for the reserve side. Now, suddenly awake, he peered over to the bed where his roommate was supposed to be sleeping, ahead of his own responsibilities in the No. 11 shirt against Celtic at Tannadice, at the start of a new season – Ferguson's first as a bona fide member of the first-team squad.

Parks could make out the silhouette of the top half of the striker's body, since he was sitting up in bed. 'I had been trying to be conscientious,' remembers Parks. 'I had been trying to get some sleep. But the garage in Monifieth, where our digs were, sold bevvy, so he had gone down and bought six bottles of K cider and a packet of fags. And there he was, having his cider and smoking a fag. All you could see was this red ember glowing in the distance. And then he just tosses the fag end at me, says I am boring.'

Ferguson – who the match programme reveals was being sponsored that season by Riddlers Coaches of Abroath – went out later that same day and scored in a rousing clash with Liam Brady's Celtic, with United again losing out 4–3 for the second competitive match in succession. Michael O'Neill describes it as the afternoon 'when Dunc came of age'. O'Neill scored twice and then Ferguson struck an equaliser for United before Celtic took the points with a late winner from John Collins. But according to O'Neill, Ferguson had been the star. 'When I first saw him, he had looked very raw and hugely left-sided,' recalls O'Neill. 'But he was brilliant that day. I remember running forward – I was playing centre of midfield – and he was taking the ball in, or knocking it down to you. He was unplayable.'

'That just summed up Dunc,' adds Parks, whose own outing for the reserves at Parkhead on the same afternoon had proved far less memorable, despite his admirable abstinence in the early hours of the same morning.

*

Dave Bowman, who played for United throughout Ferguson's time at the club, recalls hearing the striker long before being able to see him. 'He had a car, a Capri I think, with a stupid horn,' he says. He remembers Ferguson used to press it when he was outside Dens Park, home of United's rivals Dundee, just 200 yards further up the street. 'It would still be going off when he stopped outside Tannadice,' he smiles.

O'Neill has another car-related story about Ferguson, one

concerning a battered blue Escort that he drove up to Dundee on a Monday morning. Apparently, Ferguson had been out the night before and met a soldier in a club in Stirling. 'He was about to go to war in the Gulf,' says O'Neill. 'Dunc had given the boy a leather jacket in exchange for his car. It lasted about a couple of days before it conked out.'

Ferguson was one of a kind. He even had his own language. 'Instead of calling you "a prick", he would call you "a nude book" or "a nudie",' recalls O'Neill. 'That became his catchphrase.' There was a hapless element to his japery. Parks was just another youngster who felt the wrath of McLean on occasion. Now a football writer at the *Daily Record*, Parks recalls being ordered to paint a toilet block with Ferguson and then seeing their handiwork go up in flames as his cohort injudiciously pulled a lighter from the pocket of his Bukta tracksuit and lit a cigarette.

As the punishments became ever more imaginative, Ferguson must have needed to remind himself why he was in Dundee. There were times when he didn't appear to be spending much time playing football, certainly. United were installing a new AstroTurf pitch at Gussie Park, next door to Tannadice, and he is said to have helped dig so many trenches as punishment that his fellow workmen presented him with a hard hat with 'DF' written across the front. 'In the first two years I was there, he spent more time working with the groundsmen than playing, that's no joke,' says Dailly. 'He would spend a week just painting the stand or something. I did sympathise. But the groundsmen all loved him. He would buy and bring them sandwiches, even though he didn't have much money himself. He was that type of guy.'

News of this eventually found its way to Stirling. Ferguson's father harangued McLean during the course of regular phone calls to his office at Tannadice, as the impression that his son was living an Oliver Twist-type existence in Dundee began to take a grip in the media. 'His dad was a handful,' recalls Sturrock. 'Ginger hair, ginger moustache.' On one occasion, Ferguson was left out of a reserve match at Brechin for a disciplinary matter that had occurred during the week. Unfortunately for Sturrock, Ferguson Senior had travelled to watch the game. 'His old man came down from the back of the stand,' remembers Sturrock. 'He told me that if I didn't get his son on, he was going to punch my lights out!

'When I look back on it now, it was quite funny. But he was deadly serious.'

It paid to read the small print on contracts issued by United at the time. One stipulation was that the player had to be resident 'in the Dundee area while employed by Dundee United Football Club' – with this condition actually written into each contract. This radius was interpreted as about 14 miles from Dundee's city centre. Although it might have frustrated some, it does seem a reasonable way to seek to foster team spirit, and supporters like to think of players having a firmer association with the city where their club is based than training there. Many of the players were from Dundee in any case. If not, and the player involved did not have his own house, then United provided digs.

For a youngster such as Ferguson, with no funds to buy his own property, staying in rented accommodation was the only option. United had a network of homes spread throughout the city where young players would be supplied with lodgings. Even those who arrived from the club on big-money moves were not spared such an initiation. O'Neill was the club's record signing when he joined from Newcastle United in August 1989 for £350,000 and he might have expected some special treatment. But no. 'United were a club that humbled you,' says O'Neill. McLean told him: 'You'll not be staying in a hotel, you'll be staying in digs'.

'And he puts me in digs with Duncan Ferguson,' continues O'Neill. For the Northern Irishman, in the middle of studying for an A level in maths, it was far from an ideal arrangement. 'I always remember getting stuff out of my car,' he says. 'I had loads of stuff, as I had dumped everything in and driven up from Newcastle.'

Ferguson helped O'Neill unpack. He had a small bin and in it were books, rulers and pencils. 'Duncan picked up the bin and said: "What's this?"' recalls O'Neill. 'He was like, "What the fuck?" I explained to him what I was doing and he was totally shocked. He was young, probably only about 17 at the time. But he could just not comprehend that I was also intending to study.'

After a few weeks, United put O'Neill into a flat and then he bought his own place in Monifieth just inside the city limits. It wasn't that he had fallen out with Ferguson. 'We hit it off straightaway', recalls O'Neill. Indeed, Ferguson, upon learning about

O'Neill's new living arrangements, had a proposal for his new friend to consider. Understandably, the vision of being talked into erecting a doocot in his garden flashed through O'Neill's mind. But Ferguson was nothing if not unpredictable. 'He came in and had a look around,' recalls O'Neill. 'He had a suggestion: "Could I keep a greyhound at the back of the house?" I didn't really like dogs, particularly greyhounds.

'He was always suggesting daft little things like that. "Och, don't worry, I'll come in and look after it," he said. And I was thinking: that means you'd be down here everyday. That would be the worst thing ever!'

However, Ferguson's charms often proved irresistible. And most importantly, he could play. 'For a team who were basing their whole living on the win bonuses they got, that tempered their reaction to his wild ways,' recalls Gordon Parks, who, although he did not play for the first team, recalls the fuss made over win bonuses, which could be set at sums as high as £800 against Rangers or Celtic. 'The established players were just glad to have someone in the side who was as good as he was. And he was fantastic.' However, even then, Parks concedes, Ferguson could be maddeningly inconsistent, able to turn it off and on seemingly at will. 'He had an almost psychopathic approach to football; even then you could say it was almost devoid of joy,' he says. 'He was motivated by the battle. He is a complex personality, a lot brighter than many gave him credit for, and a lot more generous too. But then he had a devil on his shoulder, he could be cruel, and cut people to the quick.'

Parks got on well with Ferguson, but he quickly detected a hard, difficult-to-like streak in the player, especially during an episode that he describes as one of the 'worst things I have seen in a dressing-room', involving a young trialist from Germany who was given a less than warm welcome.

'His parents were in the army and he stayed over there,' recalls Parks. 'He was skint and they had obviously bought him a new suit – a shocker. It was a burgundy number.

'The guy turned up for training on Monday with this suit on. He was just a kid. Big Dunc terrorised him. That was the ethos at the time: if someone came in for a trial or a reserve game, they would get picked on. You'd try and make sure that they never performed, that they would not jump ahead of you in the queue for a first-team place.

'On the Thursday, when the guy was supposed to be leaving to go back home, Dunc cut the sleeves of his suit, cut his trousers into shorts, cut his shirt, his tie and shoelaces, socks. Everything.'

Whenever anything like a dressing-room prank happens at a football club, news quickly spreads. Players filed into the room. They were sitting on the benches, on the windowsill; they were waiting for the show to begin. 'This poor boy came out of the shower,' continues Parks. 'Even drying himself in front of strangers had proved difficult for him all week.

'And then he reaches for his suit. Everyone is starting to laugh. I remember thinking, there is no fun in this, it is damaging the guy. He continued to put his foot through socks, the arms of his suit fell off – I thought it was abuse, but that was the mentality. Duncan was a ringleader, it was a brutal environment.'

According to Parks, it was an extremely uncomfortable experience. 'But it meant nothing to Dunc,' he says.

'You had to be a certain type of character to survive at United at the time,' remembers Ray McKinnon, along with Ferguson, one of the most highly rated of the emerging players, and who grew up in a housing scheme in Dundee. 'The ones who succeeded were the rough-and-ready ones who could take criticism. You had to have a bit of steel.' Ferguson's cause was helped by his height, but he was also keen to improve his physique by lifting weights, and he wasn't shy in showing everyone the results. 'He'd do all these muscles poses, and so we just called him "Muscles",' recalls Christian Dailly, while McKinnon interpreted Ferguson's willingness to walk through the home dressing-room with his top off as a statement of intent on behalf of the new breed, who were pawing the ground in their determination to become top dogs at Tannadice. 'That could be misconstrued as big-headed, but Dunc had transformed his body,' he says. 'And for us young kids at the time, it was delivering a message: yes, we are coming to take your place.'

And yet the same players who complained about the strict environment also sometimes helped maintain it: brutality bred brutality. They perhaps felt that because they had suffered, others had to as well. Many had become hardened by the culture of fear. Tannadice could be a harsh, forbidding place. The young trialist from Germany wasn't the only one who left Dundee feeling traumatised.

'You would come in on trial and guys like Andy McLaren would pick the ball up and smash it off you, and not laugh,' recalls McKinnon. 'It would be like: "Here's how it is, mate, you can get to fuck – we are not passing the ball to you. Who do you think you are? You are not coming here to take my place."'

Yet it also strengthened the bond among the younger players already there. They learned to look out for one another. With Ferguson usually heavily involved, they socialised together, sometimes gathering at flats – usually Grant Johnson's – in the town for a Thursday night card school, while also often heading to Tally Ho's, a pub in the city's West Port area, for an earlier in the week blow-out (handily, Wednesday was usually the players' day off, if there was no midweek fixture). This particular bar was popular with local students, and the United players discovered that their status did not matter a jot with Northern Irish hockey players and other incomers to Dundee, and who packed the bar on midweek nights. It was a place where the players felt they could behave like any other 19 and 20 year olds. Why shouldn't they, too, be able to let their hair down?

Fionan Lynch, a barman at the time, recalls a memorable evening when Ferguson took to the stage on karaoke night, an event held each Tuesday and which was popular with United's band of young brothers because it combined discount offers on alcohol – 'we had to go to student bars because, like students, we often only had about a tenner in our pocket,' says McKinnon – as well as the promise of romance, although the cheap drink often obliterated hopes on the latter front, as Lynch recalls.

He remembers Ferguson's performance, and appearance, on one night in particular. 'Duncan Ferguson, wearing a fetching satin bomber jacket, was the drunkest player there by a factor of ten,' says Lynch. 'He kept edging nearer and nearer the stage, even though it was not his turn to sing. He was becoming more and more obnoxious, but in a gentle way, if that's possible. He never conducted himself in an aggressive manner.

'At the end of the night, he finally got up on stage, nudged whoever it was who was singing out of the way, and put the entire microphone in his mouth. Then, with arms outstretched, he let out a primal roar, with the microphone lead whiplashing around his feet. It was a memorable sight. He was becoming pretty big news by then.'

The episode is recalled with humour, even warmth. Ferguson, for all that alcohol would have contributed significantly to his lack of inhibitions, enjoyed, of course, being the centre of attention, the showman. Dailly remembers a Christmas night out which ended with Ferguson sporting a plaster on his foot after he had fallen over. Or at least it should have ended then, like it would have done with most other people, never mind a professional footballer. 'We had all gone to a nightclub and the next thing we see is Dunc on the dance floor, waving two crutches above his head,' says Dailly. 'He had gone to hospital and got a stookie put on and then come back out again!'

The next morning, the players were ordered to gather for a team meeting. 'There had been a couple of incidents, including the obvious one,' recalls Dailly. 'Jim McLean came in and said, "Where the hell is Duncan?" We were supposed to be in at 10 a.m. and it was now about 10.30 a.m., and then he comes shuffling in on his crutches. It is one of the funniest things I have ever seen. Jim McLean was just looking at him. And Dunc just said, "Sorry I am late," and sat down.'

Kicking back against the authoritarian McLean, often fuelled by alcohol, Ferguson was a confident customer. 'It was a rebellion, and the biggest rebel was Duncan – he ran the show,' says Parks. 'He thought he was untouchable; we all did to an extent back then, I suppose.' On another occasion, in a nightclub in Kirkintilloch this time, somebody threw a chair through a window. 'Big Dunc was still standing there with a pint, still with the swagger,' says Parks. 'It was as if he was saying, "There might be a riot in this bar, but it won't affect me."'

The trouble was, he couldn't stay invincible forever.

CHAPTER 6

Fisherman's Blues

Given his ability to find trouble in the quiet fishing port of Anstruther, there is little wonder that Duncan Ferguson's early career was so blighted by scrapes with the law.

Although it is, after St Andrews, the largest settlement in the East Neuk of Fife, Anstruther is no metropolis. It isn't somewhere one would normally associate with Wild West-type dust-ups, especially not those that are infused with a cross-dressing flavour. Tempers are more likely to rise in the queue for the Anstruther Fish Bar, hailed almost annually as the best such establishment in the country. The fish bar tends to be the most happening place in the area of an evening after the doors have closed at the Scottish Fisheries Museum nearby.

Anstruther, or, as it is known by locals, Anster (pronounced 'Ainster'), is the kind of place where you are alert to the silence and the stares when you walk into a bar on a Friday night. Not that the locals are unwelcoming; it is just that they are used to being surrounded by other locals, especially in the winter months, when the second-homers – normally lawyers, bankers and accountants from either Edinburgh or Glasgow – have yet to arrive. From the conversation on the night I was there, to be judged a local means having been in the area for 'mair than 20 years'.

I have been in the town fewer than five minutes before I am being pumped with questions. What is the reason for my being here, being the one most frequently asked. It is not couched in a particularly unfriendly tone, nor do my interrogators seem particularly suspicious. But then I tell them why I have come, why I have picked a blowy autumn night to stop at this particular bar.

No, I am not on my way somewhere else, as they had presumed. I am not here in search of the road out again. I am here, I explain, because I am researching a book about Duncan Ferguson. And, crazy though it might seem, the spot could mark Ground Zero in the footballer's life. The music doesn't instantly stop with the mention of his name, but it is clear that Ferguson remains a thorny topic.

'He's just a fucking nugget,' offers one customer, before returning to his game of cards.

Welcome, then, to the Royal Hotel, a rather distressed, 12-bedroomed establishment on a street that curls up from the harbour. From a quick scan of some customer-review Internet sites, it is possible to conclude that this isn't one of Fife's premier boutique hotels. 'A mortifying experience' is the first contribution, quickly followed by another less-than-satisfied guest, who writes: 'We would rather stay in our transit with the motorbike than stay here.'

Why such an unprepossessing grog-house should feature at all in a book about Duncan Ferguson is a question even he might find difficult to answer. However, there is no doubt that the bar, with its cast of Friday-night regulars and yarn-battered walls, deserves more, much more, than a mere name-check when reflecting on the prominent episodes in the footballer's life.

Everything changed for Ferguson on the night he walked into this establishment in downtown north-east Fife, with a lady's earring clipped to one of his ears and a silk glove pulled up towards an elbow. To top the look off, Ferguson also had on a pair of sunglasses and wore a flower behind his other ear. At least, these were among the revelations provided by Karen Ketchen, the then 25-year-old barmaid, when she gave evidence at Cupar Sheriff Court several months later, Ferguson having been charged with assaulting Graham Boyter, a local fisherman.

Such startling details relating to his appearance that fateful evening encouraged me to feel a bit more confident that those in the bar might recall an incident that had occurred more than 20 years earlier. If Ferguson wanted a reaction, then he got it, all right. Surprisingly, given that this was mid-season, it was a Friday. United were due to play city rivals Dundee the following day at Dens Park. Not so surprisingly, Ferguson was injured.

But why was Ferguson in Anstruther at all? Anstruther is not a difficult place to get to from Dundee: you just cross the Tay Bridge and head along the coast. It's just not somewhere you would instantly think of going for a night out. St Andrews, with its sizeable student population, would be a more attractive option for any young reveller, or perhaps even Kirkcaldy, where Jackie O's was the nightclub *du jour* and a popular hangout for many footballers in the area at the time.

In selecting Anstruther for a visit, Ferguson was surely trying to avoid bother. If this was his intention, then he failed quite spectacularly.

What he found is that he attracted trouble. This was the case in sleepy fishing towns in Fife, just as it had already been the case in taxi queues in his hometown. Even at this early stage of his career Ferguson was already fighting the public perception of him as a trouble-maker after managing to become embroiled in a violent incident with a postman on crutches while – according to the footballer – simply waiting for a taxi in Stirling with his girlfriend. But even this wasn't the first time he had been in trouble with the law. In 1991, just a few months after he had made his first-team debut for United, he was fined £125 for butting Grant Sangster, a policeman. As one reporter later noted: a policeman, an invalid and a fisherman – it was quite a hat-trick.

It was the alarming case involving the teenage postman on crutches that helped establish in people's minds the image of Ferguson as an unreconstructed lout, and it occurred on a day – 22 August 1992 – that was already turning into one to forget for the footballer. In the afternoon, Ferguson had been sent off for the first time in his senior career. Anticipating the troubles to come in his career, his offence was a supposed head-butt, this time in a flare-up involving the St Johnstone defender John Inglis. There were enough contrasting opinions to give Ferguson the benefit of the doubt on this occasion. Jim McLean was as fierce as anyone in his defence of his player. He claimed no contact had been made, and others, too, held the view that Inglis had made far too much of the incident than was justified. Nevertheless, Ferguson was red-carded.

Just as his protests fell on deaf ears at McDiarmid Park, Ferguson's plea of innocence failed to help him when he was convicted of assaulting Paul Robertson, the postman on crutches, following a street fight that took place later the same day. Ferguson had become a marked man and was a target for provocation. However, beating up someone on crutches is not an ideal way to go about restoring a reputation, given his recent history on the streets of Stirling.

As *The Scotsman* reported, the victim of the alleged assault, Paul Robertson, 19, a postman, admitted that he had gone out of his way 'to insult, goad and provoke Ferguson', who had been waiting for a taxi with his girlfriend. Ferguson retaliated, but the footballer denied punching and kicking Robertson, a Heart of Midlothian supporter, on the head and body.

During evidence, Robertson contended that a 'slanging match' had started between him and Ferguson after the footballer's girlfriend at the time, Jolene Boyle, had accused the postman of jumping the queue for a taxi.

'He had been sent off that day,' explained Robertson in court. 'I was slagging him off about that and he was slagging me off about my crutches.' Robertson required the crutches due to a recent knee-ligament operation. His leg was also in plaster to his knee, though on the night in question that was concealed by his jeans.

Ferguson, however, could hardly have failed to notice the crutches. Robertson, it was suggested, had appeared to forget his own impaired condition, though the postman stressed in court that he had not, as was alleged, been swinging one of his crutches above his head during the fracas. But he had been abusive, telling Ferguson's girlfriend to 'shut it'. In court, Robertson admitted that some months prior to the incident he had started an argument in a pub with Ferguson. On that occasion, the footballer had ignored him.

This time, however, Robertson had gone too far. He admitted that he had called Ferguson's girlfriend a 'trollop'. But, he added, he had not moved towards her in any way that could be interpreted as threatening. Ferguson's attack, he maintained, had been excessive.

The court agreed. Ferguson was convicted and fined £200.

Remarkably, even before this case had been disposed of, Ferguson booked himself a third appointment in front of a sheriff, which brings us back to Anstruther and the bar of the Royal Hotel. It had once been a much livelier place than was evident on the occasion of my visit, I am assured.

'Places are dead here now,' says Robert Thomson. 'It's the smoking ban; people don't come out. Pubs were busier back then.' In a corridor inside the hotel, Thomson, who once owned the Masonic Arms, overlooking the harbour, recalled the night Ferguson came to town and helped put Anstruther on the map.

'They phoned my wife to come up and help; it was a real commotion,' he says. 'I was in my own pub at the time. I had to stay there. But my wife, Ella, she went up. One of the local boys, Graham Boyter, had said something. A windae was smashed.'

These details are fleshed out in newspaper reports from the time. There were others involved, not only Ferguson and Boyter. The footballer had walked into the pub – he later denied that he had been dressed in the manner suggested by the bar lady – with a group that included Eddie Conville, a then teammate at Dundee United and one of Ferguson's closest friends.

Also present was Francis Downie, a leading light in the East Neuk Dundee United supporters' club. 'It's Frank – Francis is my court name,' he later points out when I visit him.

After that particular night out with Ferguson, it was the formal version of his name that he was required to give.

*

Apart from the Dundee United connection, it is not immediately apparent why Downie and Ferguson had become close. While the footballer was aged just 20 on the night in question, Downie was 48. It means he is in his mid-60s when I visit him at his home in central Fife. Like Ferguson, he has known ups and downs since that night at the Royal Hotel. He left Anstruther, the scene of the crime, in 2004. 'It wasn't because of they cunts; they couldn't get me to leave,' he assures me, a big toe sticking out of a hole in one of his trainers. 'I split up with the wife.'

By 'they cunts', I assume he is referring to certain locals in the tight-knit community who, he contends, baited Ferguson and harassed him.

I visited Anstruther early in 2011. A long time has passed since the early 1990s. An entire way of life has disappeared. At the time of my visit, the last fishing boat had just been scrapped. Over 50 herring boats once worked out of Anstruther. However, possibly because of the lack of any real competition, it remains the hub of the East Neuk, but is now more closely associated with the music scene than fishing, given the success of local acts such as King Creosote and James Yorkston.

In what might be described as Anstruther's sole style bar, I learn that natives don't tend to move far from the area. Sitting on a stool at the Bank Bar is a former brother-in-law of Karen Ketchen, the barmaid who had given such a detailed description of Ferguson – glove, earring and all – to the police. Next to him at the bar is one of Boyter's two brothers. Graham himself is harder to pin down, however; he has moved on from Elie, to Pittenweem, I am told. Later, on a visit to Pittenweem, I learn that he has apparently just moved again, back to Anstruther. Someone else tells me that he might not remember too much about the night in question. 'He was knocked out cold,' I am informed, via a text message, after I left a letter in one of the addresses given for the itinerant Boyter, who had since moved on again. One thing is clear: the night Ferguson opted for a night out in Anstruther still holds its charge in the area. More than two decades on, it's something everyone remembers.

According to the regulars in the Bank, the equally elusive Downie hasn't been back in town for a while. When his marriage broke up, he was off. To Dundee, someone proposes. Someone else offers Glenrothes. But it's on a doorstep in the former mining village of Leslie that Downie continues to tell me his entertaining story. He is wearing jogging pants and a T-shirt, which doesn't quite cover a sizeable stomach. That makes it difficult to conjure up an image of someone able to handle himself in a physical confrontation, something he is eager to portray.

'I have had a few barnies wi' that lot since then,' he says. 'I got jumped one night, twa o' them,' he continues, before proudly adding, 'Baith o' them ended up in hospital.'

Downie hasn't ventured too far. Leslie is just 20 miles from Anstruther, as the crow flies. His house is easy to find, and sits in the shadow of Falkland Hill. After knocking on the door, I become aware of another reason why Ferguson and Downie became friends. In the anxious wait before Downie answers, it is possible to detect the gentle cooing of pigeons coming from a doocot in his back garden. 'He kept pigeons and I kept pigeons,' he later tells me, matter-of-factly. 'His are racing, mine are show.'

Downie married into football and money, he tells me, as we

continue to chat on his doorstep. His father-in-law was Jock Fleming, a former East Fife chairman.

'Something else connected Downie to Ferguson, he informs me. According to Downie, the footballer briefly dated his daughter. They had met at a Player of the Year do. In those days, with United having reaped the benefit of being seasoned European campaigners, the East Neuk Dundee United supporters' club was a vibrant group, not that it exists now.

'We had boys fae Cupar in it an' all,' explains Downie. 'They used to go wi' the Glenrothes bus, but when that kind of folded they came wi' oor one.

'We used to just get a minibus; it would go from Anstruther and go to Cupar to pick up fans.'

This came to an end when Downie got 'pissed off' with McLean. Downie recalls receiving a phone call from Priti Trivedi, the manager's secretary at the time. 'She said: "Jim McLean wants to see you about Duncan."' Downie duly travelled to Tannadice to hear what McLean had to say, which, he says, can be summed up by: 'Fuckin' Ferguson – he is fucking trouble. I can't keep him out of trouble.'

'He was nipping my head,' continues Downie, who was put out, to say the least. 'I said: "Hey, you might tell your lads what to do, but you won't tell me what to do."'

On his way out, Trivedi intercepted Downie. 'Jim has asked me to tell you to phone him whenever Duncan is in Anstruther.'

Downie doesn't sound the type to obey orders. In any case, he says, on the night in question, all Ferguson wanted was a quiet evening out, maybe a few pints, a game or two of pool. But if Ferguson wished to be incognito, why the rather outré attire? Unlikely though it seemed, in the words of one newspaper report, Ferguson had apparently chosen to adopt the look of a character from *The Jewel in the Crown*, a novel by Paul Scott about the fall of the British Raj that was later made into a television mini-series shown in the mid-1980s. It turns out that Ferguson's inspiration lay a bit closer to home, however.

'You'll mind o' Victor?' asks Downie, meaning do I remember Victor Ferreyra, a somewhat unlikely Jim McLean signing from Argentina in 1991. He gained notoriety at the end of one derby game by spitting on the Dundee skipper Jim Duffy. Ferguson, however, had noted Ferreyra's penchant for jewellery, an uncommon sight among the players at Tannadice at the time. Downie says his wife, along with Ferguson, had gone to pick up teammate Eddie Conville from Tannadice after a reserve game and ahead of a planned night out in Anstruther.

'Duncan was in Dundee and wearing a fucking earring and a necklace, and he had one black glove on! It was Christian Dailly, I think, who said: "What the hell are you wearing?" And he said: "I'm Victor."

'When he came back, he still had that on. "If Victor can wear it, I will fucking wear it," he said.'

They had started drinking in the Dreel Tavern, a bar on the high street dating back to the sixteenth century. According to Downie, Boyter, a Rangers fan, and his crowd were also there. At this stage, Ferguson had already started to be linked with a move to Ibrox.

'They were nipping his head about going to Rangers,' Downie continues. 'I was saying to them, "Look, the boy is out – he wants a quiet night, it is as simple as that." My wife was there an' all in the pub, as well as my daughter. They all went home. Then Duncan says to me: "C'mon, let's go away doon the toon, to that other pub we were in one night – the Royal." So we went doon there, and who should come in again ten minutes later but Boyter and his group.

'They started again. Eventually I said, "Look, the boy is not wanting any shite," and we were asked to leave by the proprietors. So, as we were going out the door, this guy shouts out, "Aye, yer yellow bastards!"'

And then, according to Downie, all hell broke loose.

'I got hit with a broken glass and my jersey got all torn. There was fuck all about that in the papers. There was two o' them. All Dunc did was come in to get me. He came in to defend me. He skelped the boy. Basically, that's what happened. Then the next thing we left the place and we walked up to my house.'

At 5 a.m., the police knocked on the door of Downie's house. This was the last thing Ferguson needed. At Cupar Sheriff Court in August 1993, he was convicted of assault by Sheriff Charles Smith, then sentenced the following month. At one point, he asked Ferguson to write down how much he drank each week. The piece of paper was duly handed to the sheriff, who, according to one report, literally arched an eyebrow. He urged Ferguson to attend alcohol counselling. When it came to sentencing, he chose to put Ferguson on probation for a year rather than send him to jail, although he warned the player just how close he had come to a custodial sentence. 'I have discovered I can deal with the matter other than with a prison sentence,' he said.

The footballer was described as having sat 'calmly' in the dock before being driven away in an L-registration Audi. Downie's fate, meanwhile, was judged to merit only a sentence or two in newspaper reports the following day. He was fined £150, having pleaded guilty to assault.

'The sheriff jumped on it because of who Dunc was,' Downie tells me. He adds that he knows where Sheriff Smith lives now – in Scone, a village outside Perth. Sensing some alarm on my part, he explains: 'I met him three years later. I worked for Charles Gray, the builders, at the time and we were working up in Scone. We went into a restaurant for Christmas dinner and there he is, sitting in the corner.

'I went over: "Do you no' mind o' me, pal? I am the cunt you put down wi' Duncan Ferguson."'

CHAPTER 7

Like a Leaping Salmon

The gap-toothed primal passion provided by Joe Jordan had left an indelible impression on the Scotland fans, so it was understandable that the Tartan Army ached for a replacement in the same mould. The news from Dundee United about a striker emerging with both talent and a physical presence, one with the extra cachet of having been raised in Bannockburn, was bound to create excitement.

Here, perhaps, was another totemic Scotland legend in the making. Certainly, from the evidence available, Duncan Ferguson sounded capable of providing the devil that goes down well with a hard-drinking, hard-partying element of the Tartan Army, a group who have helped mythologise the likes of Jim Baxter, Jimmy Johnstone and Willie Johnston, great Scottish talents with an appealing lustiness about them. Indeed, Baxter himself handed Ferguson a seal of approval. 'I hear big Fergie likes a few pints, loves to stay out late and gives a bit of lip in training,' he said. 'In my book he has the ingredients of a good footballer.'

The Scotland supporters were desperate for a pick-me-up after the 1990 World Cup. Scotland had come within eight minutes of qualifying for the second stage for the first time, having recovered from a defeat against Costa Rica to beat Sweden 2–1. Only a late goal in the last group game against Brazil prevented them going through.

It was natural that fans would look in the direction of the Under-21s to glimpse what the future might look like. It proved a heartening exercise. Under Craig Brown, Scotland qualified for the semi-finals of the European Championships in the 1991–92 season, knocking out a strong Germany side at the quarter-final stage.

After drawing 1–1 in Bochum, they trailed 3–1 in the second leg in front of 22,000 at Pittodrie with less than half an hour remaining. Although Ferguson did not score, he played a pivotal role in a dramatic comeback, which saw Scotland score their winning fourth goal in the 88th minute. The Scots then lost out to Sweden in the last four, but there was genuine excitement at what these young players might go on and do, with Ferguson joined by players as talented as Paul Lambert, Eoin Jess and Ray McKinnon. 'It was arguably the best Under-21 team Scotland ever had,' says Brown now.

In Ferguson, Brown believed Scotland's prayers had been answered. 'I thought that we had found the best striker in Britain,' he tells me. 'He could have been Scotland's Alan Shearer: better, potentially, at the time. He came onto the scene like a whirlwind.'

Ferguson seemed to relish conspiring with new players while away from Jim McLean's ever-watchful eye at Dundee United. He enjoyed the chance to test the boundaries elsewhere. Brown, he found, was another stickler for the rules. One of the Under-21 manager's chief concerns was that Scotland should always look the part. He deplored scruffiness and the creeping vogue for accessories such as ankle tape and, his bête noire, bicycle shorts.

Ferguson's liking for the latter put him on a collision course with Brown. It was the reason he was sent home prior to an Under-21 game against the Republic of Ireland. 'I didn't like bicycle shorts because I felt they indicated an injury,' explains Brown. 'I said to the players the next day: "Anyone wearing bicycle shorts?" I never usually let them wear tracksuit bottoms, even in training. This morning was particularly cold, though. They were doing a lot of standing around. Tommy Craig was the coach and he said: "If they are going to be hanging around, we will give them tracksuit bottoms for the warm-up."'

When they took them off again, Brown saw that Ferguson was wearing bicycle shorts. 'I didn't send him away for wearing bicycle shorts, I sent him away for disobedience,' he says.

Ferguson returned to Tannadice. Brown phoned Jim McLean to warn him to anticipate his return. 'Jim agreed with me,' says Brown. 'Duncan then came back on the Wednesday to the game at Perth.

He came to the dressing-room, immaculately turned out, and apologised.'

'I am old-fashioned,' confesses Brown. He knows that some might regard his stance on bicycle shorts, which many players believed helped groin and hamstring ailments, as finicky in the extreme. 'I didn't like them and the players knew that. I got it from Bill Shankly and Bob Paisley, who had similar aversions. There were two things they never allowed – tracksuit bottoms and massages. I read about that. I have also never liked players wearing tape on their socks. I thought it made them look like a pub team.'

Brown recalls an occasion when Steve Nicol tried to put tape around his ankles. 'I said: "Steve, that is unacceptable." Players only have two words: "ah, but". He said: "Ah, but this is what we do at Liverpool."

'I told him: "This is not a pub team now. This is Scotland."'

Brown, who at the time assisted national manager Andy Roxburgh, as well as looking after the Under-21s, could get away with such an impish comment then. Scotland had qualified for five consecutive World Cup finals and, with players of Ferguson's potential having emerged, few had reason to fear this run might come to an end. Indeed, in the same year as the Under-21s reached the semi-finals of their age group's version, Scotland qualified for the European Championship finals for the first time ever. Ferguson, who had just completed his first full season in senior football with Dundee United, was included in the full squad for a warm-up trip to North America just prior to Euro '92, where Scotland had been drawn in a murderously difficult-looking group with Germany, Holland and CIS (the Commonwealth of Independent States, formed after the break-up of the Soviet Union).

Two friendlies were arranged, against the United States and Canada, with the first staged at the Mile High Stadium in Denver. The match remains notable for two things. As fans of the film *So I Married an Axe Murderer* might recall, the clash is what Mike Myers's memorably crude depiction of a Scottish father is prevented from watching due to his son's sputnik-sized cranium. He savages William for having a head large enough to obscure the television. 'Like an orange on a toothpick,' he roars.

But the match is also significant because it saw Duncan Ferguson make his international debut. In the away dressing-room after the game at the Mile High Stadium, Ferguson could have handed Myers a lesson in portraying a dysfunctional Scot.

Ferguson's contribution to the cause had been less than impressive. The match, in the film, is billed as 'world series soccer'. By Ferguson's reckoning, it seemed to rank a long way below this exalted status. Remarkably, Ferguson, aged just 20 and having entered an environment where he might have been expected to genuflect in front of seasoned pros, managed to convey an impression of indifference during the 40 minutes he spent on the field after replacing Pat Nevin, who had scored the only goal in a 1–0 victory. In truth, few had taken the opportunity to strengthen their case for a starting slot at the finals, just a fortnight away.

Ferguson in particular had struggled, spending most of his cameo appearance fighting for breath because of a combination of high altitude and baking heat.

As *The Courier* diplomatically reported, 'Dundee United's Duncan Ferguson took the opportunity, although in smaller doses, to show his promise up front.' This was a generous assessment. Nevin, who had retired to the bench in order to nurse a rib injury, was among those who watched Ferguson give a muted performance on his Scotland debut. According to Nevin, Ferguson 'basically just walked about – Scotland at the time were all about making sure the ball got upfield as quickly as possible. He just watched the ball go over his head and was kind of shrugging and half-jogging about.'

Roxburgh, a former schoolteacher, liked to assess each player's performance in the dressing-room afterwards. As was customary, he went down the line, one by one, as if back in the classroom. Nevin, who has a long-earned reputation for being among the more cerebral of footballers, admits that he felt a childish fascination at what Roxburgh was going to come up with when he got to Ferguson.

We are sitting in a cafe in Edinburgh. Nevin is relishing re-telling the story. He loved being around Ferguson. 'Weirdness seemed to be attracted to him,' he says. They aren't, it would seem, natural companions, but Nevin liked to mix with Ferguson; it seems as though he was almost studying him, trying to work out what made him tick. And he wasn't the only one doing this in the dressing-room of the Mile High Stadium, as the Scotland manager moved from player to player.

'You done well . . . you done well,' said Roxburgh. 'You done well, Pat, great goal.'

'But we weren't really listening,' says Nevin.

They all knew that Roxburgh would have to get to Ferguson. 'Even he was probably wondering what the hell to say,' adds Nevin. 'There was a real oddness about it. When he came to Duncan, he said, "What was up, Duncan?" We expected a bit more.'

Ferguson thought for a moment, looked up and said: 'Ach, these park games, I can't really get myself up for them.'

'It was his first start for Scotland!' exclaims Nevin. 'Euro '92 was just two weeks away and he says he can't get up for these park games. Because it was a friendly, Duncan couldn't be doing with it.'

Nevin recalls that there was not even a look from Ferguson towards noted jokers in the pack, such as Ally McCoist, to whom he had grown close since becoming part of the Scotland set-up. Ferguson was absolutely serious. He hadn't been able to get himself 'up' for it. It is one of the earliest and most striking examples of Ferguson's need to feel that the stakes were high, that he was competing against the very best, in order to get his blood pumping. This would be the case soon enough, though.

Ferguson had still done enough to be included in the list of 20 names submitted to UEFA when it came to the deadline for finalising squads. Aged only twenty and six months, he was the youngest of all those selected by the eight competing nations.

Asked whether he felt Ferguson needed to play in the second game of the tour, against Canada, Roxburgh replied sarcastically: 'Aye, he really needs to have his confidence boosted, doesn't he? He's sitting there trembling at the thought of a game with the big boys.'

Ferguson did, in fact, start his first Scotland match against Canada in Toronto, though he was replaced after 55 minutes by Brian McClair.

While his output on the park might have been underwhelming, Ferguson was emerging as the character of the tour. He remarked to John Robertson, the Heart of Midlothian forward, that he had scored 18 goals the previous season. Robertson disputed this, pointing out that he had actually scored only 14 times. 'So, you have been checking my records? I knew I had you worried,' Ferguson replied.

Nevin, too, was on the receiving end of some impertinence. Ferguson had been picked in Nevin's team for a seven-a-side game and watched as Nevin dummied three people before running the ball out of play. In Nevin's opinion, it had been a decent bit of skill that had gone a bit wrong in the end. It hadn't impressed Ferguson, though.

'See you, son, when you get the ball, give it to people who can play,' Ferguson told his teammate, who was nearly 30 at the time.

'I was waiting for the ironic laugh, but it didn't come,' remembers Nevin, who also recalls watching from the sidelines as Ferguson again managed to give out the wrong signals to the management, who seemed perplexed rather than infuriated. Just who the hell was this kid?

'I wasn't taking part in the training session because of my injury,' recalls Nevin. 'With Andy, it was all socks rolled up, shirts tucked in and bibs the right way round. Smart. Everyone does the right thing. This was an 11 v. 11 training game, so you are matching up with the player you are competing with for a place. It was all very reliant on order.'

At one point, the ball is launched up the right channel to where Ferguson is – or at least where he should have been.

'But Duncan is not there,' continues Nevin. 'If you can imagine the classic American college training ground – there's one small stand, and cheerleaders in the background. Duncan was on this side of the park – he was walking away.

'Normally, if you are injured, what you do is run about a bit, try and run it off, and then tell the gaffer you need to see the physio. But Duncan is just walking away, ignoring everybody.'

Roxburgh and Brown, who are standing 50 yards away, then make the ultimate mistake of shouting: 'Duncan!'

'They should have waited, talked to him privately,' says Nevin. 'It's the classic managers' rule – don't do anything in public. Duncan doesn't even turn round. He throws his hand out in a dismissive gesture. "Sare tae," he says.'

He's got a sore toe. Ferguson continued on his way and took a seat in the grandstand, next to two cheerleaders.

'He was not on this planet,' continues Nevin. 'But by this point I am thinking: "I am hanging about with him."'

Nevin says that he is attracted to 'interesting people' and Ferguson was certainly one of those. 'I just wanted to be in his company and watch the fallout,' he says.

'I immediately thought: he is not like the rest of them. What struck me was that he had this social naivety, which some people could take offence to, and did. But from people who played with him, you won't hear many negatives.'

And yet, perhaps there is no mystery as to why Ferguson was given only a very brief cameo at Euro '92, where he played for only 12 minutes in total. He replaced Brian McClair in the 78th minute for his first taste of competitive action shortly after Dennis Bergkamp had given the Netherlands a 1–0 lead in Scotland's opening game.

Ferguson couldn't help alter the situation, although he got a chance to mix with the very best. In addition to Bergkamp, the Dutch side was littered with bona fide greats of the game: Frank Rijkaard, Ruud Gullit, Ronald Koeman and Marco van Basten. Ferguson later admitted that, although he liked to convey an impression of nonchalance, he knew his place in the scheme of things.

Later, he would recall watching the game from the substitutes' bench. 'I see Gullit, van Basten; I see Koeman and Rijkaard. You are sitting there looking at them. Gullit was like a gazelle. The way he flew across the grass, I thought to myself: "Dearie me, there is a player. I am not a player. Now there is a player."'

For his part, Roxburgh wasn't quite sure what to make of Ferguson. 'He is an innocent, full of enthusiasm,' he commented at the time. 'He has shown one or two things in training even I haven't seen before.'

Later, when I contacted him to speak about Ferguson, Roxburgh put it similarly delicately. 'His enthusiasm seemed to fluctuate depending on the circumstances,' he recalls. 'He was a restless boy, he had not settled down. But then he was young.

'And you just hoped he would eventually settle down.'

The next stop for Scotland after the Euro '92 finals – they were eliminated after finishing third in the group – was Berne, where Scotland began their quest to qualify for a sixth World Cup in a row. Ferguson was again included and again he was a lively contributor – off the pitch, at least.

'At every football team there are cliques,' recalls Nevin. 'All the Rangers lads like Andy Goram, 'Coisty, Durranty and [Richard] Gough – they were characters, loads of fun and they had wee bit of devilment about them.

'It wasn't exactly Celtic v. Rangers, but in the other camp there was [Tom] Boyd, John Collins, Paul McStay – nice guys. It was a case of me looking at them and thinking: "They are the nice guys – I will hang around with them. But at the same time, it sounds a hell of a lot of fun over there."'

Over there was where Goram, Durrant, Gough, McCoist and Ferguson, the newest addition to the gang, congregated. It was pretty much guaranteed to which group Ferguson would be drawn. Scotland lost the match 3–1 and Ferguson was not called upon. He had energy, and other things besides, to burn with his new friends.

'That night after the Swiss game, one group went out and had a few – guess which one?' says Nevin. 'The other group sat in the room and had a chat. I was sitting there with John Collins and McStay, and we were talking about where it goes from here. It was an unusually serious after-match discussion.'

Those of us on the outside would imagine such post-mortems happen fairly frequently, but it's not so, according to Nevin. 'I can recall it happening only two or three times with Scotland,' he says. 'But we were so depressed by that night that we sat around and talked.

'Then, suddenly, we smelt something, and then we saw a wardrobe where it should not have been – in front of a door to a room. It was on fire. There seemed to be only one suggestion about who had been involved.

'Duncan.'

In a team meeting held on arrival at the hotel, the players had already been made aware that this was an unusual hotel. It was wood-built. 'If there was any place not to set fire to anything, then that was the one,' says Nevin.

McCoist, whose room it was and who had been relaxing in his jacuzzi on the other side of the gently smouldering blockage stacked up next to his door, refers to it as 'a prank even I would be proud to call my own'. This is high praise, indeed – but the incident didn't help Ferguson's international playing ambitions.

And yet, in the midst of a qualifying campaign in which he did not feature at all in the end, came Ferguson's finest moment in a Scotland shirt.

And a moment is all it was.

*

'It was just something a player wasn't supposed to do,' remarks Craig Levein. 'Not a Scottish one, anyway.' The former Scotland manager is reflecting on the moment Duncan Ferguson teased the Tartan Army with a promise he couldn't keep.

But then who could? Who could have lived up to the potential glimpsed when Ferguson flipped himself up into the air on a spring night in Glasgow?

On his return to earth, he discovered the world was at his feet and doors were opening before him – not closing behind him, as they soon would do. Levein does not, on the face of it, have too much to do with the Duncan Ferguson story. They never played together at the same club, and Levein's career as a stylish centre-half with Heart of Midlothian was coming to an end as Ferguson's was beginning to blossom. However, their paths did cross on one significant occasion, when Levein skippered a much-changed Scotland side against Germany, the then world champions, at Ibrox Stadium.

After nine call-offs from the original squad, the eventual starting XI were equipped with only 61 caps between them. To make matters worse, these unfamiliar international stand-ins were handed odd-looking salmon-pink and purple pinstriped change tops, worn only once before.

'Not only were we playing the world champions, we were being made to wear pink strips,' recalls Dave Bowman, one of three Dundee United players in the starting line-up. 'All we needed was the mint sauce. It was like lambs to the slaughter.'

Ferguson was fresh from scoring a derby winner against Dundee for United and, having helped dispose of the team from across the street, his scope of ambition widened to include the world champions. It was a big leap, quite literally. Ferguson being Ferguson, he took it all in his stride. Instead, it was the experienced Levein who made an uncharacteristic, game-deciding blunder, the details of which I am reading about in a café when I look up and am surprised to see a familiar-looking face.

Both my and Levein's paths have crossed and in serendipitous fashion – fortunate for me, at least. I am seated in Starbucks in what used to be the Borders bookshop in Dundee, sifting through pages of recently photocopied match reports from the night Ferguson high-kicked his way into recent Scottish football folklore. Levein is sitting at a table in another corner of the coffee shop, with a locally based football agent.

As he leaves, he stops by my table. It could be a little awkward – spread out before me are newspaper cuttings, most of them blaming Levein for the error that led to an early goal, scored by Karl-Heinz Riedle, that eventually cost Scotland the match. He spots the cuttings and recalls his slip, though his expression doesn't give much away. I explain that I am writing a book about Duncan Ferguson. Levein's response is succinct.

'Good luck,' he says, with a smile. Rarely have the two words sounded so loaded.

Levein can afford to smile. Although he would later endure a difficult spell as Scotland manager, he needn't have worried about his error that night, when he lost sight of a long ball in the glare of the Ibrox floodlights. Now, if conversation turns to this particular match, only one incident is recalled; however, not necessarily with any great accuracy.

'The match was remembered by many for Duncan Ferguson hitting the crossbar with an overhead kick,' claimed the *Evening Times* in their 'Now You Know' column in January 2010. Except now you *didn't* know. Even the Scottish Football Association's own website reports, in its archives section, that the game 'will be remembered by many for Duncan Ferguson's overhead volley which crashed off the crossbar – the closest he came to scoring in his seven appearances for Scotland'.

Compounding other basic factual errors made in relation to this match is the fact that this appearance is often referred to as Ferguson's debut for Scotland, when, in fact, it was his fourth cap. Prior to the fixture, Berti Vogts, Germany's manager, had suggested, if a little unconvincingly, that the world champions 'feared' Ferguson.

Vogts would soon taste glory, and lead Germany to the Euro '96 title before an uncelebrated stint as Scotland manager brought him back into Ferguson's orbit. Much lay in store for the striker, too.

But that night at Ibrox, he had few worries about the future. The world was one eternal now.

Nevertheless, when Tom Boyd delivered a measured ball to the back post midway through the first half, what else was he supposed to do but flip himself into the air and seek to score his first Scotland goal with a scissor-kick volley? It had seemed like the most natural thing in the world for him to attempt to do.

Ferguson had been making a habit of acting rashly, of not thinking things through. But at Ibrox, this seemed to work in his favour – almost. According to Roxburgh, 'Duncan was an instinctive player and it's sometimes difficult to coach an instinctive player – just as they often find it hard to coach other players. A lot of top managers now were decent players, but they tended to be thinking players; they were guys who had to work hard at the game. You often found that the genius player was the one who didn't have to think about it too much.'

Ferguson even helped start the move, chesting down a long pass forward and then funnelling the ball out wide to John Collins, who in turn fed Boyd. As the left-back's right-footed cross arrives in his vicinity, Ferguson shrugs off the attention of his marker and fixes his gaze on the ball, which is dropping slightly behind him. While another player might have thought to chest it down, or instead try to reposition himself for a header, Ferguson simply begins to fall back. What was he thinking? Most probably he wasn't thinking. The ball drops out of the Govan sky and Ferguson times the connection with his left foot perfectly.

As so often happens, the reality has become distorted in the intervening years. Now the accepted version is that Ferguson's spectacular effort from Boyd's cross from the left cracked off the crossbar at the Broomloan Road end of the stadium.

A re-viewing of this segment of play, from a tape of the whole match obtained from BBC Scotland vaults, confirms that, in actual fact, the German goalkeeper Andreas Kopke was equal to the spectacular effort and prevented the ball from fizzing into the roof of the net with an excellent save, high to his left. He needed no help from the crossbar. Just over three years later, Kopke again proved his worth on British soil, though once more received minimal credit, when saving Gareth Southgate's penalty in the Euro '96 semi-final shoot-out win over England at Wembley.

Even though it is more often than not inaccurately remembered today, there was considerable acclaim for both shot and save at the time. 'That would have been one of the goals of any season,' remarked BBC Scotland commentator Jock Brown when the highlights were shown later that same night.

Nearly 20 years on, even Brown is at first adamant that the shot had hit the bar. He is taken aback when informed that he, too, has misremembered it. 'What sticks with me is that, had the ball gone in, it would have been shown all around the world. Ferguson's stock would have soared, if it didn't anyway.'

It wasn't a goal, granted. But, then again, perhaps it was better than one, since it contained something even more delicious – promise.

Typically, and despite his contention on the eve of the Germany match that his 'eyes had been opened' after being charged with assault for a third time, a toe injury – rumoured to have been sustained in a bar brawl in the Menzieshill area of Dundee – saw Ferguson's season arrive at a premature end just weeks later. It meant he missed out on the crucial next World Cup qualifying fixture in Lisbon against Portugal, a game he was all but guaranteed to start – and which Scotland lost 5–0.

The result made it virtually certain that Scotland would miss out on a first World Cup since 1970, to be held in the United States the following year, while Ferguson's own momentum had been lost. After the 'overhead kick' game, Blair Morgan, Ferguson's lawyer, went for dinner with Karl-Heinz Rummenigge, then the Bayern Munich vice-president. Morgan stressed to the German legend that if Bayern signed Ferguson, and it didn't work out, they would get their money back after a year.

Meanwhile, Vogts revealed that Guido Buchwald, 'the best defender in Germany', had returned to the dressing-room looking 'shaken'. Ferguson, the Stuttgart centre-half admitted, had given him 'a lot of problems'.

In the press, Patrick Barclay, writing in *The Observer*, wondered whether Ferguson's consummate execution of one of the hardest tasks in football meant that the resemblance of the 'long, lean' Scot to Marco van Basten could be 'rather more than a question of build and style'. Several of Ferguson's teammates that night recall being just as impressed. Intriguingly, nearly all of them used the same word to describe Ferguson. He was 'gallus', an old Scottish term meaning swagger and an innate self-confidence, and it seemed to perfectly sum up Ferguson.

'It was Brazilian-like, as opposed to Scottish-like,' recalls Nicky Walker, while Brian Irvine, who played at centre-back that night, recalls someone who exuded confidence: 'In a way, it was what you expected him to do, and if it had hit the back of the net, then that would have been normal, too.'

Scott Booth watched from the substitutes' bench until appearing as a second-half replacement. 'That horrible salmon and purple strip is one of the first things that comes to mind, but I suppose it made Duncan's overhead look even more spectacular,' he says. 'There was a salmon leaping that night.

'I could maybe have tried it, but I would have fallen flat on my arse and made myself look daft. Some players are able to pull it off. Duncan was one,' Booth adds.

Ferguson had grandstanded on a night when Scotland had been meant to bow meekly in front of superior opponents. He had helped divert the threat of a massacre and turned it into a fair fight. In the days afterwards, newspapers were full of comment pieces on the wonder-goal-that-wasn't.

According to Barclay, Scotland had 'lost the match but found a star'. He added: 'It tests the memory to recall a more exciting young British centre-forward.'

When Ferguson awoke the next morning, he was a wanted man. Roxburgh expresses the wish that he had been able to call on Ferguson on more occasions, but then he is not the only manager to have felt like this. The national coach was already coming to the end of his time in charge when Germany arrived in Scotland. Indeed, he lasted only three more games, resigning after a draw with Switzerland at Pittodrie that saw the Scots' World Cup hopes finally extinguished.

Ferguson might have been aghast to see Jim McLean's name linked to the Scotland post; however, having just announced that he was vacating the management role at Tannadice, a return to the dugout didn't interest McLean. Instead, Craig Brown stepped up from the Under-21s. Ferguson could breathe again.

CHAPTER 8

Jousting with a Giant

In the years following his final parting of ways with Dundee United, making an appointment to see Jim McLean became a lot easier than it once had been. No answer at his home in Broughty Ferry, a prosperous suburb to the east of Dundee, is likely to mean one of three things: he is at the nearby bowling club, he is golfing or he is with his wife, the heroine known as Doris, in Brambles, their favourite cafe in town.

On this occasion, McLean is occupying himself with the first of these favoured pastimes, at the bowling club handily located across the road from his house, the front door of which he is able to see from the bench on which he is sitting. Interest piqued by a visitor to his door, he is already on his loafer-ed feet when I join him. In the background, the soft clink of bowls can be heard.

It is a becalmed scene, worlds away from the fractious existence of football management, its battles and worries. McLean's greeting is warm – and does not grow notably less so when the reason for my visit is explained. This is promising. For Ferguson, we know, once tested McLean's patience to such an extent that, in March 1993, he included him in the list of reasons why he was finally stepping down as manager, referring to the strain of something that he wearily termed 'the Duncan Ferguson affair'.

The title of McLean's autobiography, *Jousting with Giants*, refers to the way in which United managed to impose themselves on the European stage in the 1980s, reaching the semi-finals of the European Cup in 1984 and then qualifying for the final of the

UEFA Cup in 1987, beating Barcelona both at home and away en route. On the domestic front, along with 'New Firm' partner Aberdeen, they managed to eclipse Rangers and Celtic.

But there were other wars to wage within the walls of Tannadice Park itself. Wee Jim versus Big Dunc was one such contest that kept many enthralled at the Dundee United ground at the time. It was hardly a fair fight in terms of size – McLean had got his nickname due to his diminutive stature. It wasn't one he particularly liked, and it wasn't as if he was particularly short. Indeed, he once phoned up the sports desk at the local newspaper to complain bitterly at being referred to in print as 'Wee Jim', pointing out that he was 'five foot eight and a half inches' tall. What isn't in dispute is that he was a larger-than-life figure for more than three decades at the club.

Even after stepping away from front-line management, supposedly taking a back seat as chairman, he struggled to accept the slipping standards on the field, a new frustration and one that caused him an even more profound ache than the misdemeanours of Ferguson and his talented, wilful peers at the end of the 1980s. He continued to rail against reporters with an almost reassuring consistency. I remember being present at a press conference when he exclaimed: 'In a year I might be deid, and none of youse will be invited to the funeral!' He once predicted that he would die in the dug-out and be carried out of Tannadice 'in a box'.

A steward, clipboard in hand, once used to block the entrance to the press-box, a list of named individuals and organisations scrawled out with a yellow pen; these were those who were banned for having the temerity to question McLean's tactics or stewardship of the club. The ultimate irony is that the manager had used his joinery skills to help build the press-box at Tannadice.

Jim McLean's was the first interview conducted for this book, since so much of Ferguson's story is wrapped up with McLean. So much of the success he achieved is perhaps owing to McLean, though the player himself might find this hard to acknowledge.

Later, in their days together at Everton, teammate David Weir recalls Ferguson's reaction if ever he spotted a copy of the *Daily Record* in the dressing-room at the training ground, one brought in by either Weir himself or James McFadden and Gary Naysmith, fellow exiled Scots. 'He was always going, "What's he writing about me for?"' with reference to the entertaining column McLean wrote for nearly a decade – another irony – each Friday morning in the paper. "'Jim McLean! Is he fucking talking about me again?"' recalls Weir. 'And invariably he would be. Every second week he would get a mention. Duncan hated that.'

While McLean clashed with Ferguson, and Ferguson gave as good as he got back, they both saw their association with the club turn sour in the end. Unbelievably, given Ferguson's own scrapes with the law while at the club, it was McLean who saw the endgame arrive via an act of sudden violence. Interviewed on television after a crushing four-goal defeat at home by Hearts in October 2000, the already agitated McLean was further riled by a question about the future of then manager Alex Smith – a subject that he felt had already been made clear was off-limits. Within an hour of swinging a punch at BBC Scotland sports reporter John Barnes, he had resigned in disgrace.

It was a loss of composure in the heat of the moment, the kind of outburst that besmirched Ferguson's career, and suggests that the two, while polar opposites in many respects, had some things in common. For a start, their upbringing had been similar, raised as they were in Protestant, working-class families. But McLean was a product of an earlier era; his was a world dominated by a fierce work ethic.

As far as McLean was concerned, Ferguson's reluctance to push himself into the ground, or *be* pushed into the ground, to put his heart into training in the morning and then come back and do it all again in the afternoon on his own accord, was alien behaviour. Of course, Ferguson was not the only one who turned up his nose at something that sounded so much like hard work. But compounding the frustration, as far as McLean was concerned, was the knowledge that Ferguson had so much talent. He was wasting it. 'Duncan did just not want to make the sacrifices necessary,' McLean laments.

Having been invited back to his house, we sit in the living room, one curiously devoid of any football mementoes. 'On his day, he was unplayable,' he adds, as though describing a fast bowler.

Unplayable. Joe Royle, later Ferguson's manager at Everton, opted for this word when describing the striker to me, and several others chose it, too – but it was almost always accompanied by the caveat 'on his day'. Indeed, McLean further adds – both by the side of the bowling green and, later, when we sit in his house – that Ferguson could have been as good as the then Chelsea centre-forward Didier Drogba, and 'on his day' – that phrase again – probably was.

'He was a star, but not the superstar he could have been,' says McLean. 'Without any doubt he could have been a Didier Drogba. He was almost impossible to handle physically, unplayable at times.'

Unplayable.

But then also unmanageable.

At one point during our discussion, McLean leaves the room to take the weekly phone call from the journalist charged with turning their conversation into a weekly column for the *Daily Record* that had so irked Ferguson. Doris politely keeps the house guest company and recalls – with a degree of affection, it must be said, as though reflecting on an errant child – the grief Ferguson caused her husband.

'All I remember is Jim shouting, Duncan this, Duncan that,' she says. 'Duncan was always getting it.'

Although he could certainly be a gauche character in his younger days, it's clear Ferguson also possessed charisma. It wasn't only Doris who was susceptible to his charm. McLean would sometimes be obstructed in his attempts to keep tabs on Ferguson by the club's own landladies, of all things. Each Friday he would embark on his round of phone calls to the digs of his younger, more troublesome charges and it wasn't just to wish them 'Goodnight'.

'I remember once phoning a landlady who was also working for us at Dundee United,' says McLean. 'I said, "Could I speak with Duncan, please?" She said, "I am sorry, he's out at the shops just now, but will be back shortly. I will get him to phone you back." Right away, I realised there could be a problem.

'About 20 minutes later, the phone goes. It's Duncan. "Hello, Boss, what's the problem?" I said, "I am just checking up, Duncan. You are at home in your digs, Duncan?"

'"Yes, Boss," he says. "That's fine," I reply, but I knew he was back in Stirling. "See you tomorrow," I said, and put phone down. Then immediately I dialled the landlady back and said there were a couple of things I had forgotten to say. "Can you put Duncan back on the phone?" She had to admit he was elsewhere. He was even able to get his landlady to tell fibs for him.'

It was enough to make McLean's blood boil, but then so much

did while he was in the grip of an obsession with Dundee United. McLean didn't know when to stop, when to apply the brakes, and in the end, regrettably, it got messy. After using his column in the *Daily Record* – 'the column that packs a punch', it promoted itself, rather distastefully – to criticise new owner Eddie Thompson's tenure at the club, he had all privileges at the club withdrawn. When Thompson died in 2008 after a long battle with cancer, it was he, and not McLean, who had established himself as Mr Dundee United, a billing many had imagined would be the epithet reserved for a man who brought the Scottish Championship to the club in 1983 and who spent a total of 21 years in the managerial seat, turning the club into such a force in Europe, as well as in Scotland.

Just as Ferguson is an example of someone who perhaps didn't care enough about the game, McLean is someone who cared too much. He himself has acknowledged this in the past. 'The game means far too much to me, I know that, but it means fuck all to you,' he remembers angrily roaring at Ferguson. McLean seems rather pleased with himself when I ask whether he can expand on what he meant by this. 'There is no doubt that was one of the more accurate statements I made when I was giving the player pelters – beyond a shadow of a doubt, he has never achieved anything near what he could have done.'

It was a typically trenchant observation from the football factory floor, yet it also seems to me to be an infinitely poignant comment, one summing up two contrasting, warring personalities. It reaches to the very heart of the Duncan Ferguson enigma, as well as explaining why McLean can be placed next to the likes of Brian Clough and Bill Shankly in the pantheon of intense, passionate managerial figures who gradually began to wear something of a haunted aspect.

Reflecting ruefully on the cost to his blood pressure, McLean explains that he has been advised by his doctor to break the vow of abstinence made when he was a youth footballer eager to make his way in the game and take a few 'medicinal' sips of wine each evening. It beats the sleeping pills he once gobbled on Friday nights to ensure he was, as he puts it, at least 'a wee bit calm' before matches.

McLean simply could not comprehend Ferguson's insouciance. It was something he – and others – interpreted as arrogance. For him, such a carefree attitude represented an outrage visited on Ferguson's teammates, who, while they might not have been as talented, were 100 per cent committed to the cause. Ferguson was like Richard Gough, McLean explains. 'He was different,' he adds. Neither fitted the profile preferred by McLean, although their worth as players could never be disputed.

'Richard Gough, who was a great player for us as well, looked in the mirror and saw only Richard Gough when we won. And when we got beaten, he looked in the mirror and saw the other ten.

'People have different attitudes and different personalities. But I preferred those who were brilliant, in that they respected the other ten players in the team, as well as themselves.'

According to McLean, Ferguson did not do that, although he accepts that there were faults on both their parts. 'Unfortunately, the way he felt about football was different to the way I felt about it,' continues McLean, with considerable understatement. 'I don't want this to be a slamming exercise. He had every right not to love football. But as a manager and the person responsible for giving the supporters the best they could possibly get, we did not get what we should have got out of Duncan Ferguson on the park often enough.'

One episode in particular gave McLean reason to believe that he was dealing with someone wired very differently to the way he was. It occurred on the day David Weir made his senior debut for Falkirk against Dundee United, meaning the centre-half was up against Ferguson.

Although he would go on to become a teammate and friend to Ferguson, Weir could be described as being everything he was not. For one thing, he had just returned from the United States, having completed a scholarship degree at the University of Evansville, in Indiana. He hailed from Falkirk, little more than ten miles from Stirling, while he was also just over a year older than Ferguson. In terms of maturity, however, it is fair to say that they were light years away from each other on the day Weir stepped out into senior football. On most days, the prospect of marking Duncan Ferguson should have been a genuinely intimidating one. Ferguson, however, was sulking.

Jim Jefferies, the Falkirk manager who handed Weir his debut that day, has often spoken of the day the raw centre-half had Ferguson in his pocket. Other witnesses appear to support Jefferies' view. According to *The Scotsman*'s match report from the clash in

October 1992, seldom can Duncan Ferguson have had such a lean afternoon against any defender, 'far less a rooky who didn't even know he was playing until an hour before kick-off'.

While one manager revelled in the sight of his new centre-half dominating the striker of the moment, two more despaired. Just ten days earlier Scotland manager Andy Roxburgh had watched as his side were held 0–0 by Portugal at home in a World Cup qualifier. With another vital match against Italy looming the following month, Roxburgh had been encouraged to see if Ferguson's exclusion from the last squad – he had been included in the Under-21 squad instead – had stung him into action, and so he took his seat in the directors' box at Brockville. Ferguson, in McLean's description, was 'blazing' at having been overlooked by the Scotland manager for the previous international.

However, he didn't do what most people might have been expected to do. He didn't go out to terrorise Falkirk in a bid to show Roxburgh what he had missed. He didn't aim to make the understandably anxious Weir pay for having crossed his path that day. Rather, Ferguson was insipid, barely managing to lift so much as an elbow in anger.

'I remember going in at half-time and saying to him: "Andy Roxburgh is sitting up in the stand there, and you are not happy being in the Under-21 squad,"' recalls McLean. 'I said: "You have the perfect opportunity to show you should be in the big squad, but you have hardly kicked a ball."'

Ferguson's reaction was not what McLean expected – or perhaps it *was* what he expected, having become used by now to the player's casual attitude. He simply shrugged, telling McLean: 'I don't need to prove anything to anybody.'

The explosion that followed in the away dressing-room almost dislodged the last few bolts holding the rickety Brockville main stand together. After a brief, stunned silence, McLean roared back a response. 'I told him, "For fuck's sake, you are 20 years of age and you say you have nothing to prove! You have done nothing in the game yet. It is all ahead of you. But you have to have the right attitude. It's not you who picks the international team. It is Andy Roxburgh. You have to convince him you are the best."'

'It went in one ear and out of the other,' recalls McLean. As other managers were to learn, if Ferguson was to reach his potential, the trick often lay in making him angry.

'He could be a big, docile lad until you got him excited,' says Paul Sturrock, who recalled one particular clash against Partick Thistle in 1992–93 – Ferguson's last season at United.

It is a memorable game for students of Scottish football since it featured an infamous 'goal that never was'. United led 1–0 when Ferguson flicked on a corner to Paddy Connolly, who slammed the ball into the net from close range. The ball cannoned off a stanchion at the back of the goal and came back out. A Partick Thistle defender even picked up the ball and handed it to his goalkeeper. However, referee Les Mottram, believing the ball had struck the post, waved play on.

Amid understandably strong protests from United, the game continued. 'At half-time, Duncan was ranting and raving about not getting that goal,' recalls Sturrock. If you watch the game on YouTube, you can see Dundee United goalkeeper Alan Main launch a goalkick into the opposition box. 'It bounces on the 18-yard box,' continues Sturrock. 'The goalie comes out to get the ball and Duncan just launches himself at it – he scores a goal and poleaxes the keeper. The height he gets to is just incredible. But that's Duncan. Get him riled and he was a player.'

Clearly, Ferguson had to be cleverly handled. 'Duncan was the young player at United with the most bargaining power,' recalls Michael O'Neill. 'McLean knew he had to think twice about leaving him out. It became clear quite quickly that he was going to outgrow the club. It got to the point where McLean could not be as hardline with Duncan because he brought so much to the team.'

According to some players, McLean struggled to impose his will on Ferguson, although he himself refutes this and remembers resisting one attempt at intimidation from Mr Ferguson Senior. 'One time I came down the stairs from Tannadice after a game and this gentleman came over to me and said, "I am Duncan Ferguson's father; don't think you can speak to my son the way that you speak to him." I said, "Look, Duncan will be treated the exact same as any other player. If Duncan does not pull his weight in every single game, and every single training session, then he will get a bit of advice from me."'

According to O'Neill, Ferguson was just a chip off the old block. His father 'looked like a coal miner, and everything was black and white – he was a hard man, but he was always a gentleman. He did, though, seem to be someone who knew how to deal with things. And Duncan had the same attitude, he wouldn't stand on ceremony for anyone.'

Ferguson continued to try the manager's patience, marching boldly in where others feared to tread, literally so in one case. While in his father's presence, Ferguson was, according to O'Neill, a respectful, almost submissive figure; when it came to the authority represented by McLean, Ferguson seemed determined to issue challenge after challenge. 'He was brash and he was confident,' says O'Neill. 'He would flex his muscles – although he was a beanpole, he was quite well developed. We would play head tennis in the gym, and he loved that, and it would get quite physical over the benches. But at no time did I ever find that his way of dealing with anything was to resort to violence. If someone said something to him, he always liked to think he had an answer.'

But there were times when it got particularly tense. 'We had a dressing-room meeting, which meant every boy in the whole club had to gather in the home dressing-room,' recalls Gordon Parks. 'It was a Monday morning, and the only person who was not there was Duncan. He walks in halfway through the meeting and Wee Jim is standing there.

'The door gets pushed wide open, and there's Duncan and he is covered in oil. Jim says: "Where have you been? You are late!" Duncan goes, "Where the fuck do you think I have been? You don't pay me a decent wage and because of that I am driving a clapped-out Capri and it broke down on the way up the road, all right?"

'And Big Dunc goes and starts putting his training gear on. Jim says: "Right, everyone out of the dressing-room." So we all go out into the corridor. Everyone. Malpas, Darren Jackson, all the senior pros. All we can hear is this rammy taking place, and then one of the senior players goes in and Wee Jim is on the deck. Dunc is standing there, carrying on getting ready. Jim had had a go. Dunc just shoved him away.'

On the pitch, Ferguson was continuing to excel. A productive start to season 1992–93 saw him score United's first goal of the campaign – in a win over Motherwell. A brace against Falkirk in a 2–0 victory the following month was significant for sending United to the top of the Premier Division – a defeat to Hibs the following weekend saw them slip to fourth, and they have not reached such lofty heights again to date. Unsurprisingly, Ferguson was now starting to attract interest from clubs down south, including Everton. Their £600,000 offer managed a remarkable feat – it brought a smile to McLean's face. Or so he claimed, anyway, when explaining to a television reporter that he regarded such a valuation for the player as comical in the extreme.

Blackburn Rovers chairman Jack Walker, meanwhile, offered to build United a new stand if they sold Ferguson to the Lancashire club. Interest was coming from further afield, too.

By this time – and reflecting the player's burgeoning reputation – Ferguson had a new advisor in Dennis Roach. Now referred to as 'the first real agent', he also represented Glenn Hoddle, Paul Gascoigne and Mark Hateley, among others. Roach tended to associate himself with the biggest stars in the firmament at the time; when he first began to hear reports of Ferguson, he naturally made further investigations and ended up acting for the player. It hardly requires saying that Roach and McLean did not see eye to eye.

Indeed, it was probably best not to have been standing too close to McLean when he opened a letter addressed to him from Roach before Rangers took on Olympique de Marseille in a Champions League group match. Dated 25 November 1992 – just days after Ferguson's misadventures in Anstruther – Roach makes an optimistic request for permission to take Ferguson and his father to Ibrox because, he wrote, 'I would like to introduce him to the [Marseille] president Bernard Tapie.'

In the same letter, Roach also seeks permission for Ferguson to stay the night with his family in Stirling after the game, before travelling to Dundee for training the next morning. 'This will give us the chance to talk about his recent problems,' Roach suggests. Among these 'recent problems' was an almost comical episode that had taken place a few days earlier, when physio John Sharp was compelled to put down in writing Ferguson's latest misdemeanour. With Ferguson having been kept back for extra training to assess his fitness, Sharp informed McLean in writing that first the player refused to run, before then drawing the line 'at even walking'.

A £100 fine was imposed on Ferguson by the club for dissent, which led the player to make an official complaint to the Scottish Football League. This, predictably, led to another period of exile from the team, while it also prompted United to publicise how much Ferguson had earned in the previous twenty-five weeks, following claims that, after three years of first-team football, he still only earned £180 a week in basic pay. Not true, responded United, who took the unusual step of revealing the player had, in fact, earned £34,000, including bonuses, since the beginning of the season, or £1,300 a week.

His salary again became an issue one Friday night in January 1993, during an edition of *Scotsport Extra Time* hosted by Gerry McNee, a journalist who had fallen out with McLean on more occasions than most. McNee memorably produced Ferguson's pay-packet, which he had been given by Roach, showing that the player had been fined £400 in just one week. Not long after, the *Daily Record* reported that Ferguson had been left with a weekly wage packet of just £23.25 after fines for not spending the evening in digs and for drinking 72 hours before a game.

Roach further claimed that Ferguson was forced to eat in fast-food joints in order to sustain himself while on such meagre earnings. Furthermore, Roach stressed that the player's lodgings did not meet the standard required. On 31 January – remarkably, just months before Ferguson became Britain's most expensive ever footballer – the *Sunday Mail* published an article about complaints made by Roach on television with regards to Ferguson's room in a home owned by the Shepherd family.

United were always looking to establish a relationship with other landlords and landladies in the city in order to increase their accommodation options. Maurice Malpas, the club's Scottish international left-back, mentioned a place he had stayed, when studying for an engineering degree at the College of Commerce in the city. Ferguson moved in, but Roach quickly made known that his client was not happy. Specifically, he referred to the size of the bed and said Ferguson had been forced to move out because it was 'too short' – and he needed 'six blankets to keep warm'.

In the newspaper, landlord Jack Shepherd is photographed sitting on said bed. Beneath the headline 'The Bed that Bugged Fergie', the article includes an inventory. Listed as being present in the semi-detached villa in Union Terrace were three chairs, a wardrobe with drawers, a bedside table, a radiator and a fire, and a TV. The 76-year-old Jack responded to Roach's criticism: 'It was a real slap in the face,' he said. 'My wife Jenny is very upset.'

Days later, Shepherd died of a heart attack. It was inevitable that this tragic event would be linked with the row that had developed about the standard of accommodation that Ferguson, according to his agent, had been forced to endure. 'There was a lot of bad publicity when Duncan criticised the digs,' recalls Malpas. 'But he stayed with a lovely couple. Jack, the landlord, thought he was the next Andy Gray. Big Fergie would take Jack for a couple of pints. But it all turned a bit nasty. There was some stuff said about the accommodation in the papers. The old couple took it personally.'

It was just another spat in the continued war between Duncan and Dundee United. 'The Shepherds were stuck in the middle, unfortunately,' laments Malpas. 'Duncan did not think about who might get caught in the crossfire. Not in a million years would he have hurt them deliberately. He was young, petulant and said things he didn't realise might hurt people.'

Ferguson sent flowers to Shepherd's funeral and was said to be genuinely distraught by the episode. Before the story took such a sad course, it had provoked mostly laughter, as newspapers and fanzines depicted Ferguson shivering beneath blankets, folding himself 'like a piece of origami' into his bed. As one joke had it: he intended to ask for a continental quilt rather than a signing-on fee when he finally moved to another club.

The ongoing rows and club suspensions were disheartening for United fans, who felt that the chance of making a challenge for honours was being compromised by the mutinous vibe. The prospect of Rangers swooping to relieve United of Ferguson's services was also dismaying, and McLean was alert to the mood among the fans. Indeed, he felt much the same way.

The Ibrox club were long-time admirers, and indeed were fined £5,000 by the Scottish Football League after United reported them to the football authorities in January 1993 for making an illegal approach for the striker. Rangers players Richard Gough and Ally McCoist were even said to have taken Ferguson 'hostage' briefly following a Scotland trip, taking the player to Ibrox and making him feel at home to the extent that they pointed out where his peg would be in the lavish home dressing-room if – or, more likely, when – he made the move to Rangers.

Gough in particular was very public in his attempts to persuade Ferguson, much to McLean's anger. Even the manner of Ferguson's eventual departure from Tannadice grew to become a saga and it led to McLean falling out with Rangers owner David Murray, who embarrassed McLean when backing up a story McNee had broken about Rangers making an offer for Ferguson, which the United manager had originally denied.

United were determined to sell him anywhere but Rangers. When once the club had wanted Ferguson to base himself close to Tannadice, now they wanted their star player to continue his career as far away as possible. When it became clear that Ferguson was desperate to move on, a fee of £3,250,000 was agreed with Leeds United, while Chelsea were also in regular contact with United.

The thought of the player moving to England was acceptable to McLean. Less acceptable was what he interpreted as Rangers' covert – and sometimes overt – wooing of the player. McLean was also keen to avoid helping make a rival in the Scottish game stronger if it could be helped, even if it was clear Ferguson had his heart set on Ibrox. In the player's eyes, United's determination to move him to a team down south was another example of them interfering with his plans and ambitions. He dug in his heels.

McLean once had his own chance to join Rangers and double his wages, with the offer of a £100,000 house thrown in. Out of a sense of loyalty to the club and, he states in his autobiography, to then chairman Johnston Grant, who was ill at the time and died just months later, he turned the offer down to stay with the club he once branded a 'corner shop' when compared to supermarket giants such as Rangers and Celtic.

'As far as Jim McLean, football manager, was concerned, I made the wrong decision,' he wrote in *Jousting with Giants*. Ferguson was entitled to ask: Why did he have to suffer? Why could he not try to avoid making the 'wrong decision'?

In the end, McLean eventually relented, but he argues that when advising his board to allow Ferguson to join Rangers he did so on his own terms. In any case, he was no longer manager, having finally stepped down after a 4–1 home defeat to Aberdeen on the final day of the 1992–93 season. 'I can't spoil the habit of a lifetime: the attitude of the players was very disappointing indeed,' he told reporters afterwards. Ferguson at least avoided a final withering blast from McLean, as a result of him having missed the last six games of the campaign through injury.

McLean now had to start thinking solely with his chairman's head on, a role he had previously shared with his managerial responsibilities. Meanwhile, someone whose methods and personality could not be further removed from his own settled into the manager's seat.

Ivan Golac, the former Southampton full-back, was the surprise choice to take over. It is a matter of some regret that Golac and Ferguson never got the chance to work together; the dynamic would certainly have been quite different to the one existing between McLean and Ferguson. While McLean raged at his players, Golac took them on walks in a local park and encouraged them, in all seriousness, to 'smell the flowers'.

McLean was on holiday in America when he heard that talks between Ferguson, his agent and Leeds United had broken down. 'I had given the directors the number of the house I was staying at,' recalls McLean. 'It was a Rangers supporter's house, ironically, who was a good friend of mine. I got a phone call saying Duncan was not accepting the terms Leeds were offering, so the deal was off.'

McLean returned from America and, on his arrival back in Dundee, proposed going back on what had been a firm intention to sell to anyone but another Scottish club. When McLean had stated that there was no way he was willing to make 'one of our rivals stronger', it was clear he was referring to Rangers, the only club in Scotland with the hope of meeting United's valuation of the player. Indeed, by midway through June, Rangers, on the back of their excellent Champions League performance, had already raked in a remarkable £5.3 million from season tickets for the following campaign. 'You didn't strengthen the opposition for them to come and rub your nose in it,' says McLean, who had been initially wary of a Ferguson-bolstered Rangers returning to haunt United.

But then he began to have second thoughts. McLean wondered whether Ferguson was cut out for life at Rangers. He began to seriously doubt he could thrive at Ibrox, given his conduct at times at United. This, coupled with the prospect of being able to drive the fee up further, helped persuade McLean to reconsider the strategy of not selling him to another Scottish club. He had a hunch that Ferguson might be more hindrance than help to Rangers. 'I came home from holiday and said to the directors: "Look, I am going to fall out with you here,'" recalls McLean. "'Let's sell Duncan Ferguson to Rangers. But I would be asking for £4 million. The extra £500,000 will get me another really good player." Every one of them agreed.' And so, perhaps surprisingly, did Rangers, who met the new valuation, despite the knowledge that United had recently been prepared to accept just over £3 million for the player.

That extra money paid out by the Ibrox club took the figure up to a British record fee for a player moving between two clubs: it barely seems believable now that the transaction involved two Scottish clubs. It was particularly satisfying for McLean, who had long been anguished by the decision to sell Andy Gray to Aston Villa for just £110,000. Gray had left with McLean's best wishes, but Ferguson? Did he depart on good terms?

It was interesting that just days after I had met with McLean I arranged to interview Ray McKinnon, another talented *enfant terrible* from the 'new breed' days, in Brambles cafe. Of course being the aforementioned favoured establishment of the McLeans, it should have been no surprise when a certain former football manager walked in with his wife. McKinnon and McLean greeted each other warmly. 'He has sorted himself out now,' said McLean of McKinnon, then managing Lochee United, a junior club in Dundee. McKinnon himself acknowledged that his wild streak had presented a challenge for McLean, who, he added after his former manager had left the table, 'still puts the fear of God into me'.

There has been no such reunion between McLean and Ferguson, not even when the player returned to play at Tannadice for Everton in a friendly in 2003. By then, McLean had sold his shareholding and stepped down as director, after controversially – in light of his recent run-in with a BBC reporter – returning to the board for a brief spell in 2002.

'No, Duncan didn't show any respect to me at the end, he didn't come and shake my hand,' says McLean, after I pressed him for information on how they parted following Ferguson's transfer to Rangers.

What would happen if he one day bumped into Ferguson in the high street – as happened with McKinnon in Brambles café a few days later? 'I would say "hello" to him, but I am sure he wouldn't say "hello" to me.'

Their parting of ways was perhaps mutually beneficial; nothing further needed to be said between them. Not then, or now. 'Financially, it was imperative that we got the money that we did at the time to rebuild the stadium,' explains McLean. 'We would have been in big debt as a club if it had not been for Duncan Ferguson, without any doubt.

'But to be completely honest, he was not as big a loss as he could and should have been. I reckon he was playing fewer and fewer outstanding games for Dundee United the longer he was with us. We cashed in on a talent that, unfortunately, did not reach its full potential, in my opinion.

'I guarantee the longer he stayed at Dundee United, the worse it would have been. If Rangers cannot motivate him to turn it on every week, if Everton can't motivate him to even play, then how the hell can Dundee United with 6,000 supporters motivate Duncan Ferguson to do it?'

When you consider United had landed Ferguson for the price of a minibus, then the transfer fee received on his departure represented a spectacular deal. Why, Ferguson might well have wondered, did he need to go and shake McLean's hand? It later emerged that McLean had received a bonus of £150,000 after Ferguson's sale – he admitted this himself in an interview with the *Sunday Times* in 2004, describing it as the 'exception' after years of being paid 'peanuts' by the club (although he added that he knew such wages were all United could afford).

It is understandable if Ferguson felt strongly that he had more than paid back the club's investment in developing him as a player. He was certainly aware that his transfer fee was going to help with the ongoing renovation work at Tannadice – a new east stand was opened in 1994. The sight of such improvements prompted Ferguson to make a wry aside to former teammate Grant Johnson when he returned to Tannadice with Rangers. Spotting a bank of spanking new tangerine-coloured seats with the letters DUFC picked out in black, Ferguson turned to Johnson.

'That's no' right,' he said.

'There should be an N in it – DUNC!'

CHAPTER 9

Chewing-Gum Feet

Rangers were treading familiar ground when they signed Ferguson. Four years earlier, the capture of Maurice Johnston – newsworthy because not only was he their first high-profile Catholic signing, he had also previously agreed to move back to Celtic from Nantes – had meant that all eyes were trained on Ibrox stadium.

As with Johnston, Ferguson's arrival made the network news headlines.

The press conference took place at Ibrox Park on the evening of 14 July 1993. It was a long way from the Tuscan mountains, where many sports reporters were stranded at Rangers' pre-season base near Il Ciocco, the well-appointed training camp favoured by Graeme Souness during his time as manager. The journalists on the trip knew something was up. On the eve of departure, Gary McSwegan, the young striker who had made his name in the previous season's Champions League campaign, when scoring against Olympique de Marseille, was sold to Notts County. The decks were being cleared. The countdown to Ferguson's arrival had begun.

However, over in Italy the chatter revolved around updates on Ally McCoist's recovery from a broken leg, captain Richard Gough's forthcoming book – which was heavily critical of then Scotland manager Andy Roxburgh – and goalkeeper Andy Goram's progress after reconstructive surgery on his knee. The pending draw for the Champions League first-round qualifying tie after Rangers' exploits of the previous season was also occupying minds. What everyone wanted, however, was the story of Duncan Ferguson becoming Britain's most expensive footballer.

Ferguson had his heart set on Rangers, where his boyhood hero, Davie Cooper, had made his name. In a later interview, published in the Rangers match programme, Ferguson said: 'I got a phone call at my parents in Stirling, saying Rangers wanted to speak to me. That was it – personal terms didn't come into it. You can't let that happen if you are a Rangers man.'

How much of a 'Rangers man' he was is open to debate. His father had grown up as a Rangers supporter and, while Ferguson followed his lead, he was not much of a watcher of football. In any case, by the time he was 16 he had signed Schoolboy forms with Dundee United. Interestingly, Rangers could have saved themselves a great deal of money, having despatched a scout to watch the then 13-year-old Ferguson; however, the feedback they received advised against pursuing any interest in the teenager. The verdict: he wasn't tall enough.

Whether he had been a keen supporter or not as a child, the Ibrox side were the champions of Scotland and had begun to amass a collection of nine titles in a row. They had the further appeal of being potential Champions League participants. Arguably, they were the biggest club in Britain. At the time, David Murray, the Rangers owner, believed there was no argument. 'This is not necessarily the end of the spending,' he said at the time of Ferguson's capture. 'We are the biggest club in Britain and people had better realise it. There's no limit to our ambition.'

Of the other Scottish clubs, only Celtic had broken the £1 million barrier. None had come close to paying £4 million for a player.

Ferguson, meanwhile, wanted to live up to his reputation as the country's most promising youngster. Similarly, he wanted to live down the idea that he was the wild child of the Scottish game.

Sadly, he failed on both counts.

At the time, football was in the process of a startling metamorphosis. After the tragedies and the hooliganism of the 1980s, it was becoming gentrified. Fans in the '90s found themselves sitting in shiny, new plastic seats rather than standing on ancient, rickety and often unsafe terracing. Structures like the all-seated 'Duncan Ferguson Stand' at Dundee United were rising from the rubble of terracing all across the land.

Ferguson was a most unlikely poster boy for this new era. And yet that, briefly, is what he became when Murray told his manager, Walter Smith, that he had agreed to meet Dundee United's valuation of the striker. You suspect he was secretly pleased that United had proved robust negotiators; it meant Rangers had broken a British transfer record, with all the publicity – and puffery – that this guaranteed. Although, how robust United had been is open to conjecture; as Jim McLean suggested in the previous chapter, he had simply advised upping the asking price by £500,000 and seeing what transpired.

'Walter had identified him as a signing target and Duncan desperately wanted to come to the club,' recalls Murray. 'We were up there with the best. Even prior to that we had signed Trevor Steven ahead of Manchester United. We had signed Terry Butcher, the England skipper, just before I came. That's why we were able to compete with other clubs to sign Duncan Ferguson.'

'I remember the day he signed, coming up the stairs at Ibrox with his father,' adds Murray, nearly 20 years later. 'I shook his hand. He was a very amiable young man. He'll have been, what, 22 years old, 23?'

In fact, Ferguson was just 21.

The previous record transfer fee between two British clubs was the £3.4 million Blackburn Rovers had paid Southampton for Alan Shearer, a month before he turned 23. On the night before Ferguson joined Rangers, David Platt, the then England captain, had become the most expensive British footballer, when he joined Sampdoria from Juventus for £5.2 million. Just days after Ferguson's move, Roy Keane signed for Manchester United from Nottingham Forest for £3.7 million – but this was still only described as the 'second highest transfer fee between two British clubs'.

Platt was in Italy and was already an established player, who had excelled at the World Cup. Ferguson was the most expensive native footballer operating in the British Isles and he was still relatively unproven. It meant he also became the most closely scrutinised player in British football at a time when he was already finding it hard enough to pass unnoticed on evenings out.

Over in Italy, with the transfer saga nearing its end, Walter Smith was finding it similarly difficult to escape the notice of others. He had received the command to return to Ibrox but wished to avoid the rumpus caused by sports reporters who would naturally want to know where he had gone, and why. In a scene bursting with symbolism, a helicopter was hired to fly him across the Tuscan hills from Il Ciocco to Pisa. 'I got the call that we were ready so sign him, that we had completed everything,' he says. 'I had to get a small helicopter from the hotel – I will never forget it – down to Pisa, and it was a horrifying journey over the hills.'

It was also horrifying for those reporters he had left behind in Italy, or at least most of them. Stewart Weir from the *Evening Times*, a Glasgow newspaper, was the one who landed the exclusive story. The night before, the press corps had been invited for drinks and a meal with Smith and the Ibrox backroom staff, including assistant Archie Knox and coach Davie Dodds. However, when they turned up at the appointed hour, only Knox, Dodds and Andy Goram were there to greet them. There was no sign of Smith.

'According to Archie, he had travelled to the draw for the Champions League, where he would meet up with [club secretary] Campbell Ogilvie, so the details for the ties could be sorted on the day,' recalls Weir. 'It seemed a perfectly plausible explanation.'

The reporters slipped away at regular intervals in order to file a story back to their newspaper desks about Smith rushing off to Switzerland for the draw, and then returned to continue imbibing and eating in what were very convivial surroundings.

Weir's deadline was the next morning. He awoke early, if groggily, and delivered his own version of the 'Smith departing for Switzerland' story via a copytaker. He then went down for breakfast, where he was given a message: he had a call to take in his room.

'Before the first edition had gone to print, my late colleague John Quinn received a call from Tommy Gilmour, the boxing promoter, who informed JQ that he had just flown up from London on the first shuttle,' says Weir. Next to him had been sitting none other than Walter Smith. It was obvious why he was returning to Glasgow. Weir had his exclusive.

Smith returned to Italy and Rangers' pre-season training camp. Only this time he had someone else with him, valuable cargo in the shape of Ferguson.

With the star signing on his way, Weir had the good fortune to stumble upon a small gathering of Rangers players playing cards. Here the journalist glimpsed the kind of wind-ups Ferguson needed to prepare himself for, with McCoist and Ian Durrant the main practitioners. Another Ferguson, the midfielder Ian, was a victim, along with Mark Hateley, the player who was now facing a fight for his first-team jersey – or so it was assumed.

'Durrant was baiting Hateley about his age, his transfer value,' recalls Weir. McCoist meanwhile was directing his best shots at Ian Ferguson, or 'Fergie', as he was known. Would he still have that nickname with Duncan around, McCoist pondered.

'I was here first,' claimed Fergie.

'But two Fergies is confusing.'

'There's only one. Me!'

'Aye, but the fans will decide,' McCoist teased. 'They'll go with who is most popular. And that will be the goal-scorer, the big new signing.'

If there could only be one Fergie, there was also a feeling that there could be only one tall, physically imposing centre-forward at the club. 'Ally McCoist and Mark Hateley were doing really well together, but there were all these rumours in the papers that Hateley was going back to England,' recalls Smith. 'And I thought: if we are to continue to get the best of Scottish talent on offer, then we have to get Ferguson.'

As he explains now, Smith knew the price had to be high, given United's tough bargaining stance, and it was driven up by circumstances – what David Murray refers to as 'market forces'. However, Smith also knew it was a lot of money and was likely to prove 'problematic' for the striker, not least within his own peer group of players at Rangers, who were waiting – and willing – to ridicule him on his arrival in Italy in traditional dressing-room no-holds-barred fashion.

The initiation process was a bruising one for Ferguson – not that he appeared to help himself. Smith returned to Italy with his prize possession and quickly noticed something that secretly delighted him: a competitive edge was already forming between Ferguson and Hateley.

On the Friday, observed by Weir high on the mountainside training pitch, Rangers went through various training drills, one of them a routine where the striker played a series of one-two passes between the midfield and the wing, then sprinted forward into the penalty area, where he was expected to connect with a crossed centre.

What emerged was an insight into the rivalry between the two 'target' men, with undertones of: 'Anything you can do, I can do better.'

Hateley went first, finishing off the move with a side-footed volley. Ferguson did the same, producing an almost identical shot.

When the Englishman then converted a header, his new teammate mirrored the move – crashing a header into the net. Hateley's next assault on the vacant goal saw him hurl himself full-length, as he powered a diving header into the rigging. Unsurprisingly, Ferguson copied this, then saw Hateley repeat his earlier performance, emerging from the turf, his sweaty face matted with grass and hair.

'Another two!' came the call from the coaching staff. Ferguson made his pass, then made his move, but just eased up on his run as the centre looped in. If Hateley had been impressive in full flight, Fergie decided to go one better, positioning himself so he could leap and twist in mid-air, crashing an acrobatic scissors kick between the goalposts. 'It was not unlike his effort against Germany at Ibrox,' says Weir.

Hateley's last effort was a ferocious left-foot volley, full of venom, that smashed the bar, while Ferguson's session ended tamely, with a fresh air swipe at a badly hit cross ball. It was 1–0 to Hateley.

'It was evident that even in an uncontested passing-and-finish manoeuvre that both these guys were going for broke,' recalls Weir, who was again a privileged witness as the Rangers welcoming committee went to town on Ferguson later that night.

A bus had been hired to take the party to their destination, an open air bar/disco called Skylab in a nearby town, and it was on their journey there that Ferguson made the mistake of informing his new teammates that he was there 'to take them to the next level'.

Unsurprisingly, this didn't go down too well. Without Ferguson's help, the players had managed to go 44 games unbeaten during the course of the previous season, had won the domestic treble and had also come within an ace of reaching the final of the Champions League, being pipped by an excellent Marseille team (who were subsequently stripped of the title due to match-fixing allegations).

Durrant was the first to react. 'You, you big skinny drip of watter. You're only here so the big man [Hateley] can have a day off now and again,' he shouted down the bus. Ferguson replied by mentioning the goals he had scored at Dundee United. That didn't go down well either. 'You?' questioned Durrant. 'You've won fuck all apart from your BB Youth shield and Forfarshire Cup – I could play keepie-uppie in a telephone box with a beach ball and you widnae get a kick at it,' he added, to cheers and hilarity in the bus.

Ferguson wasn't backing down. 'I didn't win anything because Dundee United didn't win anything,' he shot back. Coach Davie Dodds, who had been assigned as mentor to Ferguson, presumably on account of their Dundee United connection, stepped in. Weir recalls that Dodds 'jumped out of his seat, kneeled on it and looked back up the bus, pointing an accusing finger at Duncan'.

'Dundee United never won anything?' roared Dodds. 'Dundee United never won anything? I've got two League Cup medals and a Scottish championship medal, and I played in a European Cup semi-final. And Dundee United never won anything? It's because of the likes of you that Dundee United haven't won anything!'

Weir recalls Dodds's impassioned tirade being interspersed with expletives and interrupted by cries of 'Gon yirself, Doddsie' from McCoist, Durrant and co. Others were reduced to tears of laughter. Weir also sensed there was considerable bite in some of the comments: 'Given how Ferguson had been put in his place, it was clear to me that the Rangers squad were far from convinced they needed him.'

Still, it was true that young, talented Scottish players were now at a premium due to the ruling that clubs could play only three foreign and two 'assimilated' players in European competition.

Rangers were forced to operate in a sellers' market. It is why Scottish clubs did so well out of Rangers, Murray tells me. We are speaking in 2012, shortly after the club was voted out of the Scottish Premier League following their financial implosion, which led to the club being forced to make their way up from the lowest tier in Scottish football. Given all of which, the former owner and chairman is surprisingly bullish: 'I'll say this now, although many clubs are not pro-Rangers at the moment, I wouldn't mind adding up how much money we gave other Scottish clubs over the years. It will be tens of millions of pounds – and you can quote me on that. Dundee United did a good deal after Walter had identified Duncan as a signing target who could benefit the club, because of the foreigner rule.'

At the time, Murray said he was 'happy' that the money for

Ferguson would 'circulate within this country'.

The landscape had changed because of the player-quota system adopted by UEFA in 1991. It had done Rangers few favours. An English contingent comprising Gary Stevens, Trevor Steven and Mark Hateley remained from the Souness-inspired revolution of the mid-to-late 1980s. Significantly, these players were now regarded as 'foreign' for the purposes of European competition, where Rangers, having won five successive domestic championships, had now fixed their sights.

Difficult though it is to believe now, especially given Rangers' fall, Murray's ambition was to win the European Cup – or the Champions League, as it had only just become known. 'It was an entirely different environment at that time; we'd just had a financial downturn, there had been a blip in the economic world,' he says. 'But we were filling the ground, we were selling season tickets. We were getting European Cup football on an every-year basis. We had to endeavour to try and buy the best Scottish talent.'

The Ibrox side had to look to their own backyard, even when it came to stand-ins. Fraser Wishart has an entertaining story to tell about joining Rangers. After Ferguson's arrival, he was next man in.

As a 28-year-old out-of-contract full-back whose most recent club had been Falkirk, he feared his best days were behind him. Then, out of the blue, came a call from Walter Smith. He needed some cover for David Robertson and Gary Stevens at full-back, and Wishart was invited in for signing talks the next morning. For his part, he knew there wouldn't need to be much talking. But it presented Smith with a headache. 'I have just had Britain's most expensive footballer in here; what the hell am I supposed to do with a free transfer from Falkirk?' he asked, when Wishart walked in through his door.

There wasn't much left in the pot for Wishart. 'I got the dregs,' he smiles.

Both Ferguson and Wishart made their competitive debuts for Rangers against Celtic at Celtic Park. Ferguson had missed the first two league games of the season because of injury. It was only ten days until he was due to attend Cupar Sheriff Court to stand trial for the alleged assault on Graham Boyter and, perhaps predictably, the home fans had already composed a song for him: 'He's tall, he's skinny, he's going to Barlinnie, Duncan Ferguson, Duncan Ferguson.'

On the occasion of his debut, not only did Duncan Ferguson fail to score, but so too did both teams. It was the first scoreless result between the sides for nine years.

'Finally,' wrote Kevin McCarra in his match report for the next day's *Scotland on Sunday*, 'there was a chance to consider just what Rangers have bought in Duncan Ferguson.' The writer noted that Smith had been keen to play Ferguson in order to remove some of the 'mystique' surrounding the striker, who was in danger of becoming the most expensive non-playing British footballer in the land. This was August 1993; Ferguson's last competitive appearance had been in April, when he had turned out for Dundee United for the last time, against Falkirk, in front of 3,000 spectators.

After another four first-team appearances without a goal, it was beginning to look like an inauspicious start to his Ibrox career: Rangers had drawn with Partick Thistle and Dundee, and lost to Kilmarnock and Aberdeen. There were further challenges ahead, but Murray recalls Ferguson with sympathy, even affection: 'He admits himself that he was a raw young boy at the time – but you could not meet a nicer fella. He was polite, mannerly. He had an edge to him, but the edge is what made him a good football player. He wasn't a shrinking violet on the football pitch, was he?'

In a perceptive article published the day after Ferguson arrived at Ibrox, Hugh Keevins, writing in *The Scotsman*, asserted that 'in a game that is admittedly prone to hyperbole, it is no exaggeration to say that his behaviour over the coming months will shape the rest of his life'.

And so it proved.

Smith says he thinks Ferguson joined Rangers 'one or two years too early'. Murray seems to agree: 'All of a sudden he goes from earning £200 a week at Dundee United, where he is just finding his way, to becoming a record signing. That is a lot of pressure for a young man. In most professions, one's apprenticeship is much longer; in most professions, people get to the top after a much longer length of time. It happened very quickly for him.'

It didn't take Rangers long to realise that they had bought the entire Ferguson package, injury problems and court obligations included. His Cupar Sheriff Court appointment came after just six appearances for Rangers. Speaking at the time, Murray expressed his confidence that the player had learned his lesson. 'These events happened prior to him coming here,' said the Rangers chairman. 'He has been made fully aware of the discipline we expect. Hopefully there won't be a repeat.'

A foot injury sustained against Aberdeen two days after being placed on probation for a year put Ferguson out of first-team action. A combination of flu, and knee and hamstring injuries then kept him sidelined until the new year. His return in January 1994 for a 'mini Old Firm' clash at Ibrox attracted a post-war record crowd of 20,331 for a reserves match. Rangers had to open an extra stand to cope with the numbers, something that led to a ten-minute delay to the kick-off.

The Celtic fans then gleefully seized the opportunity to remind the striker that he was still to score a goal for Rangers. The away fans ridiculed him as he mis-kicked in the six-yard box, and then cheered as Mark McNally made sure he had to wait a little longer for a goal, heading an effort off the line. Finally, 12 minutes from the end, it came: Duncan Ferguson's first goal in a Rangers shirt. He swept in a cross and then perhaps closed his eyes and pretended that this was a first-team fixture, one that really mattered.

Afterwards, he was offered some unlikely support from a member of the opposition. 'He did not ask to cost £4 million. Who is worth that kind of money?' said McNally, the defender who scored Celtic's goal in the 1–1 draw. Of course, herein lay the problem – everything Ferguson did was viewed in the context of how much he had cost. He was booked early in the match for, according to one newspaper report, being rather too free with his '£4 million elbow'. He was a '£4 million this' and a '£4 million that'. Everything he did was set in the context of this number.

His second-string Old Firm goal did not help clear a path into the first team. As if it wasn't enough to try and dislodge Hateley, another rival had emerged on the scene. Gordon Durie was signed in November to help cope with Ferguson's absence and he was stringing together both games and goals. Ferguson was left frustrated.

'At Rangers, he was coming to a club as a big-money buy and, all of a sudden, after playing every week at Dundee United, he was being left out,' recalls Smith. 'He didn't like being left out of the team and said that to me often. I tried to explain to him that he needed to take his time.' Smith describes him as 'impatient', adding,

'But then, you couldn't hold that against him.'

In spite of everything, Ferguson was popular among the majority of his teammates. Despite the cutting nature of the banter that met his arrival in Italy, he was highly rated by the players – most of them, anyway. McCoist, for one, would have relished the chance to establish a partnership with him. 'As with Mark Hateley, he would have been better for me than I would have been for him,' he says. 'They were incredibly similar: strong, brave and selfless. On his day, Duncan was an incredible tower of strength to have beside you.'

McCoist repeats the oft-heard contention that Ferguson was far better with the ball at his feet than many gave him credit for at the time. Wishart, too, is keen to emphasise this, and laughs as he recalls Ferguson being quick to let people know that he was about more than just power. 'He used to say to us: "Just call me chewing-gum feet – just play it in to me, I am chewing-gum feet, it just sticks."'

The trouble was, the ball wasn't always played to his feet. Even at Rangers, the temptation was often too strong to play it high and long to Ferguson, rather than along the ground. 'Having a British spine made us tougher,' reflects Murray. 'But we were maybe not as sophisticated football-wise; it was more direct.'

Rangers were by now perennial title favourites in the Premier League, where Celtic were a diminished force. In Europe, where Murray was desperate to succeed, their deficiencies were stripped bare. Ferguson only appeared in two European ties for Rangers, both of which were lost over two legs.

The first disappointment arrived against Levski Sofia in the qualifying round for the Champions League. Everything Rangers were doing at the time was geared towards progressing in Europe. Here, however, they fell at the very first hurdle. Although Hateley scored twice in the first leg – a 3–2 win for Rangers – Ferguson was a hapless presence wide on the left, where Smith had positioned him to the bafflement of many Rangers supporters. When Rangers lost the second leg 2–1, going out on the away-goal rule after a last-minute strike (Ferguson was absent, injured), they were left to concentrate on their domestic ambitions with a team worth many millions of pounds.

Even the reserves, for whom Ferguson played more often, were probably capable of winning the Scottish title. Wishart recalls playing in a second-string match where McCoist and Ferguson were up front, and Russian and Dutch internationalists Alexei Mikhailichenko and Pieter Huistra were on the wings. All had been left out of the previous Saturday's team. It summed up Scottish football's problems, and possibly meant that Rangers were left exposed on the European stage. At the time, and in the absence of a serious challenge from Celtic, Rangers' 2nd XI were probably the second-best side in Scotland, although Aberdeen and Motherwell did push them hard in Ferguson's only full season as a Rangers player, finishing respectively three and four points behind the Ibrox side. The striker's own contribution to the championship success was one goal in ten league appearances.

Ferguson's trials and tribulations proved fertile ground for humorists. 'Ever since he was a young street urchin surreptitiously smoking 20 a day behind the bike shed, Ferguson has craved the opportunity to play reserve-team football at Ibrox,' wrote Bruno Glanvilla in the parody column that entertained readers of the Scottish football fanzine *The Absolute Game*.

Another edition of the same fanzine featured a cartoon with Ferguson on its front cover. He is leaning, in delinquent fashion, against a post. A nearby policeman asks him, 'Aye, aye, Ferguson – what are you up tae?' Ferguson's reply? 'Och, nothin' – just trying tae nick a goal, officer.'

Both McCoist and Wishart make the same remark during conversations I have with them about Ferguson. They tell me that the first thing they do when someone mentions his name is break out in a smile. They don't mean it in a mocking way. Both genuinely warmed to Ferguson, McCoist in particular. 'The biggest compliment I can pay Duncan is that if someone mentions him, then I smile. That's the first thing I do: I smile. I loved him.'

Nights out were invariably made more entertaining by Ferguson's presence, although he didn't always engage his brain. At one players' Christmas party, he had to be gently persuaded that sporting a convict's outfit might not be the brightest idea. Instead, he turned up in a suit of armour. 'You could see the indentation on his shoulders for about a fortnight afterwards,' says Ian Durrant, shaking his head. Sometimes it does not feel as though the reason for Ferguson's injury-plagued career is such a mystery. Another time, he turned up in a Pink Panther costume. 'He didn't realise it would be roasting inside,' says Wishart. 'He had to carry around this Pink Panther's head under his arm all night.'

There was, though, some genuine rivalry between the striker and Hateley, whom he had been bought to replace in time. The English international rose to the challenge, embarking on the most productive spell of his career. Smith reflects on the effect buying Ferguson had on Hateley. Although it's difficult to argue that the club got value for money from Ferguson, the manager points out that Hateley's reaction was to become a £4 million-rated player himself, finding a new level of performance in his early 30s. He won both the Football Writers' and PFA Player of the Year awards in a season when he was supposed to start making way for Ferguson. Instead, he was reinvigorated.

When I contacted Hateley, I felt there might have been some sense of disapproval of Ferguson in his comments. Possibly it is a case of once a rival, always a rival.

'I think the fact that Rangers paid £4 million for Duncan meant Duncan automatically thought he might get straight into the first team,' says Hateley. 'But that wasn't the case. It was a case of coming in and waiting for your opportunity, and taking it when it came. Unfortunately for Duncan, he could not get his head around that.

'Duncan paid the ultimate price at the end of the day, with his off-field antics. It really did spoil what he was doing on the pitch.'

Hateley had also made a big move as a young player, joining AC Milan from Portsmouth. He had risen to that challenge, too. He might have wondered: what was Ferguson's problem? The big transfer fee was one thing, but he had moved 30 or so miles from where he grew up, and to a team that he knew all about. It wasn't like going to a different country, as Ian Rush is said to have remarked on leaving Liverpool for Juventus.

Unlike Hateley, whose young family moved with him to Milan, Ferguson didn't already have two children. Except for putting the ball in the back of the net at regular intervals, he didn't have responsibilities. But then neither did he have someone like Ray Wilkins, who joined Hateley in Milan, to act as a sobering influence. Those such as McCoist and Durrant, infectious personalities though they are, were not ideal chaperones; they, too, were wired for fun.

Ferguson did have Walter Smith, someone who has since gained a reputation for taming troublesome players, most notably Paul Gascoigne. Smith even invited Gascoigne round for Christmas lunch one year upon hearing that his midfielder was in the middle of some family-related distress. Ferguson, says Smith, was harder to get to know – even though, as with Gascoigne, he managed him at two different clubs, first Rangers and then Everton.

While clearly fond of Ferguson, Smith admits that he 'didn't really get close to him'. It is possible to detect that Smith feels he failed Ferguson, a sense that he might be annoyed at his own inability to make sure Ferguson fulfilled his potential. 'Everyone says to me that I am good with players like that, players who need a bit of guidance, and support,' he says. 'But as a player, I would never have said I got close to him. There are some players you could get a bit closer to than others; that is natural in any walk of life.'

In the absence of genuine achievement at Ibrox, myths and fabrications fill the void. There is the one involving Mark Hateley's Versace suit and a pair of scissors. Another has Ferguson whispering what he earned each week in the ear of opposing defenders, in a bid to take their mind off marking him at corners.

Hateley flat out denies the Versace suit incident. Ian Durrant admits Ferguson might have put it on – along with Hateley's pants, socks and shirt: '£4,000 quid of designer gear – and he still looked like a tramp,' smiles Durrant. But there were no scissors involved, apparently.

In his autobiography, *Blue and White Dynamite*, Durrant does mention a fistfight between Ferguson and Hateley at the Rangers' pre-season camp in Italy. 'I'd have backed Hateley,' he writes. Not everything, it seems, was cordial between the pair, therefore. Indeed, the England centre-forward is supposed to have reacted to news of Ferguson's signing in bolshie fashion: '£4 million? That's an awful lot of money for a sub.'

Hateley sounds slightly more sympathetic now. 'I was towards the finished article, while Duncan was just starting off,' he says. 'Walter looked at Duncan's attributes and saw a lot of early signs that he could become the player that I was, and add to his game.

'I think the money paid for Duncan probably put far too much pressure on him, especially coming to one of the Old Firm, where it is a unique place,' he adds. 'We have seen plenty of players come and really not handle the mental side of what is required.' Hateley echoes Smith: 'I think, at Duncan's age, it was probably a couple of years too early for him.'

Ferguson scored five goals for Rangers in total. His one league goal in the 1993–94 season was followed by another on the opening day of the following campaign, against Motherwell. His other goals came in a hat-trick burst, at Gayfield Park, home of Arbroath, in a 6–1 League Cup win for the visitors. It is unlikely that Ferguson has kept the match ball for posterity. His second and final European appearance for the club came in a second-leg clash with AEK Athens in another Champions League qualifier in August 1994. Still it appeared as though he and Hateley were incompatible, with *The Independent* noting that they were 'guilty on several occasions of going for the same ball', as Rangers lost 1–0 at home after a 2–0 defeat in Greece. The financial ramifications of again being knocked out of Europe so early were to impact on Ferguson.

At Ibrox now, there is little to mark the day the club broke the British transfer record. Wander down the corridor in the Bill Struth main stand, where hang photographs of those who were capped while playing for Rangers, and you won't see a framed picture of Duncan Ferguson. He is not there because he did not play for Scotland during his 15-month stay at Ibrox, which is remarkable, considering the fuss that surrounded his arrival and his own contention that he wanted to establish himself in both club and international sides. Walking down this Ibrox corridor, I sense another absence in the Duncan Ferguson story, another blank space.

And yet, despite the underwhelming return in the form of goals, despite the limited number of appearances and lack of an international cap, it is incorrect to say he made very little impression at Ibrox. On the contrary, Ferguson did manage to create history while wearing the light-blue shirt of Rangers.

CHAPTER 10

Where Were You Looking, Kenny?

Jimmy Nicholl, the Raith Rovers player-manager, wasn't quite sure what he had seen, and afterwards played down the incident. So, too, did Walter Smith, who, after the match, said he had been moving down from his seat in the directors' box to the dugout when the flashpoint occurred.

To be fair to the Rangers manager, this was a trait of his in both of his spells in charge at Ibrox. It is a switch he normally makes about five minutes before half-time, meaning there is always a chance something significant might happen as he descends the stairs inside the stand. He's been known to emerge from the tunnel having managed to miss goals. The incident around which so much of this book hinges took place in the 35th minute, approximately, of the league fixture between Rangers and Raith Rovers. And Smith was not the only one who claimed not to have seen it.

Referee Kenny Clark chose an inopportune moment to turn his head, after awarding Raith Rovers a free kick following a tangle between Duncan Ferguson and Jock McStay, the Kirkcaldy side's right-back. The Rangers player, frustrated by the award going against him, and also McStay's continued close attentions, then looked to have propelled his head towards his opponent, who fell to the ground, clutching his face. There was a brief flurry of elbows, a tug of shirts. Then silence.

Clark later claimed he had turned his back in order to point back up the field after awarding the foul to Raith Rovers, having determined that Ferguson had been the initial aggressor. He told this to newspaper reporters and, later, he repeated it in a court of law. Words, statements, opinion and condemnation quickly followed Ferguson's clash with McStay. But in the direct aftermath a hush fell upon Ibrox, suggesting that the majority of the home fans in the 42,545 crowd – a gathering which included Bill McKinlay, the future governor at Barlinnie, who was taking his godson to his first football match – knew that their man had erred.

The void, however, was soon filled once more with voices; the game resumed, as if nothing had happened. However, something *had* happened. Jock McStay, the second actor in the drama, was nursing a small cut inside his lip. He knew it could have been worse. Part of him wished that it had been. Part of him wished that he hadn't flinched and had instead received Ferguson's forehead square in the nose.

At least then it wouldn't have gone unnoticed; a bit like McStay was destined to do, when jettisoned by Raith Rovers soon afterwards to begin a gradual disappearing act from the game altogether. At least then he would not have been mocked for going down 'like a sack of spuds'. He very quickly became damaged goods, he reckoned. His card had been marked, his image and reputation forever tarnished by his brush with Ferguson. And that is before we get to the psychological scars he suffered purely by virtue of being an unwitting contributor to one of Scottish football's most controversial episodes.

Even though he made fewer than 20 competitive appearances there, a case could be made for classing Ibrox Stadium as the most significant football ground in Ferguson's life: he made his senior debut there for Dundee United and, undoubtedly, made his name by *nearly* scoring a goal – which, perhaps, sums up his career. But he also made his greatest mistake there.

When Ferguson was handed a rare start for Rangers on 16 April 1994, he was eager to impress and conscious that he was in danger of going down in Scottish football history as a multimillion-pound misfit. He had yet to score a goal after more than 700 minutes of football for Rangers and was clearly on a mission to please fans, who were beginning to have concerns that the club had forked out £4 million for a malingerer.

Ferguson was alert to this mood among the supporters, and perhaps the club were, too: he had been chosen to be the subject of the profile piece in that afternoon's match programme, in which he pleaded for some tolerance. He acknowledged the unease that existed among the supporters. 'The fans are bound to get impatient, but I'm feeling just as bad as them,' he said.

He knew it was time he made his mark.

*

By the time we meet to discuss his part in the Duncan Ferguson story, circumstances have planted Jock McStay at Celtic Park, news that might excite conspiracy theorists from all those years ago, who suggested that Ferguson versus McStay was a contest which, like so many conflicts in the west of Scotland, had another context, and a depressingly familiar one at that: Rangers versus Celtic, Protestant versus Catholic.

The McStay name will be forever linked with Celtic due to the success of Paul McStay, Jock's elder cousin. But the association between the family and the club goes back further than this, to Jimmy and Willie, Jock's great-grandfather and great-uncle. Both captained Celtic in the 1920s. Jock follows on in the McStay tradition of being Celtic through and through, this despite the family's ancestral seat being Larkhall, of all places, the South Lanarkshire town known for its large Protestant population and also a reputed aversion for shop frontages painted green.

McStay has long accepted the fact that, despite his own achievements in the game, it is an association with someone else that defines his career. It is just that, understandably, he thought it might be his cousin Paul's shadow that would linger over him as he sought to plough his own furrow at Motherwell and Raith Rovers; Paul, meanwhile, gathered honours and international caps at Celtic.

Jock McStay was sometimes miffed at having to live so much in Paul's shadow. However, it was no slight to be regarded as existing in someone such as Paul McStay's slipstream; most of those who played football in Scotland in the 1980s and early '90s suffered this fate, including Paul's own brothers, Willie and Raymond. All had to accept that, in the talent stakes, Paul McStay, known as 'the Maestro' by Celtic fans, was the yardstick against which few could compete. Their closeness in age – just ten months separated them – meant Jock and Paul played together at a boys' club in Larkhall and also for the school team, although there was little doubt who would go on to star for Scotland. At just 15, Paul captained the Scottish Schoolboys side against England at Wembley and was 'man of the match' as Scotland triumphed 5–4.

Paul was one in a hundred. Jock, by his own admission, was like the majority of the other 99 players: committed, rugged at times, but in love with a game that had given him everything, including a trade.

'How come you want to talk about football all the time?' his friend and, for a spell, flatmate Gordon Dalziel would ask him, when the pair were holed up together in Motherwell in their late 30s. McStay was attempting to put a divorce behind him and was now assistant manager of Albion Rovers, where he continued to feel persecuted.

Referees and linesmen were, he felt, prejudiced against him due to his involvement in such a high-profile case as the Ferguson one. 'I was definitely a marked man,' he says, bleakly.

McStay's own association with Celtic as a footballer was never anything more official than training with the club as a youngster, when he was known by his 'Sunday' name of John. Currently, though, he has achieved something he was not able to as a player; he is now employed by Celtic. As the club's maintenance painter, he is contracted to keep the stadium looking spic and span. He sits down while still wearing his white overalls on a cold, grey day in early January, having led me to a table in the Jock Stein suite on the first floor of the main stand at Celtic Park.

It has proved easier than expected to get McStay to agree to meet. I had been initially pessimistic about the likelihood of obtaining an interview, aware that he had been hesitant when asked to speak in detail about the incident with Ferguson when approached by *The Observer* in 2003. 'It has cost me in so many ways,' is all he would say to them on the record. The passage of several more years has perhaps helped soften his stance; he returned my call and invited me to meet him during a break at work.

McStay is a fuller figure now, though the mop of dark hair is still intact. Below, in the car park, there is the usual bustle of activity that continues even on non-match days outside Celtic Park, as people queue to buy burgers and the shirts of those players currently in vogue.

His cooperation is a relief since he is the flip-side of the coin in this story, the man whose tale is every bit as intriguing, if much less known. As with the two faces of a coin, McStay and Ferguson have never actually met: at least not properly, the way people normally do, via formal introductions.

If they ever did get the opportunity to reflect while in each other's company on what happened that day, then McStay would tell Ferguson that he is sorry the consequences of their clash turned out to be so grave for him. But then, he would add, it was not only him who suffered. Despite feeling the force of Ferguson's head-butt, McStay endured more than just a cut lip. He felt as though he'd had his chair kicked from underneath him; he says, when he'd attempted to sit down again, after the dust had settled, 'I fell on my arse.' There was no support network for him and, with his contract weeks away from ending, no guarantee of income.

Does he have any feelings at all for Ferguson?

'Nothing really,' he shrugs. 'I was the victim that day. It was definitely me who had it hardest. All right, he spent some time inside. But I don't think I had much to do with that. He made a lot of money out of the game from not really playing that much.'

McStay, on the other hand, was, in his own words, 'dropped like a brick' by Raith Rovers following the incident. Having served just two clubs for over eleven years – his Raith spell alone spanned seven seasons, close to testimonial territory – his career grew to become a peripatetic one, taking him from a month's trial with Falkirk to Clyde, Portadown on to East Fife, Clydebank and then into the junior game in Ayrshire.

McStay's senior career had begun with Motherwell at the age of 16, when Jock Wallace was manager. It was Wallace, who later took charge of Rangers, who insisted that McStay should also undertake an apprenticeship, and he did, training to become a painter and decorator. McStay played a handful of games for Motherwell; however, it was at Raith Rovers that he did most to create for himself an identity away from Paul. 'I have two medals,' he says, before adding rather pointedly, as if aiming a rather belated dig at Ferguson, 'Better players than me haven't won two medals.'

McStay was already at Raith by the time Jimmy Nicholl arrived to inspire an upswing in fortunes, something he kick-started by insisting the club made the move to become full-time ahead of season 1991–92. These were wild, high times in Kirkcaldy. 'That's why we were a good team,' smiles McStay, who didn't have to be asked twice to go on a night out. 'Fans could associate with the players then. The gulf is getting wider, even at that level. We used to know every fan's name, and spent a few nights out in Kirkcaldy. The night we won the league [in season 1992–93] we were up there for about three days.'

McStay played a pivotal role in that championship team and then played the majority of the games in the Premier League, too, as Raith battled to survive the drop. He even scored against Rangers in a 1–1 draw at Stark's Park earlier in the season. By the time Raith travelled to Ibrox for the seventh-last game of the campaign, they were in need of a miracle. In the end, they were relegated, along with Dundee and St Johnstone, nine points adrift of safety – a considerable distance in the final season of two points for a win. 'If Ferguson had been sent off, then who knows?' McStay says.

But Ferguson was not sent off. He wasn't even booked. Not for this incident, at least. And therein lay one of the problems. Rangers were already a goal up when Ferguson and McStay tangled in the south-west corner of the stadium, between the main stand and the Broomloan Road stand. Later, in court, they were located rather more precisely: 'ten metres in-field and twenty to thirty metres from the Raith Rovers goal-line'. According to McStay, Ferguson reacted 'after a bit of argy-bargy', as they battled for the ball. This spot of 'argy-bargy', as McStay terms it, set in motion a devastating chain of events, the most serious of which was Ferguson being met by a charge of assault on what was reported to be the instruction of the procurator fiscal in Glasgow, Andrew Normand. Although he did not ever make a formal complaint to the police, McStay was formally questioned nine days after the incident. Indeed, according to Jimmy Nicholl, two policemen had turned up at Raith Rovers' next game, at Kilmarnock. 'We were just going out for the warm-up,' Nicholl recalls. 'It was about five past two on the Saturday. Someone came to the dressing-room door and said: "The police are here. They want to speak to you and Jock McStay."'

Nicholl remembers the police officers as being from Govan police station. 'One of them said something along the lines of: Just to let you know, the procurator fiscal wants you to testify against Duncan

Ferguson, and he wants Jock McStay to say "Yes, he did it" in court – do it officially. I said: "Get yourself on, what time is this to come here? It's five past two on a Saturday.'" It was explained to Nicholl that the timing was simply because they knew that this was where McStay would definitely be present.

While he has always admitted that the wounds were hardly career threatening, McStay remains adamant that he was struck in a forceful manner by Ferguson. He interprets the silence in the immediate aftermath of the incident as denoting shock at what had just happened. He also argues that it was a tacit acknowledgement from the fans that their player was in the wrong. Indeed, McStay still cannot believe he had to spend so much time trying to convince people that there had indeed been contact. But was there intent on Ferguson's part? That is another, more difficult and loaded question to answer.

'There was one picture in the paper; I always meant to get a copy of it,' he says. 'You could see him grab my shirt and pull me towards him. You see the strands of my hair going back. And yet people still say to me: "He didn't touch you!"'

McStay wasn't a completely innocent party; he admits that he briefly traded on the notoriety and the exposure that he gained. However, he wasn't to know how the situation was going to develop. To him, and to almost everybody else, it was a flash point in an otherwise unremarkable football match.

McStay played what ended up being his final competitive game for Raith against Dundee United on the last day of the season, a week before the Tannadice club met Rangers in the Scottish Cup final. 'We beat United at Tannadice,' recalls McStay. 'Afterwards I asked Craig Brewster for his top because we were going away on an end-of-season piss-up and I wanted to wind a few of the Rangers fans up.' It was how McStay came to be wearing a Dundee United top in a bar in Magaluf when Brewster, of all people, scored the winning goal. 'It was quite funny that,' adds McStay, recalling a game in which Ferguson had made an appearance from the substitutes' bench 14 minutes before the end, to little avail.

McStay was soon cast as a witness rather than a victim in another notorious incident in Scottish football. Just four months later he looked on from the substitutes' bench as Craig Levein threw a punch at Hearts teammate Graeme Hogg during what was laughably termed a 'friendly match' between Raith Rovers and Hearts at Stark's Park. On this occasion there was little debate as to what had occurred – Levein delivered a haymaker, which was caught on camera, and broke Hogg's nose. Afterwards, he was handed a ten-match ban. In contrast to Ibrox, both players were sent off by referee Bill Crombie, with Hogg shown his red card as he was being stretchered from the field.

Indeed, it was an episode that Rangers would later submit as evidence that much, much worse than the brush of heads between Ferguson and McStay occurred on football pitches and yet was ignored by the police and the courts. In actual fact, police did look into the clash between the Hearts players, but chose to take no action, despite the flagrant nature of the crime and the extent of Hogg's injuries.

Whatever other criticism could be levelled at Hogg for his part in the flash point, it was not possible to accuse him of faking it. However, this was the accusation that dogged McStay. He received a small cut above his lip, but it might have made things easier for him had there been more obviously serious damage, scars that would take longer to heal, like the psychological ones have done.

McStay felt people dismissed him, doubted the extent of the impact that saw him tumble to the Ibrox turf. Kenny MacDonald, then working for the *News of the World*, recalls McStay showing him the cut just after the match; there was no question, according to the journalist, that contact had been made. MacDonald, who already knew McStay, waited behind outside Ibrox to speak to the player in person – the only journalist to do so.

'What I think did for him [Ferguson] in the court was the club doctor's report,' says McStay. 'There was a cut above my lip, it confirmed. When I look back now, I wish I had kept my face there: he would probably have broken my nose. You can see the sweat; it's spraying off me!'

As for Ferguson's motivation, McStay remains at a loss: 'I just don't know why he did it. People always ask, "What did you say?" There was nothing. The ball was put in the corner and we were running for it. I turned him and took the ball away, and he was holding my arm. I was trying to get away from him. I didn't elbow him, just tried to get away from him because he was pulling me back, and pushing. That was it.'

McStay remembers Danny Lennon running towards the referee

and furiously gesturing to him that his teammate had been felled by a head-butt from Ferguson.

'The referee later said that if he had seen it he would definitely have sent him off,' McStay says. 'Well, where were you looking, Kenny?' If the referee had been looking in the right direction, if he had brandished the red card there and then, who knows what might have happened? Who knows what could have been avoided?'

*

So where was Kenny looking? Just 32 years old, Clark was in his second full season as a top-grade referee. Great things were expected of him; however, he now admits to fearing that his career was almost over before it got started. That would have meant concentrating on his day job – as a criminal-defence lawyer.

'It was not a game which was fiery; there was not a lot of angst or confrontation between the players,' he says now. 'I suppose in one way that is the best excuse I can offer for having missed it.'

The referee heard later that there had been some 'verbals' going on between Ferguson and several members of the opposition that afternoon – possibly Ferguson again whispering in the ears of defenders how much he was earning compared to them.

'In a cauldron like Ibrox, unless you are actually standing on top of the players, you are not going to be aware of what they are saying,' continues Clark. 'Things happen between players all the time; you turn a deaf ear unless it contains particular menace. But I wasn't aware of any build-up.'

Clark's defence sounds well rehearsed. It sounds as though he has delivered it a million times before, to friends, colleagues and, on one occasion, to a packed Glasgow courtroom.

'It wasn't as if it was a serious foul that had been committed,' he says of the initial tangle between Ferguson and McStay. 'It was a run-of-the-mill foul, if anything.

'Instead of pointing back up the pitch over my shoulder, I actually turned to give the direction of the foul, and that was in order for there to be no dubiety about to whom I was giving the foul. But in doing so I looked away at the crucial moment.

'I looked back; McStay was on the deck.'

It's very clear who McStay considers to be the villain of the piece.

Not Ferguson, whose act of aggression might have been out of order, but was and is not uncommon on a sports field. Not even his manager Jimmy Nicholl, who he accuses of being unsupportive from almost the minute the game finished. Rather, it is Clark who McStay has least time for; it is the referee who he believes, even now, has got the most to explain.

'It happened in a corner – he's walking towards there, the linesman is there,' says McStay. 'Where else is the referee looking?'

He continues: 'It's crazy. The ball was right at my feet. The strange thing is you could hear the crowd take a big intake of breath. It was right down by the enclosure. You could hear the silence, as if they were saying: "I don't believe he has just done that."'

McStay would later run into Clark on occasion as his career continued further down the league, and as the referee strove to get his own one back on track, after what he describes as a 'worrying silence' from the Scottish Football Association's referees department, one that he felt 'spoke volumes'. Clark, too, complains of lack of support. McStay recalls one game at Montrose, when he was playing for Albion Rovers, and Clark was battling to redeem himself at a lower level.

'I was having a dig at him, and he was having a dig at me,' says McStay. 'I gave him a right hard time: "Oh, so you saw that one, did you?" I was really winding him up. Because I really felt bitter against him.'

Up until the fateful day at Ibrox, McStay had been playing for Raith every week, doing what every other player at his level did. He consulted his marks out of ten in the tabloid newspapers on a Sunday and then had a laugh about them with his teammates at training on a Monday morning. He was reasonably well known, not only because of his attention-catching surname. He was a hero in Kirkcaldy, for what that was worth. He was married to Pamela and had a son, Jonathan, and a young daughter, Kirsten. His contract was about to end, but he remembers having no real worries on that front. It was reasonable to suppose that if he had been considered good enough for the Premier League then he would be able to cope with life back in the First Division.

However, he wasn't given the chance, discarded not at the first opportunity, which would have at least given him the summer to fix himself up with a new club, but at the last.

'Jimmy Nicholl left me in limbo,' he complains now. 'My contract was up and we had been relegated. While I had done all my pre-season work with Raith, I hadn't signed any contract yet.' Raith, with McStay included in the travelling party, went on tour to Ireland. 'The manager told me that the chairman was coming over to Ireland and we'd get the situation sorted out then. It got to the day before the start of the season, the Friday,' continues McStay. Raith were due to play St Johnstone the following afternoon. Nicholl called the defender into his office after training and told him he was being freed. 'It left me snookered, because all the other managers had already picked their sides,' says McStay.

It also meant that he missed out on the club's greatest day, just four months later, when Raith Rovers, despite their lower-division status, overcame Celtic in the League Cup final, winning 6–5 on penalties after a 2–2 draw. With Hampden Park out of commission at the time, the game was played at Ibrox, of all places. McStay looked on from behind the goal, where he sat with the Raith fans, as his cousin, Paul, missed the decisive penalty. 'I knew he was going to miss,' he smiles. 'I knew there would still be a McStay having a say in Raith winning the cup.'

Unsurprisingly, Nicholl disputes McStay's contention that he was left 'to hang out to dry' by the club and then abandoned completely. As far as I can make out, he offers little evidence on which to base an accusation that he was – or remains – unsympathetic to McStay's plight.

I met the likeable Ulsterman when he was assistant manager at Aberdeen. He drew up a chair and cast his mind back to a time when he was among the most talked-about young managers in the country. We sat facing each other in the old boot room at Pittodrie. His face is more lined, while the once trademark curly hair has receded further. He might well have felt that he didn't need to offer an explanation for why he dispensed with McStay's services. Nevertheless, he attempted to give one, although it remains clear that McStay's departure could have been handled more sensitively, and been more helpfully timed, certainly as far as the player was concerned.

'It certainly had an effect on him,' he begins, referring to the Ferguson affair. 'It turned sour on him. I am not saying it was the main reason . . . but I had to go and get someone better, who could use the ball better. He had lost his confidence a bit. You could not fault his enthusiasm, or his appetite for a game of football. That's the type of lad he was. He wasn't a nasty one, or vindictive.

'I would not sympathise with him as much as I do if he had been loving the notoriety and had been going round saying: "Yeah, Big Dunc stuck the head in me."'

Nicholl is alert to the football and religion-related tensions in Glasgow. Not only did he play for Rangers in two different spells in the '80s, but he was also brought up on a housing estate on the outskirts of Belfast.

McStay's frustration was further underlined when he was forced to attend a rescheduled SFA disciplinary meeting after he had failed to turn up for the first appointment on the advice of his club, who had been informed by lawyers that attendance meant the risk of prejudicing the forthcoming court case. However, Rangers and Ferguson had complied with the SFA's wishes in the end, which left Raith Rovers with a threatened suspension from the league and McStay facing a *sine die* ban.

When the hearing took place, McStay was again left with the impression that he was on his own. 'At the SFA we sat in this wee room, me and Jimmy [Nicholl],' recalls McStay. He remembers Campbell Ogilive, the company secretary at Rangers, being present. Tony Higgins, who was the Scottish Professional Footballers' Association secretary, also accompanied Ferguson. 'I was a union member too, so why was he there with Ferguson?' wonders McStay.

In the end, Ferguson was handed a 12-match ban by the SFA, a then unprecedented suspension in British football and one that enraged Rangers, who complained on the not unexpected basis that Ferguson was already an 'accused person' and such a punishment meted out by the football authorities might be considered prejudicial to any impending court case. Rangers quickly appealed the ban, which meant Ferguson was allowed to make what turned out to be such an unmemorable contribution to the Scottish Cup final against his former team, Dundee United, while McStay, wearing a United top, watched in a bar in Spain.

If the consequences of the head-butt episode had not been so serious, then aspects of the saga would be considered laughable. Perhaps the most comical of all moments those that unfolded on the afternoon at Ibrox itself.

At long last, Ferguson had achieved something that he had struggled so long to do: he had finally scored a first-team goal for Rangers. Taking a pass from David Robertson in his stride in the opening minute of the second half, he took a slightly heavy touch as he bore in on goal. However, he then managed to clip the ball over Scott Thomson, the advancing goalkeeper.

Delirious, he ran to the fans at the Copland Road stand to celebrate. When he returned to the pitch, Clark was waiting for him. The referee then proceeded to take out the yellow card from the back pocket of his shorts.

And what was Ferguson's crime? What had finally provoked some action from the referee? He had committed the heinous crime of leaving the field of play without permission.

*

However much the official Rangers magazine, *Rangers News*, sought to gloss over the head-butt, it was clear the controversy was not going to blow over any time soon. 'You Nutter' was the headline on the back page of the *News of the World* the morning after the game. Yet, in the best traditions of *Pravda*, the Rangers magazine highlighted only the positives of Ferguson's display for the next edition, concentrating on the fact he had finally scored his first goal for the club. It wasn't quite a case of, 'Head-butt? What head-butt?' but it came close to a complete whitewashing of the incident.

The match report included in the magazine did make mention of a 'flash point' between Ferguson and McStay. However, it notes that referee Kenny Clark was 'content to deliver a lecture to both men'. It added that both managers 'also played down the altercation', instead preferring to dwell 'on the more positive aspect of the game'. Indeed, neither Jimmy Nicholl nor Walter Smith had been particularly outspoken afterwards, while Ferguson himself hardly seemed to be fretting.

The striker even felt good enough about himself to consent to being interviewed. Now chief football writer with the *Scottish Mail on Sunday*, Fraser Mackie was then a young reporter making his way in the world of journalism. He was offered a way-in via the

Rangers News, which, like the *Celtic View*, has helped launch several careers in sports writing. Not yet tainted by a link to the established written press, he was able to interview Ferguson after the match and recalls thinking that the player didn't seem overly concerned by what had happened. The thought that he had carried out what could be viewed as an assault in front of over 40,000 witnesses and while already on probation had yet to impinge on the thrill of having scored his first goal for Rangers.

Remarkably, it was Ferguson's first competitive strike of any sort since he had been on the scoresheet for Dundee United in their 3–2 defeat by Celtic in March 1992, over a year earlier. The most expensive native striker in British football had gone over 12 months without scoring a goal. Perhaps there is little wonder he was so determined to celebrate.

Why spoil his mood, reasoned Mackie, who, seizing on Ferguson's giddiness, managed to draw some precious words from the player. Ferguson was leaning against a wall in the corridor, still clutching a can of lager as he tried to wind down. Outside in the street, McStay was inviting a journalist to have a look at his cut lip. A few feet inside the main entrance at Ibrox, a referee was preparing to make his journey home, where he was met by quizzical looks from his wife. Her gestures suggested she was alert to the gathering storm. 'My wife pays very little attention to football in general,' says Clark, 'but she was looking out the window and spreading her hands, as if to say, "What happened?"'

Elsewhere in the city, a referee supervisor called Mike Delaney was getting ready to write a report criticising Clark's performance, while another report, this time compiled by Strathclyde Police for the benefit of the procurator fiscal, would also soon be completed.

But inside the main stand, a 22-year-old striker was beaming with pride and getting on with the task of beginning the night's refreshment.

'Big Dunc, McEwan's Lager can in hand, was kind enough to give me some words of wisdom on his first goal for Rangers,' recalls Mackie. 'On the flash point with McStay, I think what he said was "the boy made a bit of a meal of it"! But, being loyal to the cause, we just brushed that under the blue carpet and I did the interview with him talking about everything else but that incident.'

The line that the magazine decided to take focused on Ferguson's pride at finally scoring his first goal for the club and how, with his father watching from the stand, it had been a dream come true for the player.

'I always saw Walter Smith on the Monday lunchtime for his news and he asked what I was doing about Dunc, as I'm sure the storm was just starting to brew up in the daily newspapers,' continues Mackie. 'I mentioned that I'd spoken to Dunc and would just have him talking about his goal and the injury woes that were now behind him, as if the head-butt hadn't existed at all. That was considered to be fine.'

The piece Mackie had prepared was, however, leaked to the *Scottish Sun* newspaper, which ran with quotes that, set in a context other than the club's own magazine, looked horrifyingly insensitive, as well as triumphalist.

'Hope you are proud of me, Dad!' screamed the headline.

'Duncan Ferguson has spoken out for the first time since his disgraceful head-butt on Jock McStay,' the piece begins. 'He told the *Rangers News*: I hope I made my Dad proud on Saturday.' *The Sun* cranked it up, for all it was worth.

'Ibrox hit man Fergie broke his goals duck in the 4–0 romp against Raith Rovers – but that strike was overshadowed by the one that left Raith ace McStay with a bust lip,' the article continued. 'That controversial incident is virtually ignored by the club's official newspaper. There is no apology from Ferguson, nor any comment on the butting from Rangers manager Walter Smith. Indeed, the feature on Fergie dwells on his first goal for the club.'

Ferguson is as expansive as he has ever been, either before or since, as he gushes about what it meant to have his parents in the stand at Ibrox for his big moment. 'My mum and dad were here today from Stirling and they're absolutely delighted,' he said. 'My dad's been watching me play football since I was nine. It's him who's pushed me along and helped me from day one. If I'm playing, he'll come along, so I have to perform to keep in his good books. It was a great day for him. I hope I've made him very proud. He's a big Rangers man, so I hope this is the start of great things.'

There was even a reference to the yellow card he earned for leaving the pitch to celebrate his goal – 'I wasn't too worried about that, I had got my goal and that was me delighted' – but nothing at all on what *The Sun* described as his 'loutish behaviour'.

Instead, Ferguson even tried to claim he had been vindicated. 'It was an amazing feeling and a great weight off my shoulders,' he said. 'It was very important for me to shut a lot of people up.'

Just four months after their altercation at Ibrox, fate deposited Ferguson and McStay back at Ibrox Park. They sat like two china dogs on opposite ends of the mantelpiece, in their role as substitutes in a League Cup tie between Rangers and Falkirk, the club with whom McStay was seeking to reboot his career. Jim Jefferies, the Falkirk manager, handed McStay a month's trial after the player was freed by Raith Rovers on the eve of the new season. Almost inevitably, Falkirk were drawn to play Rangers in the second round of the first cup competition of the season, and Jefferies was alert to the delicate circumstances.

He made a point of checking with McStay that he was comfortable being included in the squad for this return to Ibrox, so soon after being installed as Enemy No. 1 in Govan. 'I said: "Why wouldn't I be?"' recalls McStay, never one to shirk a challenge. In the event, unlike Ferguson, who came on as substitute late in a game that Rangers surprisingly lost 2–1, he never made it onto the pitch. McStay hasn't played at Ibrox since the fateful day in April 1994.

There would be one further on-field meeting, a postscript to their tangle at Ibrox. It occurred at Recreation Park, in Alloa, where Rangers played their reserve fixtures at the time. In this unlikely setting, amid the old timber terracing, their paths crossed once again.

The incident had cast a long shadow over the pair of them. Here they were one evening in Alloa, playing for the stiffs, condemned men.

Had anyone bothered to occupy the press seats for this reserve league clash between Falkirk and Rangers A teams, then 'round two' would have had extensive coverage in the papers, particularly since it included another clash between the two main protagonists.

McStay contends he was again the victim of Ferguson's temper. While hardly welcome, perhaps this was the right place for scores to be settled, by dint of going in that bit harder, by blurring the lines between foul and fair play, the way competitors have done since sport's inception. Better to sort it out here, back out on the pitch, than in the courtroom.

McStay, perhaps, had most reason to consider jabbing a fly elbow into Ferguson, but his opponent got there first. This time, however, there were no television cameras, and no procurator fiscal itching to get involved. This time McStay's face bore the very obvious evidence of physical impact, something that might have helped had it been the case at Ibrox.

'I was left with a smashed face,' says McStay. 'Two black eyes. It was an elbow at a corner. Ferguson smashed me right across the face with it.' In reply to my inevitable next question, he pauses, before adding: 'Oh, yes, I think he meant it all right.'

CHAPTER 11

There's a Derby Match Tomorrow, Dearie Me

By the time his latest assault case came to court, Duncan Ferguson was no longer Rangers' problem. The striker was originally set to stand trial in August 1994, the year in which he was charged with assaulting Jock McStay. By the time of the second adjournment – which was requested by Ferguson's legal team when Blair Morgan, the player's lawyer, had to depart for Australia suddenly because a close family member was seriously ill – he was an Everton player, though only on loan.

Weeks later he moved on a permanent basis to a club where the core principles were set out in the motto, *Nil satis nisi optimum*: nothing but the best is good enough. This might have amused Jim McLean, among others. However, any rare smile on the Dundee United manager's face would have disappeared as soon as it dawned on him that Ferguson had once again become a source of frustration for him, 16 months after leaving the club.

United had been due to receive a dividend from Rangers when Ferguson made a number of appearance targets. However, these were proved to be wildly optimistic. In their contract agreement with Rangers, the Tannadice club had insisted on the inclusion of several add-on clauses, as was becoming the norm at the time.

When Ferguson reached 50 first-team games, United would receive £100,000, and after 100 first-team games, another £100,000 would be paid to his old club. After 150 first-team games, it was agreed that United would be due a smaller – and final – sum of

£50,000. For the avoidance of doubt, on the contract itself it is spelled out: a first-team appearance meant being included in the squad of thirteen on a match day, back in the days when only two substitutes were permitted.

Even then, Ferguson did not reach the first target of games. He left Rangers having made just 23 appearances. While the prospect of his imminent appearance in a court room certainly speeded up his exit from Ibrox, Rangers had endured a bruising week at the start of the 1994–95 season when, as well as the Champions League qualifying loss to AEK Athens, they were beaten by Celtic and then knocked out of the League Cup by Falkirk. Given the uncertainty surrounding Ferguson's future prospects, never mind his poor return in the form of goals for Rangers, David Murray could be satisfied with the sum agreed with Everton – £4.25 million. It wasn't a case of cutting losses. Rangers managed to make their money back. 'He drove a hard deal,' recalls Peter Johnson, the then Everton chairman. 'We were not in the best position, so we had to accept it. We had to get Everton kick-started.'

'Duncan gave Evertonians a feeling that maybe the club wanted to do things,' adds Johnson. 'It didn't have a good reputation for doing things. They hadn't done anything since '87, when they won the league. OK, they had been runners-up for the double twice. Since then, the team which won the European Cup-Winners' Cup in Rotterdam had really faded from the scene.'

It was felt by many that the Goodison Park club were taking an enormous risk in becoming associated with Ferguson. For a start, there was no guarantee that they would be able to avoid handing the player over to the custody of the Scottish Prison Service, whether this be sooner or later. Everton officials perhaps felt they had little choice but to take their chances on this count.

Had the club been given any assurances about Ferguson's future? Johnson, who had taken over ownership of the club the previous summer, doesn't recall that being so. 'We knew it was a possibility he might go to jail,' he says. 'My own personal view was that he wouldn't have gone to prison. I mean, in the climate of the moment, you could punch someone in the street, be convicted of grievous bodily harm and still not go to prison.'

In any case, what assurance could Everton expect? No one could possibly second-guess how a sheriff would treat Ferguson, although there was a very real fear on the part of the player's representatives that he would be sacrificed as an example to others. Those with less reason to be loyal to Ferguson simply surveyed his lengthy charge sheet and predicted the worst: in February 1992, a conviction for assaulting a constable in the execution of his duty, and then, in March and August 1993, two further convictions for assault.

In any case, Ferguson's relationship with Everton was not initially designed to be anything other than a temporary measure. It was simply hoped that it would prove to be a mutually beneficial arrangement when the three-month-loan deal was agreed, in October 1994. In the time since the clash with Jock McStay that defined his spell at Ibrox, Ferguson had made only ten further appearances for Rangers. He was back on the bench mostly and, with Rangers again having exited Europe early in the following season, it seemed prudent to trim the wage bill.

It was clear that 'Ferguson and Rangers' was not working out as both parties had hoped, although neither seemed quite ready to give up on the other. On the day the loan deal was struck with Everton, Walter Smith, the Rangers manager, insisted to reporters that Ferguson would be returning to Ibrox 'at the earliest opportunity'. The player, for his own part, planned to use the time at Goodison Park as an opportunity to force his way back into the first-team reckoning at Rangers, as he explained to Kenny MacDonald of the Scottish *News of the World.* 'When I originally went south in October, I viewed it purely as a chance to play first-team football,' he said. 'I never gave the prospect of it being a forerunner to a permanent move a second thought.'

Everton, meanwhile, were in dire straits. Intriguingly, the link with Ferguson was the product of a trip Johnson and some boardroom colleagues had made to Ibrox to gauge ways to increase hospitality income streams. They went in search of catering tips and came back with a taster menu comprising of Duncan Ferguson and Ian Durrant, the Scottish international midfielder who was bidding to overcome horrific injury problems. It perhaps said everything about Ferguson's struggle to establish himself at Ibrox that the attention was mostly centred on Durrant. Everton's preference had been to sign Durrant and Trevor Steven, their former midfielder who was now also at Rangers, on permanent deals, and sign Ferguson on loan. However, the Steven move fell through, and Durrant's future prospects were deemed to hinge on the results of a medical examination.

Much was made in the Merseyside press of the players being foisted on Mike Walker, the then under-pressure Everton manager. When I spoke with Johnson, he said little to indicate otherwise. He remarked that Walker was not complaining when he phoned to say that as well as some tips on serving three-course meals, he had picked up a couple of players from his trip to Ibrox. Walker had his sights set on a striker, having been rebuffed once already when making enquiries north of the border.

'To be honest, I first suggested that we try and sign Mark Hateley,' says Walker. 'But we were told he was reluctant.'

Top of Walker's wish list had been a tall, physically dominant striker, something of a tradition at Everton.

'Hateley was the first choice and then I had a chat with the chairman and said, well, the only other one I would want up there is Duncan,' adds Walker. According to him, Johnson was wary. '"He's a bit of a bad lad," he told me,' says Walker. 'I replied, "He has had that much gyp, that's a reason for him to want to get away!"'

Johnson is eager to take some of the credit, too, unsurprisingly, given the part he later played in the player's departure.

'One of my colleagues on the board had met David Murray and we had agreed to go up and have a look at their facilities and match-day boxes,' he explains. 'We had a very good day, and we also met up with the manager, Walter Smith. And the conversation moved on to loan players.'

At this stage, Everton still hadn't won a match, despite being ten games into the season. Things were getting desperate. 'So I rang our manager and said to him: "How would you like a couple of players on loan?"' recalls Johnson. 'He didn't seem to mind. He thought it was worth a try. When you are bottom of the league and your chairman says how would you like a couple of Scotland internationals, you don't complain, do you? Anything is worth a try.'

Walker is annoyed that he was made to look foolish after originally denying all knowledge of the transfer, as they had agreed. Walker promised not to make mention of the Ferguson deal until after that weekend's game. Johnson flew to Scotland to finalise arrangements, and Walker took the team for a league match at Manchester United, after which he was surprised to be asked by journalists about rumours of a move for Ferguson. He quickly rubbished them. 'It only turns out the chairman had told them, so, of course, the story came out that the chairman's signing players behind Walker's back,' he says now.

Whatever the truth of the matter, and whoever's idea it was first, a distinct lack of enthusiasm greeted the signings back on Merseyside, where neither Johnson nor Walker were flavour of the month in any case. Both were being held responsible for Everton's appalling start to the season. Here they were, preparing to risk further damage to their reputation on a couple of players from Scotland who appeared to define the term 'damaged goods'. Headlines such as 'Farce' and 'Loan Rangers Fiasco' greeted Walker and Johnson when the story broke, after a 2–0 defeat at Old Trafford.

Indeed, the whole messy affair just seemed to outline what had gone wrong at the club. Poor communication was simply another symptom of the sickness.

If anything, it was Durrant who promised most, given his reputation as a box-to-box midfielder for Rangers and Scotland. A sickening injury sustained to his knee in a clash with Aberdeen's Neil Simpson in 1988, still regarded as the principal source of enmity between the clubs to this day, halted his progress, but he had scored twice in Rangers' Champions League run two seasons earlier. However, his rehabilitation had faltered again and he found himself on the sidelines at Ibrox, much to his frustration.

Durrant struggled in the medical, but it was agreed that they would see how he fared for a month, before deciding how long to keep him. Ferguson, meanwhile, signed up for a stint of three months. Both players were of the same opinion: they'd come down to Everton, get some game time, and then return to Rangers and seek to win back their places in the side. That might have been Walter Smith's wish too, but as the manager drove the pair down to Liverpool in his own car, he had a suspicion that Ferguson's career would be better served by leaving Scotland, even if, in public, he was saying the precise opposite.

'I had to go to him and say, "I think this is the best thing for you,"' he recalls. 'He went to Everton on loan, and he seemed to strike a chord with everyone there. I think leaving Scotland was a relief for him.'

Ferguson, though, didn't appear to have thought too deeply about the move. Perhaps only Duncan Ferguson could turn up for a press conference to announce his loan signing at Everton wearing a scarlet blazer.

'I had a blue one on; I'd read the script,' says Durrant now. 'It happened so quickly. You know what he is like. He just wasn't thinking. It was remarked upon in the press conference by the local scallies: "Who was this player who had turned up to sign for Everton while wearing red?"'

Liverpool Echo football reporter David Prentice was one of those 'local scallies' present and he recalls Ferguson's 'completely inappropriate' choice of jacket – though the word choice implies some thought had gone into the process of selecting what jacket to wear, when clearly it had not. 'It just smacked of him thinking he would not be around very long,' adds Prentice.

At the press conference, Durrant did most of the talking. However, it was Ferguson who pulled on an Everton shirt first – although it was still not a blue one. Everton were in the middle of a two-legged Coca-Cola Cup tie with Portsmouth when the signings were made, and Ferguson was pitched in to the second leg at Fratton Park, with Everton required to wear their change strip against their blue-shirted opponents. Everton drew 1–1, which meant they were eliminated from the competition, having lost the first leg 3–2 at Goodison Park.

With the club due to face Southampton on Saturday, the team stayed down on the south coast, as did Prentice. In a hotel he made his first acquaintance with someone who would frustrate members of the Merseyside-based press for years to come. On this occasion, Ferguson, then unaware that Prentice was a member of the dreaded press corps, was a bit more forthcoming.

'He had got injured that night, predictably enough, and his ankle was encased in a huge block of ice,' recalls Prentice. 'He was just chatting away generally. I don't think he knew I was a journalist at this point, which is perhaps why he was indulging me.

'I said to him: "It's only a loan period, do you think you will hang around when the three months are up?"

'He just looked at me. It wasn't sneering exactly, but it was almost like, "Nah, I wouldn't have thought so." He never said it, but you got the impression that he thought Everton were a bit beneath him.'

Everton's crowds had dipped as low as at any point in recent history; they attracted only just over 27,000 when Ferguson made his home debut, against Coventry City. In Scotland, Rangers were playing in front of home crowds of over 40,000, and there was the added attraction of almost guaranteed Champions League participation, even if the Ibrox side had fallen at the first hurdle in both of Ferguson's seasons there.

Everton, sitting in last place in the league, were not quite so appealing. Paul Rideout, who had made the same journey from Ibrox to Goodison, articulated the contrast between Rangers and Everton at the time when he greeted Durrant on the player's first morning at training at Bellefield, the club's training ground: 'Jesus Christ, Durranty, what the fuck are you doing here? Do you not realise the state we're in?'

It would get worse for Everton before it got better. Three consecutive league defeats against the hardly fearsome trio of Coventry, Southampton and Crystal Palace placed Walker's position in further jeopardy, and he was sacked following a 0–0 draw at Norwich, of all places. 'Duncan never scored for me,' Walker laments now. 'If he had, I might not have lost the job – who knows?'

Walker, a Welsh former goalkeeper who had played for Watford and Colchester United, is given little credit when the subject of Ferguson's early days at Everton are under discussion. In fact, most people associate the player's arrival on Merseyside with Joe Royle. Walker is eager to set the record straight; again, this is understandable, given the way his reputation has been traduced on Merseyside following an undeniably successful spell with Norwich City, whom he led to third place in the Premier League. Few have a good word to say about him at Everton, however – not even Neville Southall, who, despite being Welsh and, like Walker, a goalkeeper, could not get the measure of him, branding his former manager 'clueless' in his autobiography, *The Binman Chronicles*. 'Instead of someone who loved football, we got someone who loved his suntan,' Southall adds, witheringly.

Ferguson's own commitment levels had begun to be questioned: Did he really want to be in Liverpool? It wasn't solely Ferguson's responsibility to bail out a struggling manager – and he certainly didn't manage that. Walker recalls the player doing 'everything but score'.

'Who knows what might have happened if he'd scored a couple?' he wonders now, from his home in Cyprus. 'But I wouldn't blame him for that. He did what he did. We didn't have a very good team at the time, trying to rebuild. But then the ironic thing was that in the first game after I was sacked, he scored. Maybe that was an omen.'

It wasn't altogether certain that Ferguson was taking his Merseyside sojourn entirely seriously. He and Durrant were holed up in the Moat House hotel on Paradise Street, where Walker, unusually, also stayed during his time on Merseyside. According to Durrant, he was even informed by Walker at a disco in the hotel that he was not being kept on at the club, in what was further proof of the club having become dysfunctional.

It meant Ferguson had lost a valuable ally. 'I was a slightly older head than him; he was hard work at times,' recalls Durrant, who has retained an enormous amount of affection for Ferguson. 'We did a tour of Liverpool nightspots.'

Ferguson loved going to the Cavern, the venue made famous by the Beatles. 'Unfortunately, next to the Cavern there was an amusement arcade, and Duncan loves his amusements,' recalls Durrant. 'He would be in there playing the "puggies" and then we'd go for an Italian or a Chinese. When you are in a hotel, it's about finding things to do. He didn't have a car, so I was his chauffeur. I was at his beck and call, "Let's go here, let's do that." He was like a kid.'

That month, Durrant recalls, the footballers from out of town were 'basically living with each other'. They were even in rooms next to each other at their hotel. 'We formed a special relationship; ever since then he's been like a lost brother to me,' says Durrant, whose relationship with the player had certainly improved since those early days together at Rangers, when he mercilessly taunted the expensive newcomer.

Walker, however, was not Durrant's cup of tea. 'Elusive,' he reflects. The manager's first words to Durrant at training were hardly encouraging. 'So, where do you play, son?' he asked a player who had already made several appearances for Scotland.

It didn't augur well, and neither did the misprint on Durrant's shirt for one of the five games he played while down south. 'Durant' was the name arced across the back, above his number, 22. He has kept it as a souvenir of his experience in Liverpool. Many sensed that Ferguson might not be very long up the road behind him, as Everton continued to struggle and the new striker failed to find the net.

In fact, of course, it was Walker who was next to leave. An international break meant Everton had some time to consider the options, and when they did, one particular choice stood out. Joe Royle had distinguished himself as manager at Oldham Athletic and, having scored over 100 goals in 275 appearances for Everton, it was helpful that he still enjoyed a strong connection with the Goodison Park faithful, something Walker was never able to command. And there was another reason to appoint Royle, according to Johnson.

'We hoped that a big old English centre-forward would be able to motivate a big young Scottish centre-forward,' he says.

In Liverpool, it was difficult to avoid bumping into renowned No. 9s, it seems. Ian Rush was still excelling at Anfield in his second spell at the club and had clocked Ferguson's arrival across Stanley Park. Before long, the two were enjoying a beer together in a bar.

Without Durrant, Ferguson would sometimes seem a bit lost. He did, though, find a friend in Mark Ward, who had left Everton for Birmingham City at the end of the previous season. The diminutive midfielder was from Liverpool and liked a night out, so he returned home often. On one such occasion, he bumped into Ferguson. 'He was charming, even though he had been out drinking all day and was drunk,' recalls Ward. 'He was out with the night porter from his hotel.'

According to Ward, Ferguson 'didn't seem to have a friend in the world' in Liverpool. Ward had been at the races, where he had met Rush. As seemed often to happen in Liverpool, the footballers and their respective parties all congregated in the same bar at night. Ferguson was there too, and he and Rush got talking. 'I will always remember Rushie probing Duncan: "So, how many are you going to score, then, big man?"' says Ward. 'Duncan was such a gentleman. "Not as many as you, Ian. I'd settle for half you scored."

'He was very humble,' continues Ward. 'Obviously Rushie is one of the greatest centre-forwards that ever played. I turned round and said, "He'll do a lot more than score goals; he'll make a lot, too." But it was just fascinating to see these two centre-forwards from across the city coming together, chatting about football while at different stages of their careers.'

The night grew sour, however, when the girls who were with Rush began to get 'a bit lairy', to use Ward's description. 'They started to badmouth a great friend of mine, Maurice,' explains Ward.

Maurice? I repeated the name, wondering if he was talking about the person I thought he was talking about. 'Maurice Johnston, I played with him at Everton,' confirms Ward. As if the night was not pregnant enough with strikers, another one had joined the throng – in spirit, at least. 'Duncan saw what was going on and said, "I don't want you talking about my mate when he's not here." The girl looked at him, and said: "Who the fuck are you?" It could all have got a bit nasty. That's when Duncan told her to "shut up" and we left the bar.'

Later, at a press conference at Hampden Park, I met up with Johnston, then manager at Toronto FC in Canada, and brought up the subject of Ferguson with him. They had never played together at Everton – Johnston left the year before Ferguson joined – but I presumed two such controversial Scottish strikers had come across one another before, particularly having heard Ward's account of the night when Ferguson seemed so determined to speak up for Johnston. However, it turns out that Johnston had never met the person who defended him so vigorously in a Liverpool bar. 'I have heard a lot about him,' he says. 'He's a strong character, a good drinker – all the stuff I like. It's just unfortunate that you don't always cross paths with the players you might want to.'

This incident helps portray a picture of someone who didn't seem too concerned about heeding the advice of various Scottish sheriffs, who warned Ferguson to avoid potential flashpoints. Here he was, prepared to risk landing himself trouble in defence of someone he had never even met. Ward says he had only admiration for Ferguson, perhaps attracted by the loyalty shown towards a fellow *enfant terrible*. 'From that moment on, we became friends,' he recalls. They met up again the next day after Ferguson had finished training and headed to a bar owned by Ward's brother.

'After he arrived, he was never going anywhere,' recalls Ward. 'Guys were not going back to work, kids were crawling all over him. We had to shut the doors. He just sat there all day, signing autographs.'

Duncan Ferguson [far left, front row] while playing for Grangemouth-based boys' side ICI Juveniles, now known as Syngenta Juveniles.
(Pic courtesy Willie McIlvaney)

Ferguson [second from right in front row, arm around friend] featuring in the Bannockburn High School team before a game against the teachers, circa 1985.
(Pic courtesy David Halcrow)

'The New Breed' - the Dundee United youth team after lifting the BP Youth Cup following victory over Hibs in 1990. Ferguson stands at the back looking imperious.

Also included are Tom McMillan [far left, back row], Christian Dailly [crouching, directly in front of Ferguson] Gordon Parks [in white tracksuit top, front row], Eddie Conville [far left, front row], Grant Johnson [third from left, front row] and Andy McLaren [holding the trophy]. (© DC Thomson)

Ferguson beats Graeme Hogg to the ball to send in a flashing header against Hearts in September 1992, at the start of his last season at Dundee United. (© Dave Martin, Fotopress)

Ferguson on the day in July 1993 when Rangers broke the British transfer record to secure his £4million transfer from Dundee United. Ibrox manager Walter Smith stands with his hands on the then 21 year-old's shoulders. (© Paul Reid)

Ferguson jousts for possession of the ball with Jock McStay, the Raith Rovers full back, in the 35th minute of a Scottish Premier Division fixture at Ibrox stadium on 16 April 1994.

After referee Kenny Clark blows for a foul against Ferguson, the Rangers player turns and confronts McStay and then propels his head towards his opponent.

McStay collapses to the turf, holding his face.

After receiving treatment, McStay points to where he says he has been hit. The game restarts with a free-kick to Raith Rovers. Ferguson is not even booked.

With his loan move to Everton from Rangers having been made permanent two months earlier Ferguson celebrates in memorable style after scoring the winner v Manchester United at Goodison Park in February 1995. (© Trinity Mirror)

At the end of his first season at Everton, Ferguson is presented to Prince Charles before the FA Cup final at Wembley in 1995. Ferguson appeared as a second-half substitute in the 1-0 win over Manchester United. (© Getty Images)

Just five days after winning the FA Cup at Wembley Ferguson is at Glasgow
Sheriff Court to hear the verdict in his assault case for head-butting Jock McStay.
(© The Scotsman Publications)

Ferguson in court – an artist's impression. (© The Scotsman Publications)

In August 1996, nine months after being released from prison, Ferguson returns to the Scotland side for the first time since his conviction to win his sixth cap in a World Cup qualifier against Austria in Vienna. He made one further international appearance. (© Eric McCowat)

Ferguson completes his surprise transfer to Newcastle United in November 1998 and is welcomed to the club by manager Ruud Gullit. He returned to Everton in August 2000. (© North New and Pictures)

Ferguson finally scores a goal at Hampden Park - for Everton in a 6-0 friendly win over tenants Queen's Park in July 2002. It was the only time he scored at the national stadium for club or country. (© SNS)

Ferguson grabs Leicester City player Steffen Freund around the neck in March 2004 after he had already been sent off for two bookable offences. Unsurprisingly Everton chose not to appeal the extra four game ban and £10,000 fine he was handed by the English FA. (© Action Images)

Ferguson stoops to head home the winning goal for Everton against Manchester United on 20 April 2005. On the same evening an orchestral piece inspired by his life was premiered in Helsinki. (© Getty Images)

The Last Goal. Ferguson celebrates with a supporter after scoring the equaliser against West Bromwich Albion in the 90th minute of his final appearance in professional football. (© Getty Images)

Ferguson returns from exile in Majorca to be inducted in the Gwladys Street Hall of Fame at a ceremony held at the Adelphi Hotel, Liverpool, in March 2009. (© Jamie Williams)

News came of a child on the estate in poor health. 'He got into someone's car to go and see him,' recalls Ward. 'The man has a heart of gold, as far as I am concerned.'

Had more information been available in the run-up to Royle's opening match – against Liverpool, of all opponents – then the hope that Ferguson might buck up his ideas would surely have seemed forlorn. Ferguson, whose place of residence remained the Moat House hotel, did not believe the change in management necessitated a major change in attitude. He remained hopelessly unprofessional in his outlook.

Ferguson has since given a hair-raising and unusually expansive account of his chosen method of preparation for his first Merseyside derby – and Royle's debut match in charge. On the Saturday night before the Monday night's televised encounter with their derby rivals, he hit the town, managing to attract the attention of both a female carouser and members of the Merseyside Police force. A girl was sitting in the passenger seat of his car as he headed back to base. He was over the alcohol limit. Ferguson just didn't help himself. If one wishes to remain inconspicuous, it isn't advisable to drive through a bus station after midnight, having ignored a 'no entry' sign. This is particularly true if you happen to be the centre-forward for one of the city's two professional football teams, and someone valued at many millions of pounds. Something else should have given him pause for thought: an imminent court case for an alleged assault charge committed while already on probation.

Ferguson himself takes up the story. Speaking from a safe distance of nearly 20 years later and in front of an adoring, non-judgemental audience, at a sportsman's dinner in Liverpool, he recalls: 'It was quite funny – well, it was not funny – I had been out on the lash, know what I mean?' He remembers knowing he was doomed when the policeman involved turned out to be a Liverpool supporter.

'Have you been drinking?' he asked.

'No, no, no, I haven't been drinking,' Ferguson replied.

He was taken to St Anne Street police station. Naturally, the girl in the front seat next to him was concerned by this turn of events. 'Where are you going, what's happening?' she asked. Ferguson gave her his hotel room key. 'I will be back,' he told her. 'I don't know when, but I will be back.'

At the police station, Ferguson was put in a cell. Fortunately, some 'bluenose' police officers, hearing of their striker's predicament, got involved and handed him jugs of water through the latch while a doctor was called. According to Ferguson, he was only 15 milligrams over the limit, though this surprised him. 'I don't know how that happened – I had drunk five bottles of red wine!'

Ferguson then asked why a doctor was needed. 'Because you only blew 15 milligrams over the limit. We are going to do a blood test,' he was told.

'I am thinking to myself: "Dearie me, take my blood?"' says Ferguson. 'I was on the lash on Saturday, on Friday, on Thursday. Don't take my blood, whatever you do . . . '

They let him go at six in the morning. 'I am sure some of you have been there, like. They gave me my shoes back, I put my laces back in.

'And I am thinking: "I have a derby game tomorrow night, dearie me."'

It wasn't just any old derby. It was Ferguson's maiden Merseyside derby, his first match under a new manager. He returned to the hotel, got a key from reception and then went to his room. 'And the girl is only still there, isn't she?' he smiles.

The next day is derby day. Ferguson is feeling rueful, particularly since so much is at stake. 'I feel like I have let everyone down,' he says. 'I have had a drink, and I shouldn't have had a drink.'

The sense of regret helped 'fire me up', he recalls, as did an awareness of the significance of the occasion for Royle personally.

'I am really going to have to pay this fella back,' Ferguson pledged.

It was the night when Ferguson, famously, became the legend before he had become the player. This was Royle's take on things after the goal that cemented Ferguson's love affair with Evertonians, and made it seem inconceivable that he would not come to the club permanently. The striker left the field with fans hanging off the sleeves of his jersey. 'Like the Pied Piper of Hamelin,' recalls David Prentice. It had seemed a portentous evening. A streaker made an appearance in protest at some comments that had been made by Brian Clough in relation to the Hillsborough disaster. The gentleman – 'though a cold night, it was just about possible to make this out' – was the first streaker at a derby match since 1979, noted the *Liverpool Echo*.

Ferguson kept his own shirt on this time. Indeed, he threw himself onto his knees at the Gwladys Street End, in front of an advertising hoarding promoting Carling Black Label. In Royle's eyes, while scoring his first goal for the club, Ferguson had simultaneously written his own epitaph.

'I meant it nicely,' Royle says, when I ask him about the 'legend before the player' comment, one that seemed to become ever more perceptive with each passing year of Ferguson's career. 'He'd hardly kicked a ball for the club before I arrived. Until about 50 minutes in against Liverpool on my debut game, I have to confess I was wondering what all the fuss was about.'

Then Everton had a stroke of luck. Neil 'Razor' Ruddock, the Liverpool centre-half, kicked Ferguson from behind. This tended to have the same effect on the Scot as a tin of spinach had on Popeye. 'He got angry and he became unplayable,' recalls Royle. Indeed, to use the former Everton manager's own description, Ferguson 'went to war'.

'Duncan had immense ability,' he adds. 'And here he was, at a club where the striker has been revered since Dixie Dean, and before. They love their No. 9s. Alternatively, they can be incredibly hard if you don't fit the bill. Unlike a lot of gangly boys, Duncan could jump. He could jump, all right.'

On that night, in the 56th minute, Ferguson rose as high as the crossbar, out-jumping both goalkeeper David James and Ruddock, to connect with Andy Hinchcliffe's corner and give Everton a 1–0 lead.

'That very first night he scored, he changed the match, and probably Everton's season,' recalls Peter Johnson. 'Blackburn Rovers went on to lift the Premier League title. It was a great opportunity for Liverpool to do something – the Manchester United stranglehold had not yet started. And here we were at the bottom of the league, winning 2–0 on a night of raw emotion, with the lights on and the Sky cameras there.'

Few Everton players can have picked such optimal conditions in which to make their mark: a Merseyside derby, live on television, at the famous home end of the ground. To put a seal on the evening, Ferguson then set up Rideout for the second goal with an astute pass across the box.

Royle recalls contemplating taking Ferguson off at half-time. Had he done so, what would have become of him? Already viewed as more trouble than he was worth at Rangers, the news about the drink-driving charge, combined with another goalless appearance which saw him replaced after 45 unimpressive minutes, would surely have seen Ferguson condemned as a waster and a liability in the eyes of the Everton supporters. He might so easily have been packed back off to Ibrox the following morning, with a tag that read, 'Thanks, but no thanks.' It could all have been so different.

Indeed, it looked like he would be returning to Rangers in any case. The news that Ferguson had broken his duck at Everton prompted more questions about his future. 'After his three-month-loan spell has ended, Duncan is coming back to Ibrox, it's as straightforward as that,' insisted Walter Smith the following day, but whether he really believed this at the time only he can say. Ferguson's loan deal had just over a month to run. He scored against Leeds United in his next-but-one game and signed a permanent deal with Everton shortly before Christmas.

But Royle is aware that he might not have been given the green light to sign Ferguson had the striker been unable to redeem himself against Liverpool. Royle was told about the breathalyser incident just before they went out on the pitch, his informant being the club physio at the time, Les Helm. Ferguson's opening-half performance did little to alter the less-than-favourable first impression that was already forming in Royle's mind.

'He'd been so anonymous in the first half that I had it in my mind to replace him,' says Royle. 'I was looking at him, thinking: "Is he *still* suffering from the drink?"

'Thankfully, I left him on,' he adds. 'It was one of the best decisions I ever made.'

Ferguson scored six further times before facing Manchester United for the first time. Again, the game was at Goodison, although on a Saturday afternoon this time. Again, Ferguson leapt remarkably high to score with a soaring header from a Hinchcliffe corner at the Gwladys Street end of the ground. Although another fine finish, and one that had seen him easily beat Roy Keane to the ball, the manner in which he celebrated the goal that gave Everton a vital 1–0 victory is more firmly lodged in the memory. The striker tore off his shirt, before veering towards the Goodison Park main stand family enclosure. His right hand is clutching his top, which he swings like a lasso above his head, his milky-white upper torso exposed to the chill of a Merseyside afternoon in February. After transferring the shirt to his left hand, he flexes a bicep for good measure.

'I remember Duncan later describing it as "twirling" his shirt above his head,' says Steve Jones, an Everton supporter. 'That stuck with me. It was a Scottish description, not one we'd use on Merseyside.' One reporter wrote that Ferguson's half-naked sprint was a 'frenzied display of triumphalism'. It landed the player with a warning from the English FA, who deemed the celebrations to be 'excessive'.

Royle later joked to the press that they were free to speak to Ferguson, 'if you can catch him'. Of course, he did not appear. But perhaps his half-naked gallop up the touch-line had spoken eloquently enough; his shirt swinging above his indie kid mop of brown hair, his upper body lean but ripped: it was as if he was showing the world that he was in top condition, as if he wanted everyone to know he did not have a care in the world. And perhaps he didn't. Not then, not right at that moment at least.

A phenomenon which Ferguson himself later referred to as 'Dunc-mania' was clearly building; Grant Johnson, Ferguson's old teammate from Dundee United, felt it for himself just over a fortnight later after he travelled south to visit his grandmother in Warrington. 'Why not take the chance to see Dunc?' he thought to himself. Conveniently, Everton were playing at home against Newcastle United in the quarter-final of the FA Cup. Ferguson sorted Johnson out for tickets and invited him to the team hotel on the eve of the fixture. 'He was just as usual, his dad was there also and he made sure everyone was sorted for drinks, and ordered food on his tab,' recalls Johnson. 'At the game the next day, it was unbelievable. He was obviously a legend already.

'At Goodison at the time they must have had an indoor warm-up area because the Everton players didn't seem to come out to warm up,' he adds. 'They must have done it all inside. We were there about an hour before kick-off and everywhere you looked there were Ferguson No. 9 shirts and "Big Dunc" T-shirts. The Newcastle players came out and did their warm-up. And then at about quarter-to-three out comes Duncan with a ball. He does a few keepie-ups and the place goes nuts, and then he walks back in.'

Everton reached the semi-finals after Dave Watson's goal handed the home side a 1–0 win. 'Dunc was brilliant,' recalls Johnson. 'He was up against [Newcastle centre-half] Darren Peacock, and smashed him all over the place.'

Ferguson was in the first XI for the following match against Manchester City, but because of a hamstring injury he started only once more that season. Among the matches he missed was the semi-victory over Tottenham Hotspur. Despite being patently unfit, and with his preparations having been further disrupted by the small matter of a criminal trial just a few days earlier, he was named among the substitutes for the FA Cup final against Manchester United, for morale-boosting reasons as much as anything else, Royle later admitted. It meant that he was guaranteed not to play the full 90 minutes of a national cup final for the third time, although even the time he spent on the pitch felt like a bonus. Ferguson still managed to make his presence felt when barging goalkeeper Peter Schmeichel over in a typically robust effort to get to the ball after coming on in the 51st minute to replace Paul Rideout, whose headed goal on the half-hour mark turned out to be the winner.

Ferguson was conspicuous afterwards, having taken possession of a fan's comedy blue nose, which he wore on the lap of honour. And he didn't stint on the celebrations later that evening while wearing a kilt of ancient Ferguson tartan at the Royal Lancaster Hotel, overlooking Hyde Park. Not that he had been pleased to see two of his countrymen earlier that afternoon. In the days before what he describes as 'noise-cancelling, journalist-cancelling headphones', a sports-writing colleague Gordon Waddell recalls encountering Ferguson in the Wembley tunnel after the game, along with a colleague from another Scottish paper. Figuring that Ferguson might at last be willing to offer some on-the-record thoughts in the giddy aftermath of victory, Waddell called out to him.

'Big man, big man . . . Dunc, over here!'

Ferguson looked across, narrowed his eyes.

'Can you spare a word for the Scottish guys, big yin?'

'Aye, I'll spare you two – fuck yeez.'

CHAPTER 12

It's Good to Kill an Admiral from Time to Time

A year that stands as a defining one in Duncan Ferguson's life began in ominous fashion, with the striker's first red card in English football. Earlier in the same week Ferguson had walked away from court, having been told that his trial for on-field assault had been adjourned for a third time and would now take place in May.

It's fair to assume that his legal team would have advised Ferguson to stay out of trouble until then. *Best keep your nose clean. Best not do anything that might attract further negative and unhelpful press attention.* At least that would have been the usual advice given to a client, never mind one operating so clearly in the public eye. Ferguson, however, managed only five days.

It was that very weekend, on 14 January 1995, in the 52nd minute of a Premiership clash against Arsenal at Highbury that Ferguson is described in newspaper reports as having 'lashed out' at Arsenal's Danish midfielder John Jensen in the centre circle, thereby gaining his first red card in English football.

According to *The Independent*, 'the ball was yards away'. Everton manager Joe Royle was furious with Jensen, who he said had made the most of what was only a 'shove'. Not everyone agreed. 'Dunc struck him clean,' recalls Donald Walker, a journalist colleague who was in the crowd at Highbury that afternoon. 'I can still see the long blue sleeve coming round like the arm of a windmill.'

Violence on the football field – or even just off it – was set to become an even more topical subject. Football was not in a good place. Match-fixing allegations concerning former Liverpool goalkeeper Bruce Grobbelaar had recently emerged. Only 11 days after Ferguson's dismissal against Arsenal, Eric Cantona decided to leap into the stand at Selhurst Park in order to have his vengeance on a foul-mouthed Crystal Palace supporter who had rushed down several rows of seats to scream abuse at the Manchester United player as he headed towards the tunnel after being sent off.

Parallels were quickly drawn with Ferguson's on-field clash with McStay, although Cantona's offence seemed more flagrant and, if taken on its own 'merits', more serious as well. The following morning every newspaper in the land featured the same photograph of the famous kung-fu kick.

Although manager Alex Ferguson vowed to stand by Cantona, the club issued their own punishment. As early as the next morning, chairman Martin Edwards confirmed that Cantona would not play for United again that season, which meant missing a minimum of 16 games. The suspension stretched to 20 games when the Old Trafford side reached the FA Cup final, where they met Everton, of course – and Ferguson.

The English FA, meanwhile, doubled Cantona's suspension to six months, banning him until the following September, while the possibility that he would face a jail sentence – he was charged with common assault – also remained a threat. In March 1994, at Croydon Magistrates' Court (the district where the offence occurred), Cantona was told by the chairperson of the bench that for someone looked up to by so many, 'the only sentence that is appropriate for this offence is two weeks' imprisonment'. However, United complained that he was being 'punished three times for the same offence', since he had already been fined by his club two weeks' wages, as well as being handed club and FA bans. Cantona appealed and saw his original sentence commuted to 120 hours of community service, a popular punishment at the time for disgraced sportsmen.

The decision was greeted with approving nods by Ferguson's legal team, as they prepared their own case, since it was a precedent of sorts – or so they thought.

Ferguson's own trial was eventually set for 9 May 1995. By the time the case was heard, 12 months and 24 days had passed since the head-butt incident. Many felt that it proved an unhelpful stay of execution for Ferguson. The delays allowed the incident to become established in people's minds, while additional incidents in the intervening period, such as the Arsenal sending off, were not likely to help Ferguson. Neither was the drink-driving conviction handed down to him at the end of the previous year.

An act of aggression that lasted a few seconds had been given a full year to become firmly established in the public consciousness. Replayed again and again on television, it had assumed an enduring quality. Cantona's case had been disposed of within weeks of the offence being committed; Ferguson, by contrast, had been left in limbo. The anguish was drawn out.

Even Ferguson was aware that anyone found guilty of assault on three occasions had to be prepared for the sound of prison doors clanking shut behind him. I asked Donald Findlay, QC, to describe how Ferguson must have felt as he continued to play football – when fit enough to do so – against such a background, while managing to seem so unconcerned about his looming court commitments. According to Findlay, who helped prepare Ferguson's case, there was turmoil inside the footballer's head, even if it wasn't always obvious as he galloped up the side of a football pitch swinging his shirt above his head. Findlay produces a vivid description of how Ferguson felt while continuing to live life in the shadow of a very possible prison sentence. 'It was as if someone had put his thumbs on a desk and hit them with a sledgehammer,' he says. 'The gnawing pain would just not go away.'

Contrary to how many remember events now, Findlay did not represent Ferguson in the actual case. At the time of the head-butt, he was the vice-chairman of Rangers. He had been present at the game against Raith Rovers. 'I could not represent him, since I was technically a witness,' he explains, in response to those Rangers fans who queried why their vice-chairman – a well-known and clearly very accomplished lawyer – had not acted for Ferguson from the start. There was a feeling at the time that Ferguson had been abandoned by the Ibrox club.

'Looking back, I am pretty sure that the trial would never have come about had the referee seen the incident or been assisted with the incident by his linesmen and had taken action against Duncan during the game. However, there was an enormous media clamour. I have no doubt that the police and the fiscal reacted to this. You would have to ask the fiscal why.'

No official complaint was made by Jock McStay, at least not before he was obligated to give a statement to the police. In comments made to the press afterwards he simply wanted to establish that he had been hit, and that he hadn't dived. Neither was there a complaint issued by Raith Rovers Football Club. It later emerged that Dick Barton, described in press reports as a 'zany' Glasgow publican, had written to every police station in Scotland demanding that Ferguson be charged over his clash with McStay. 'I was angry when some top copper said they couldn't act unless a member of the public complained,' he explained. However, after being summoned as a witness he began to feel guilty and withdrew his complaint. He turned up outside Glasgow sheriff court during the trial wearing a 'Dunc's No Punk' sandwich board after reaching the conclusion that Ferguson was 'no worse' than the customers who drank in the pub he owned.

It is understood that it was either the procurator fiscal's office or the Crown office who instructed the police to carry out an investigation. 'It was a third party, one who had not been at the game,' I was told by a source close to Ferguson's legal team, who continued: 'The prosecuting service wanted to remind the public that actions on the football pitch were not immune to prosecution and they wanted a high-profile case to emphasise that.' Although Andrew Normand, the regional procurator fiscal for Glasgow and Strathkelvin region at the time and now a sheriff in Glasgow, declined the opportunity to speak to me, I did have it communicated to me that he had not been present at Ibrox on the afternoon in question; some reports from the time suggest that he had been. In Scottish criminal case reports, the trial is still referred to as *Duncan Cowan Ferguson* v. *Andrew Christie Normand*.

Findlay accuses the media of creating an atmosphere where the procurator fiscal felt he had no choice but to take action. 'I appreciate I am no great lover of the Scottish media,' he concedes. 'But until the Scottish media began to demand that something was done about the incident, I am not sure whether there was a lot of will to take it further.'

He understands how it is possible for an ill-thought-out act to impact on a person's career – and life. The QC's own time with Rangers came to a controversial end after he was filmed singing songs identified as sectarian in nature at a supporters' function. The episode made front-page news in Scotland and his career at Rangers was quickly terminated. He resigned from his position at the club in May 1999 and attributed his own downfall in a large part to the media, although he also admitted his conduct was 'not acceptable'.

He has since revealed that he fell prey to suicidal thoughts after stepping down from his position at Ibrox. Findlay knows how one wrong move can indelibly stain a life and he knows that when his obituary comes to be written, reference to this incident will be there somewhere, just as the word 'head-butt' will feature in a similar account of Ferguson's life. 'And that is an appalling thought,' he says

With his trademark whiskers, dress coat and fob watch attached to his waistcoat, Findlay looks like a Victorian mill-owner. His roots are firmly planted in working-class turf, however. When the mines began to close, one by one, in Fife, his father, a miner, moved further up the east coast to Dundee, to become a church beadle. Findlay, however, is an atheist, although he clearly has a keen interest in justice. He felt great sympathy for Ferguson, who had 'the whole mechanism of the law' thrown against him. 'To some extent, he was the wrong man in the wrong place at the wrong time.

'He was only a big daft laddie,' he adds. Findlay believes that Ferguson was sacrificed as a warning to others who might have been tempted to form a view that a sportsfield provides immunity to the law. To make his point, he quotes in French from Voltaire's *Candide*: 'Dans ce pay-ci, il est bon de tuer de temps en temps un amiral encourager les autres.'

Translated into English, the saying goes: it is good to kill an admiral from time to time, in order to encourage – in this case, encourage is used ironically, and actually means to discourage – the others. It is a quote that is often cited in legal textbooks in situations when a punishment is far heavier than the offence warrants, perhaps imposed in a politically motivated attempt to prevent others committing the same offence and, sometimes, to deflect blame. In short, it identifies scapegoats.

What he perceived as the 'singling-out' of Ferguson pained Findlay because he had grown to like him very much. And he also liked his family, who shared his Presbyterian outlook on life. He describes them as 'down to earth'. Ferguson, meanwhile, 'just wanted to play football and look after his pigeons'. And it was becoming increasingly likely that he wouldn't be free to do either, for a spell at least. 'When it comes to Duncan, I am quite happy to wear my heart on my sleeve,' he says. 'I must tell you this, he was the kind of boy I liked.'

Sadly, it wasn't Findlay who Ferguson needed to win over. In the High Court in Scotland, and in serious cases in the Sheriff Court, if the accused denies the charges, a jury comprising 15 people will sit and hear the evidence before deciding whether he or she is guilty. In less serious cases, which Ferguson's was deemed to be, the sheriff alone reaches the decision.

The man who held Ferguson's fate in his hands when the trial finally began was Alexander – or Sandy – Eccles, a sheriff then in his early 60s. Their backgrounds could not have been more different. As is often the case with sheriffs and judges, Eccles was the product of the public school system. He was educated at Loretto, on the outskirts of Edinburgh, before going on to graduate from Cambridge University.

Eccles was a keen sportsman, which offered some encouragement to John Baird, who was installed as Ferguson's defence counsel. Perhaps it was possible that some common ground could be found. Eccles played rugby for Scottish universities and then Durham, where he played alongside future English internationalists Stan Hodgson and Mike Weston. Eccles himself was unfortunate not to be capped for Scotland and is thought to have suffered for playing much of his club rugby in England. 'I was slotted in to do the case because I had been reasonably good at sport in the past, and was interested in sports,' says Eccles.

These sporting ties helped earn him the best seat in the house. If not quite the trial of the century, then it was still set to have a huge impact on the governance of sport, as well as on a pair of young footballers' lives. McStay, who had turned 29 by the time the trial began, says he felt like he was joining Ferguson, 23, in the dock, despite being the victim of the alleged assault; he was, as far as the official language of the court was concerned, the complainer. In the official statement he gave to a Strathclyde police officer a month after the incident, he had clearly accused Ferguson of deliberately head-butting him. However, by the time the case came to court, McStay now intimated that he felt the clash might have been accidental.

Time had helped to metaphorically as well as literally heal the wounds. In a bleak, windowless room inside Glasgow's Sheriff Court, McStay remembers feeling as though 'the walls were coming in' on him as well. Understandably, he felt a certain amount of unease at being held partly responsible for sending a fellow professional footballer to prison. On the first day of the trial, he was warned about the consequences of lying in court. After giving his name to the court – '*John* McStay,' he said – he was asked several times by Alasdair Youngson, the depute fiscal, to give his impression of the incident. McStay answered by saying 'the two of us clashed and there was a clash of heads'. According to reports, Youngson had to ask McStay twice whether he thought it had been an accident. Eventually, he answered: 'At the time, no.'

Youngson then pointed out that in his statement he had said that Ferguson had 'suddenly lunged' at him and head-butted him in the mouth. He was reminded that he was under oath and he was there to tell the truth, and he was asked whether he understood the word 'prevarication'. There was a risk that he might be charged with being in contempt of court. 'That is a very serious offence,' Sheriff Eccles reminded him.

'The whole point of giving a statement to the police was because people had said I had cheated,' McStay explained in reply. 'I wanted to establish that contact was made.'

McStay was clearly under pressure. It was only natural that he was considering the flak he was already enduring in the street, and which would only get worse if Ferguson was jailed.

'I did indeed feel sorry for McStay,' says Findlay. 'He was a perfectly nice lad. He too was caught in a situation not of his making or choosing. But when the legal machine comes towards you it tends to grind everything, and everyone, in its path.'

Although still playing part-time football with Clydebank, McStay gave his occupation as a painter and decorator when asked in court what he did. Having been ushered out of the door so quickly by Raith Rovers, his own post-head-butt career had included a month's loan at Northern Irish club Portadown, based in a predominantly Protestant town. It was a problematic posting for this Celtic-supporting son of Larkhall, whose greatest claim to fame was – in the eyes of the Rangers supporters, certainly – as an agent provocateur in the downfall of a record signing.

When sitting together with McStay so many years later, it remains easy to sympathise with what he had to put up with. By his own definition, he was just a working-class, journeyman footballer who had been thrust into a harsh spotlight that he had not sought. In Portadown, he had the danger to his own personal welfare spelled out to him in a bar. 'I was there one night and there was a spot of bother,' he recalls. 'This guy came over to me and said: "I am going to finish off what Ferguson started."'

'The usual crap, which I got from the Rangers fans, was that I was the one who got Ferguson the jail,' he adds. 'But it was nothing to do with me. In fact, it seemed like I was the only one *not* trying to put the knife into him.'

That was the problem for the witnesses who were asked to take the stand; 20 in total, including the Raith physio, Gerard Docherty, who, to use a phrase Ferguson will be familiar with, put the cat among the pigeons when he claimed that McStay, while he was being tended to on the ground following the clash, told him: 'He's done me.'

Everyone knew what were likely to be the consequences of what they were saying. Even photographers were summoned to appear. Eric McCowat was then working for both the *Daily Express* and the *Sunday Express*. Negatives of the photographs that he took that afternoon while sitting just by the edge of the 18-yard box, behind the Raith goal-line, were taken away by the police and used as evidence in court. He, too, was called as a witness and remembers it being a 'nerve-racking' experience, particularly since he knew he would likely cross paths with Ferguson again in the future in the course of his work. He also recalls McStay 'furiously backtracking' as he realised just how serious this was all becoming.

As a sports photographer, the onus was on McCowat not to miss the big moment. And he hadn't, which was why he was obligated to take the witness stand. The same applies to referees; they too are expected not to miss the big moments. However, Kenny Clark had to live with the fact that he had missed the incident. And he had to admit this error in court again and again.

Like Ferguson, Clark had been in such a setting before. However, as a criminal defence lawyer, he would normally have been the one pacing about in front of the sheriff, asking questions, placing others under pressure or else attempting to put them at ease. 'I knew what it was all about,' he says. 'But it didn't make it any easier for me.'

Clark knew he had erred on the day in question. Even now, the direct aftermath of the incident is singed on his mind. He hadn't seen the pivotal moment, but he remembers Danny Lennon, one of McStay's teammates, jumping up and down, and shouting, 'He's just nutted him, he's just put the heid in him!' Lennon was the Raith Rovers player nearest the scene, so was called as a witness. Ally McCoist and Gordon Durie, two of the nearest Rangers players, were not.

At half-time, just over ten minutes after the head-butt had taken place, Clark and his two linesmen reconvened in their dressing-room. According to Clark, they spoke about what had just happened. 'The far-side linesman, a guy called Willie McKnight, said he was not well positioned to see, and anyway, there had been other bodies between him and the incident,' says Clark. 'The stand-side linesman, Jim O'Hare, said it looked pretty bad to him. He said it looked as though Ferguson had lunged at McStay.'

Not unreasonably, Clark wondered why he had not then alerted him to this by raising his flag. 'I asked him, "Well, why did you not tell me that?"' recalls Clark. 'He said that, from his angle, he could not tell if there had been contact, and if so, how much contact. He was pretty much looking at Ferguson's back. I could sympathise, I suppose.'

When Clark saw the incident again on video in court, he confirmed to the sheriff what action he would have taken had he seen it at the time with his own eyes – a straight red card, for violent play. Mike Delaney, who had sent off the then Rangers player-manager Graeme Souness on his Scottish Premier League debut against Hibs in 1986, was the Scottish Football Association's referee supervisor at the match and was also called as a witness. He said he had seen Ferguson butt McStay in the face. In his opinion, it had been an 'aggressive' butt 'delivered deliberately'. He had, he said, expected the referee to order Ferguson off.

McKnight stood up in court and said he had seen Ferguson's head go towards McStay but originally claimed that he would not describe what happened as a butt. He also felt there had been a delay before McStay collapsed to the turf. However, after viewing the incident on video, he agreed that there had been no delay in McStay's fall. He also agreed that it had certainly been a head-butt. O'Hare was of a similar view.

It was not looking good for Ferguson.

*

Richard Elias was sitting in the press gallery watching all this unfold and furiously writing notes, which he turned into reports for the *Daily Post*, the Liverpool newspaper. He was 32 years old at the time and an avid Everton supporter – he already had his ticket for the upcoming FA Cup final against Manchester United. He had celebrated along with Ferguson and over 30,000 other Evertonians when Ferguson had scored the winner against Manchester United just three months earlier. Yet here he was, chronicling what looked set to be the downfall of his favourite team's star player.

'I always remember that Duncan was such a physically big presence that he towered over everyone else,' says Elias. 'Even outside the Sheriff Court, when he was being mobbed by press and photographers, he seemed to sail almost serenely through the crowd, that parted before him as he strode through.

'He was always with his dad; his dad accompanied him everywhere. Duncan seemed to take it in his stride. I think he was resigned. He was used to having run-ins with the authorities and I think he knew it was going to end badly.'

While Elias chooses the word 'resigned' to describe Ferguson's demeanour, Sheriff Eccles opts for 'arrogant' and 'surly'. He was aware of Ferguson but had to set aside what he already knew about his past and focus on the episode on which the charge of assault hinged. Eccles had presided over more straightforward and less high-profile cases, that much was sure. However, he wasn't new to the concept that sport could turn ugly.

'I can remember playing for Edinburgh Wanderers against Stewart's Melville FPs when, just as I was about to put the ball in the scrum, it broke up in a tremendous flurry of fists,' he says. 'And then I saw the hooker clutching his ear, and I looked down and there was a bit of ear on the ground. Our hooker had bitten his ear. He was suspended for a number of weeks.'

But that incident, despite being so gruesome, hadn't become the subject of a criminal trial. 'No, it certainly did not,' replies Eccles. And this was the point that Ferguson's legal team pursued most doggedly: there had been innumerable examples of violence on a sporting field that had not progressed to a criminal trial. Indeed two of the three delays to the trial beginning were due to this reason. Findlay sought more time to wrest television pictures of other outbreaks of on-field violence from Scottish Television [STV].

Specifically, this was the tape of a game between Glenafton and Largs in the OVD Junior Cup final, played just weeks after Ferguson's clash with McStay, at Ibrox, of all places, and shown live by STV. Even given the Ayrshire juniors' propensity for violence, this clash had proved exceptionally bad-tempered and saw four players sent off amid a flurry of punches, a dive and, yes, even a head-butt – one which, on this occasion, was seen by the referee and a red card was duly administered.

As well as obtaining this footage, Ferguson's lawyers also finally succeeded in getting their hands on a tape of the bust-up between Hearts teammates Graeme Hogg and Craig Levein during a pre-season friendly fixture against Raith Rovers – the one which McStay watched from the substitutes' bench. Although Eccles granted permission for brief video excerpts from these games to be shown in court, the sheriff took the perhaps surprise view that both examples were 'irrelevant' because the incidents 'took place in play and immediately from continuing play, unlike the present case'.

For Eccles, the crux of the matter was that, when Ferguson's forehead made contact with McStay, play had already been stopped after the award of a foul for the tugging of shirts and use of arms immediately preceding the lunge central to the case.

'Looking at the TV film of it, it didn't look as if it was done in the heat of the moment,' Eccles explains, in the sitting room of his home in Fife. The retired sheriff, I discovered, is now based only a few miles from Anstruther, one of Ferguson's old stomping grounds. I was not sure whether he would welcome my visit. After all, he is now in his early 80s. A long time has passed since he presided over the case. Even the most sharp-minded octogenarian's recall might not be what it once was.

Although I presented myself on his doorstep without warning, he is pleasingly hospitable. With a limp that I later discover is traced back to an old rugby injury sustained while playing for Perth Accies, he leads me into an attractive cottage that sits on the corner of a road running through a quiet village in Fife. At mention of Ferguson's name, a knowing smile helps crease his face further. It is almost as if he had expected that the day would come when a biographer of Ferguson would appear at his front door.

There are two cases in his career that stick out most clearly in his mind: Ferguson's and the time a farmer brought two horses into his courtroom – as witnesses. 'He led them in, clomp, clomp, clomp,' says Eccles, shaking his head. 'They left evidence in the form of their business on the floor.'

Ferguson was in need of witnesses able to provide output that was slightly more helpful to his cause. Strangely, some powerful allies were left sitting on the proverbial substitutes' bench. One of Ally McCoist's greatest regrets is that he was not asked to speak on behalf of Ferguson in court.

Speaking today, he expresses his frustration. His eyes light up at mention of Ferguson, but he becomes more serious when the subject turns to the topic of the so-called head-butt and its consequences. 'I have to say something, and it's something I have never said before, but if I have one regret about the big fella, it's that he never asked me to go to court for him,' says McCoist, a popular and highly credible witness; with a gift for charming almost everyone he meets, he could have proved an effective weapon.

'I would genuinely have stood up in a court of law and said Duncan did not head-butt Jock McStay,' he adds. 'The sheriff would have looked at me and asked: "And where were you, Mr McCoist?" And I would have said: "I was the Rangers player nearest the incident when it happened."

'"Are you sure Mr McCoist?"

'"I am 100 per cent sure."

'I wouldn't tell him a lie,' adds McCoist. 'I would tell him the truth, because it is what I feel and I would be under oath.'

Who can tell what effect McCoist's contribution might have had. Strangely, Findlay does not recall whether recruiting the Rangers striker was ever an option that was considered.

Ferguson himself spent a total of 29 minutes in the witness stand, giving his version of events. He could not avoid being quoted here. Those in the press gallery eagerly jotted down his comments. In Ferguson's view, it all boiled down to a misjudgment. 'It's hard to recall because it all happened so quickly,' he said. 'Mr McStay turned round to square up to me. I stepped forward and we collided.'

Ferguson explained that he had only 'tried to show some aggression' in response. 'I misjudged my distance and collided with his head,' he added. 'I was clumsy with my head.'

Answering questions from John Baird, who was conducting his defence, Ferguson agreed that he felt under pressure at the time, as he had yet to score a goal for Rangers. Asked if he had drawn his head back and then struck McStay in the face 'as if he were heading a ball', Ferguson replied, 'No.' He added that he hadn't felt the need to apologise to McStay at the time because he didn't think the clash was 'severe enough' to warrant an apology.

'I was clumsy with my head' was later included as one of the quotes of the year by *The Guardian*, alongside Eric Cantona's memorable observation on his return to football after his own courtroom dramas. Describing the feeding frenzy in the media that resulted from his personal anguish, the Frenchman was at his enigmatic best when he stood up during a press conference and said, 'When the seagulls follow the trawler, it is because they think the sardines will be thrown into the sea.'

'I was clumsy with my head' did not have quite the same poetic resonance, nor did it help dissuade the sheriff from taking a dim view of the incident.

Unfortunately for Ferguson, footage, which can still be viewed today on YouTube, underlines how actions speak louder than words. The clip was shown during the trial on large television screens again and again. The head-butting action was there for all to see, even if the intent was harder to assess. Did even Ferguson know what had gone through his head? The case hinged on one man's interpretation of what had happened. The sheriff remarked that the incident had to be viewed 'in the heat of a game in a very highly charged atmosphere, in a game which involves a considerable amount of body contact and aggression'.

Ferguson and his legal team's spirits sank as Eccles looked at the footballer and added: 'Bearing in mind the backgrounds to this matter, I believe it was not accidental but deliberate.' Sitting in the press seats, Richard Elias noted that Ferguson 'took a deep breath and then shook his head'.

He knew what was coming.

The guilty verdict made headlines all across the world, not only in Scotland and Liverpool. A professional footballer had been jailed for the first time for an on-field offence. As more than one newspaper noted, Ferguson, once worth a British record transfer fee, was again making history. But with sentencing adjourned until later in the month, Ferguson was free to go. Elias recalls wandering into a lift that was taking people down to the ground floor and being aware of a presence beside him. He looked round and saw Ferguson and his father standing there, waiting to be delivered to the ground floor as well.

'I thought this is my opportunity,' he recalls. 'I was a young, enthusiastic reporter. I knew I had to just go for it. So I said, "Duncan, do you have any words for the Everton supporters back home?"

'He said, "Aye."

'I thought, this is it, I have nailed it, I have got my first quote from Duncan Ferguson. And he just looked at me and said, "Can you shut the doors?"'

Not even the fact that he was facing jail could erode the young man's gallusness. Elias remembers Ferguson looking as though he was not completely 'tuned-in' to the goings-on in the courtroom. 'He was listening, but you didn't get the impression he was fully engaged,' he says. 'Often in court the defendant is writing notes and passing them to his legal team. But there was none of that.

'It was as if he thought that it was the last thing he would have to do in common with Scottish football – and Scotland. It was almost like he was saying: "Get through this, then that's me done with Scotland. I am in a bigger league now, what am I doing here?"' According to Elias, Ferguson was already nursing a sense of resentment.

Perhaps this demeanour in court helps explains why Eccles found him so cocksure. Maybe it was just a coping mechanism. After all, Ferguson had an FA Cup final to prepare for just days later. He shook Prince Charles's hand before the match and accepted a cup winner's medal from him afterwards, before then donning a blue clown's nose and cavorting around the pitch. Perhaps Eccles was right; here was a man displaying few signs of genuine remorse. But then it was also understandable if Ferguson wanted to milk the Wembley win for all it was worth since he suspected the walls were about to close in on him again.

He returned to Glasgow just five days after the victory, for sentencing, wearing a dark suit, black waistcoat, dark-blue shirt and yellow patterned tie. He wore no clown's nose in Court 15, where it was so busy that Peter Johnson and Sir Philip Carter, Johnson's predecessor as Everton chairman, were forced to stand outside and wait for news of the developments.

Donald Findlay conducted the mitigation with his usual *élan*, pointing out that in the 1993–94 season in Scotland more than 120 players had been sent off and a third of this number were red-carded for violent conduct. Not one of them had been ordered to appear before a sheriff.

Sheriff Eccles was unmoved by this, just as he was by a letter written by Johnson, which detailed Ferguson's regular visits to children's hospitals and the time he spent coaching youngsters on Merseyside. He also decided against heeding the advice contained in a social inquiry report from the Lancashire Probation Service, one Eccles had specifically asked for, which recommended community service rather than a custodial sentence. Instead, Eccles told Ferguson that he would be 'imprisoned in the public interest' and that 'such behaviour cannot be tolerated'. He said he was compelled to 'bring home' to Ferguson that he was in a prominent position, as a footballer who was looked up to by younger people. Although the maximum sentence available to him was six months in prison, the sheriff decided to restrict the period to three months in view of the fact the injury sustained by McStay was not a serious one.

When it had come down to it, Findlay, for all his oratorical flourish, had been unable to do what he needed to do, which was turn back the hands of time and prevent Ferguson from entering a hotel bar in Anstruther – or even heading to the town at all on that fateful night. As Eccles pointed out, 'This is not the first time you have been convicted of an incidence of violence and I am taking into account your previous convictions.' Ferguson was being sent to jail primarily because the clash with McStay occurred while he was seven months through a year's probation. As the *Sunday Times* noted, 'The truly shaming part of Ferguson's record lies with the three assaults in taxi ranks and a pub.' The last of these incidents had occurred nearly three years earlier, in November 1992 – when he was still with Dundee United.

Still, he was left with some hope. Ferguson was released on bail when his lawyers made a successful application for appeal to Eccles. 'I imagine he is relieved,' said Findlay. Ferguson left it all behind to attend the wedding of Everton teammate Daniel Amokachi in Tunisia. 'Do you fancy going over, just for a weekend jolly?' Ray Parr, a friend, recalls Ferguson saying to him during dinner one night shortly after he was sentenced. Their subsequent adventures included a pub crawl around the town of Gammarth in the company of an African prince and his son, as recounted by Parr in the book *Tales from the Gwladys Street* by David Cregeen and Jonathan Mumford.

This was a long way in every sense from the Supreme Court in Edinburgh, where Ferguson's appeal was heard five months later before the Lord Justice-General Lord Hope. He was joined by Lord Allanbridge and Lord Osborne in a formidable front three, representing the Scottish establishment. Indeed, Eccles and Lord Allanbridge were near contemporaries at Loretto. Were the appeal judges really likely to reach a different conclusion to Eccles? 'I was more hopeful we might do something in the appeal court,' says Findlay. 'I thought by then things might have stepped back a bit.'

Richard Elias returned to Scotland to report on the events and was immediately struck by the stark contrast between the setting for the trial and the setting for the appeal, in the capital. 'The Sheriff Court in Glasgow is a very modern, anodyne building, while in Edinburgh it was more traditional and grand,' he says. 'It was a lot darker and I remember the acoustics were dreadful. You could barely hear a word.'

Ferguson's lawyers had appealed initially against both the conviction and sentence. However, they later abandoned the appeal against conviction and sought to proceed solely with an appeal against sentencing on the grounds that 'there were available alternative forms of disposal other than a custodial sentence'. Ferguson's legal team also questioned the sheriff's description of the footballer's previous legal convictions as a 'quite appalling record of . . . violent offences'.

However, Lord Hope upheld Sheriff Eccles' original sentence, commenting that 'the most important factor' was that the footballer was already on probation when the offence they were now dealing with was committed. The sitting judges felt that he had been dealt with 'leniently' in the most recent case at Cupar Sheriff Court and so viewed the committing of 'the same kind of offence while on probation as a most serious matter' so the punishment 'cannot be described as excessive'.

Lord Hope did add that he felt it was a 'particularly unfortunate case'. There was one minor victory for Ferguson, however. The judges accepted that Eccles had 'overstated the matter' when describing

Ferguson's previous record of offences as 'appalling'. Not that it really mattered now.

'It was done and dusted very quickly,' recalls Elias. 'And because you could not really hear, it felt like a delayed reaction. Duncan suddenly stood up and off he went. I always remember he just wandered off. He barely batted an eyelid. There was no outcry. One minute he was there, and the next he wasn't. An hour later he was being led into a van, handcuffed to a police officer.'

Now, finally, had come the time for Ferguson to make the latest high-profile transfer of his career – from a well-appointed Edinburgh courtroom to a prison cell in Glasgow.

On my visit to interview Eccles in Fife, just a few miles from the scene of Ferguson's Anstruther troubles, I wanted to establish whether the now retired sheriff considered the sentence to have been excessive, if the passage of time had changed his view. After all, just weeks before I turned up at his door, a bronze statue – a *statue* – of Zinedine Zidane propelling his head into Marco Materazzi's chest during the World Cup final between France and Italy had been unveiled outside the Pompidou Centre in Paris. It is titled, simply, *The Headbutt*. The same act that saw Ferguson sent to prison has been glorified in this instance.

For Eccles himself, the period when he was involved with the Ferguson case was not a particularly happy time. He received a sack full of offensive letters to his sheriff's office in Glasgow, the majority of them bearing a Liverpool postmark. 'Some quite nasty stuff,' he recalled. The two burning questions I had come to his sitting room to ask such a long time later were very simple ones.

'Do I have sympathy for Ferguson?' he replies, repeating my first question before allowing the room to fall silent for several moments. 'No, not really.'

This pattern is repeated with my next question.

'Would I have done it differently?' he wondered, again taking his time to answer.

'No, I really don't think I would.'

CHAPTER 13

Birdman of Barlinnie

There is no first floor in Barlinnie's D Hall. It goes from ground to second floor, and then from third to fourth. It is on the last of these, on the floor once used as the holding area for those prisoners awaiting execution, that Duncan Ferguson spent the majority of his stay in what is regularly termed the country's most notorious jail.

Indeed, 'notorious' is the word ITN used to describe Barlinnie in their evening report on *News at Ten*, filed by Glen Oglaza from outside the Court of Session in Edinburgh on the day Ferguson began his sentence. Oglaza then concluded his story to the camera, saying, 'He was once Britain's most expensive footballer – tonight he is just another prisoner in one of Britain's toughest jails.'

While the Scottish Prison Service sought to maintain the public pretence that they were dealing with just another prisoner, the reality was something else. It wasn't just that Ferguson was a high-profile footballer, one recently signed for over £4 million. This, on its own, was reason enough to guarantee his physical welfare was given serious consideration. It was because his elder sister, Audrey, worked as a physical-training instructor at Glenochil Prison, near Alloa, that further caution was advised. 'It would not have taken a great deal of thought for someone to want to put a notch on their belt by slashing or assaulting Duncan Ferguson,' a prison officer informs me when I visit.

Although the authorities stressed again and again that Ferguson would be treated like any other prisoner, the intention often perished on the cold slab of stone called practicality. In the words of *The*

Guardian, the Scottish Prison Service was welcoming 'its most famous customer since Rudolf Hess'.

Certainly, no other prisoner was getting bags full of mail sent to him each day, something that prompted a quick change of lodgings for Ferguson – to a slightly bigger cell, one where the already limited space was not completely swallowed up by the mountain of correspondence. However, the special treatment did not extend to ensuring this new cell was ready to welcome its celebrity occupant.

Most recently, the cell had doubled as a storeroom. 'It had not been used for years,' says David McCue, who was employed as a prison officer at Barlinnie at the time of Ferguson's incarceration. 'Ironically, it was full of pigeon shit. And it stank,' he continues. 'It was filthy – full of old beds and mattresses, too. It was degrading. It was Duncan's own responsibility to get it cleaned up. He spent days emptying it all and finding places for the crap before he moved in.'

According to McCue, the difference between his first cell and this new one was the equivalent of 'living in Southfork compared to a flat in Glasgow's East End'.

Home sweet home. Ferguson had only recently moved into a new house in the Lancashire village of Rufford, on a street called – unbelievably – Flash Lane. It was reported that he had spent £20,000 on a pigeon loft. In his cell in D Hall, a little rickety table was one of the few items of furniture.

All the time, the letters kept coming: 'Santa Claus-style bags full of them,' according to McCue. 'Duncan was getting probably ten times more correspondence than the whole hall,' he adds. It wasn't always only letters. On one occasion, a pink blow-up sex doll was delivered to him, sent to him by Dick Barton. He was the same eccentric bar owner who had written to every police force in Scotland to demand that Ferguson be charged for his on-field assault of Jock McStay.

'I felt so guilty when I read how lonely he was in his cell that I sent him my favourite blow-up doll,' Barton was quoted as saying in press reports from the time. Though the gift put a smile on the faces of the prison officers, it was confiscated from Ferguson.

Despite overcrowding issues, the footballer was given his own cell, which meant he did not have to suffer the indignity of defecating and urinating into a chamber pot – known as a 'slop bucket' – in front of another man, or 'co-pilot', as cellmates are termed at

Barlinnie. McCue describes it as 'inhumane' – and that was as true for the average prisoner as one worth a few million pounds on the football transfer market.

Describing the mechanics of the practice known as slopping out, McCue explains, 'It was just a small pot. About eight to nine inches in diameter, eight inches high. Excuse the French, but it dealt with your number ones and twos.' Ferguson was fortunate in that he was in D Hall. 'By and large, it was single-cell accommodation because it was full of semi-trusted or fully trusted prisoners,' explains McCue.

'Had Duncan been in any of the other halls, he would have been doubled up, meaning he would have had to do the toilet in front of another human being.' Instead, reports McCue, each morning, while under supervision, Ferguson would slop out the contents of the pot in an area known as the 'arches', the name given to the toilet and washroom facilities in Barlinnie. 'It was still especially degrading,' points out McCue.

This practice was actually banned under the European Convention on Human Rights, which only came into effect in Scotland in 1998. Thousands of prisoners have since won damages totalling more than £10 million for being forced to carry on slopping out, as the Scottish Prison Service struggled with the logistical headache of fitting toilets and washbasins in the hundreds of solid-stone cells dating back to Victorian times.

Although considered to be the preferred destination of the five halls at Barlinnie, D Hall was, and is still, an intimidating building to enter for the first-time visitor. Above the main entrance is a painted crown; inside, the walls are white. 'Prison is a terrible place for anyone, especially a place like Barlinnie,' continues McCue. He recalls once bringing his mother and wife to his place of work. 'They felt sick at what they saw, and trembled when a prisoner said "Hello" to them,' he remembers. 'For someone coming in as a prisoner for the first time, it would be horrendous for them.' He recalls seeing the 'terror' in Ferguson's eyes.

Although it was refurbished in 1998, D Hall retains a haunting aspect. Despite the overcrowding issues, on the ground and second floors there were cells that were deliberately left empty. Known as contingency cells, they were only to be used in case of riots in prisons elsewhere. It is a reminder, if any is needed, of the fragile social ecosystem that exists within a prison.

The empty cell across from Ferguson was firmly out of commission, riots or otherwise. This was the 'hanging shed' or 'execution chamber' and had not been in use for decades. Indeed, Ferguson's double cell was the same size as that used to house prisoners enduring the grim wait to be executed by hanging. Between 1946 and 1960, ten convicted murderers were put to death, the bodies buried in unmarked graves outside D Hall. They were still there in Ferguson's time, even though the hanging shed's own days were numbered.

The footballer's arrival was not the only reason for excitement in D Hall in the autumn of 1995. The authorities had allowed the Scottish film-maker David Graham Scott to record a short, somewhat chilling film just prior to the dismantling of the execution scaffold.

'I remember being told there was a famous footballer in one of the cells at the time,' Scott says, before directing me to a website where the film can be seen. Entitled *Hanging with Frank*, it features a retired Barlinnie death-watch officer called Frank McKue returning to the prison. At one point he is filmed outside D Hall – it is strange to consider that Ferguson could have been just the other side of the thick wall. Walking alongside the grave plots, McKue reels off the names of each hanged prisoner, like someone reciting the players in their favourite football team.

Barlinnie is deeply rooted in the Scottish public's consciousness; in fact, even further afield the name still holds a charge. The prison suffers from the lazy stereotyping of Glasgow as Britain's most violent city. If that is indeed so, the thinking goes, then what must its largest jail be like, this repository where many of the city's most hardened criminals are deposited?

Barlinnie – often referred to as 'the big hoose' – is the largest penal establishment in Scotland and is located in the north-east of Glasgow, four miles from the city centre and adjacent to the junction of the A80 and the M8, the busiest road in Scotland. Tens of thousands pass by the prison every day. The top of the sandstone-brick walls can be seen from the dual carriageway, as can the distinctive blunt chimneys. Beyond Barlinnie, the next most imposing structure on the skyline is Celtic Park, home of Celtic FC, and referred to by their supporters as 'Paradise'. When lit by floodlights, this place of hope can seem as though it is bathed in a celestial glow, providing a stark contrast to nearby 'Bar-L' – or 'Bar Hell', as it is also sometimes known.

As they thunder past on their daily commute, few people will give a thought to what lies within the walls of the prison on the horizon. Indeed, for many of a certain vintage, the most enduring image of Barlinnie is traced back to photographs that appeared in newspapers from the riot of 1987, when prisoners, wearing sinister-looking balaclavas improvised out of blackened pillowcases, managed to scale the roof after taking members of staff hostage. Newspapers carried the iconic image of two prisoners silhouetted against the sky. They are standing on the chimney cowls with their arms aloft, as though having just scored a goal.

Even when the sun is shining, Barlinnie can seem a dark, bleak place. When the prison first opened in 1882, newspapers remarked on the light colour of stone used to build it. According to Robert Jeffrey, in his book *The Barlinnie Story*, the prison used 'to shine in the summer sun'. No longer is this the case, however. The stone has since turned grimy black, darkened and pitted with age. As if a prison needs to look any more forbidding.

Originally, the prison comprised four blocks, each designed to house 200 prisoners. A fifth block – D Hall – was built later, but even that dates back to 1884. These same five blocks constitute the five halls of the present-day establishment. The Victorian impression is hard to shake, even if the outlook of those in authority has become more modern in recent times and ideas about penal punishment more enlightened.

While much about Barlinnie has changed since Ferguson's time, many other crucial aspects have not – as Bill McKinlay points out with a flourish of a hand while we sit together in his governor's office on the occasion of my first visit. Gesturing towards the window, he says, truthfully, 'They're still the same walls.'

Life continues on as normal on the other side of these walls, which are wound at the top with barbed wire. Down on the street below, Smithycroft Road, there is a launderette, newsagent, betting shop, tanning salon, several takeaways, as well as a pub and, near the gates of the prison, there is an Orange Lodge. So familiar is the backdrop to those freely going about their daily business that few will give much thought to the hundreds of men inside a building that once sat amid a farmer's fields. And it *is* hundreds and hundreds of men – as many as 1,200 at its peak in the mid-'90s.

It wasn't difficult to make room for just one more inmate when the gate shut behind Ferguson at just after 3 p.m. on 11 October 1995. He had been driven to Saughton jail in Edinburgh, before being transferred to another van for the journey along the M8. Since Ferguson had appealed the sentence rather than the conviction, prison staff had been prepared for his arrival for some time. Even the footballer's legal team, it was felt, had reached the conclusion that he was going to prison; it was just a question of how long for. After all, they had focused their efforts on shortening the sentence at the appeal. According to one prison officer I spoke to, 'There was little possibility of that happening.' In fact, the perception inside the Prison Service was that he would get the term increased. 'We all knew for some time that he was coming,' the officer adds.

Although described as a maximum-security prison, Barlinnie specialises in accommodating short-term prisoners. This term usually applies to those serving four years or less. In Barlinnie, the majority are serving four months or less. At the time, the prison was running at 132 per cent capacity, meaning the majority of its 1,135 inmates had to share around 860 cells. Disabusing anyone of the notion that Barlinnie was not befitting its reputation as somewhere best avoided, even by criminals, was the programme screened the night after Ferguson's arrival by BBC Scotland, alleging brutality by staff at the prison.

The Scottish Prison Service was still recovering from a series of significant convulsions in the '80s. Specifically, the riot at Barlinnie eight years earlier cast its shadow. 'That really traumatised the place,' says Roger Houchin, who was governor at the time of Ferguson's incarceration. At one time, he estimates, as many as 130 staff members out of 600 would be off sick on a daily basis. Even then, the churn of people throughout the year is remarkable. As many as 18,000 prisoners pass through its gates in a year, visited by over 500 people a day.

Barlinnie is a city within a city, with its own walkways, a gymnasium, a hospital ward and a church, as well as halls, residential units and workshops. 'That's not to say it is anything other than an alien environment for first-timers,' says McKinlay, Houchin's successor. For a start, you are no longer identified by name. Ferguson swapped his No. 9 jersey at Everton for a unique prison number: 12718.

Numbers are not re-allocated, so it remains his to this day.

On his arrival, the footballer was welcomed by those on the back-shift rota, operated by what are known as Second Division staff. He was allocated a cell in D Hall because of his assessed low-risk status.

This hall housed category C and category D prisoners only, with Ferguson originally classed as category C. Within a week of his admission, he was downgraded to D – the lowest-risk category of prisoner. Having been convicted on three separate occasions, there was an expectation among the prison staff that Ferguson would be given category B status. 'It could be further argued that it was also highly unusual for Duncan to be granted D-category status so soon after prison admission,' adds David McCue.

Nevertheless, Ferguson still had to go through the formalities on arrival. He was held in a holding cubicle, known as a 'dog box'. He was then escorted through a succession of interviews and medicals, which aimed to establish, amongst other things, whether he was a suicide risk and whether he was concealing drugs or any other foreign object on – or indeed in – his person. 'It isn't particularly dignified,' one prisoner officer tells me. It was here that the photograph used on his identity badge was also taken.

On my visit, I am permitted to bring in a tape recorder, but no mobile phone. Fortunately, I am spared the dog box.

Insult was added to injury for Ferguson when he was relieved of his civilian clothes – Ferguson had worn a suit with a waistcoat that was buttoned up high, almost to his collar, in court earlier that day. Now he was handed a Liverpool-red sweater, the colour marking out convicted prisoners from those on remand, who wear Everton-blue. He was also handed a red-and-white striped shirt. 'It was a struggle getting one long enough for Duncan,' one prison officer tells me. 'We were always asking him to tuck it in.'

He was also given what proved to be an ill-fitting pair of dark-blue denim trousers, into which he struggled on that first, desolate morning when he opened his eyes and realised it had really happened: they'd put him in Barlinnie.

Even though he had been measured up against the height chart on arrival, the trousers he was handed were a few inches too short for his 6 ft 4 in. frame. Although the length of his trousers was the least of Ferguson's worries at the time, it was an extra dose of humiliation on top of the understandable mix of fear and apprehension felt by the footballer. McCue suspects he was 'bammed up' – another prison term, this time for when someone is the brunt of a joke, often the crueller the better. And this one had been played on him not by his fellow inmates, but by wardens.

The 'news' quickly spread that Ferguson had been given trousers worn by the actor Eric Cullen, the last well-known figure to serve time in Barlinnie. Cullen, who made his name playing 'Wee Burney' in the first three series of the BBC Scotland comedy *Rab C. Nesbitt*, served only the first fifteen days of a nine-month sentence for child-pornography possession before being released on appeal. He was housed away from most of the other prisoners, in the prison hospital – a sensible precaution by the authorities, given the nature of Cullen's offences. The fact he was only 4 ft 4 in. tall, as a consequence of being born with the syndrome achondroplasia, a type of dwarfism, was another reason why he might have been targeted; it also explained why it was being put about that Big Dunc was wearing 'Wee Burney's breeks', Cullen having been released several months prior to Ferguson's arrival.

McCue is not absolutely certain that the issuing of the ill-fitting trousers had been done on purpose. After all, Ferguson was taller than the average prisoner and longer-legged denims might have been at a premium. Plus, because of his sister Audrey's role in the Prison Service, Ferguson was viewed as 'one of their own' by the majority of prison officers. But McCue also learned that Ferguson had not been given any blankets, or 'itchy greys', as they are termed in Barlinnie. 'He just thought that was the norm in prison – you didn't get any sheets,' McCue says. 'It seems too much of a coincidence to think it wasn't done on purpose.'

While Ferguson was always a ringleader when it came to dressing-room pranks, this was something different. At Dundee United, he had delighted in cutting up a young trialist's suit, but in Barlinnie, according to McCue, Ferguson resolved to keep his head down.

'He was getting pelters that first morning going down to feeding because of his short trousers,' recalls McCue. 'In the first few days, Duncan did not know how to react to the banter. I told him: "You cannot be aggressive, you cannot react."'

The man who had already been sent off twice in his short Everton career was advised to turn the other cheek. Otherwise, McCue told him, 'You risk losing all the perks you have.' McCue also encouraged him to accept he was 'going to be a victim'.

Within a few days, Ferguson's confidence grew. 'He began to acknowledge and respond to the banter, which was fine,' McCue says.

Born in 1968, David McCue was just a few years older than Ferguson, and he proved a helpful ally. Remarkably, his face should have been familiar to the footballer. Indeed, it might have reminded him of better times had he not been the worse for wear the last time he saw it. Just three years earlier, in far happier circumstances, McCue had bumped into Ferguson in a bar in Sweden. McCue was there as a member of the Tartan Army, having travelled to cheer on Scotland in their first-ever European Championship finals appearance. Ferguson, the youngest player at the tournament, didn't have a care in the world as the players celebrated after their group stage exit, when they had signed off with an emphatic win.

Following a 3–0 victory over the CIS, the players were intent on letting their hair down. 'It was nice to see the Scotland team,' recalls McCue, who adds that Ferguson, out of the 20 or so who were there, was partying 'harder than anyone'. McCue still has an old photograph from the evening; Ferguson is at one end of a table cluttered with beer bottles. Kevin Gallacher is sitting opposite, while Stuart McCall is next to him. Other teammates such as Derek Whyte, Dave Bowman and reserve goalkeeper Gordon Marshall look on. Ferguson – a mere 20 years old, remember – appears to be holding court.

How could anyone have imagined the circumstances under which McCue and Ferguson would come to be together in a room again? This second time the windows were not large and neatly paned for a Georgian-style sash effect, as in the photograph McCue hands me. Instead, they are thin and dirty and have bars running up and down them, as well as grids to prevent anything being thrown-out – plastic bags full of faeces, specifically – or, indeed, being thrown in. Suddenly, the digs in Dundee did not seem so bad, with their too-short bed and single-bar electric fire. Ferguson could even perhaps reflect wistfully on what he had thought was a strict regime at Dundee United, although he learned that not all prison officers were as dogmatic as Jim McLean, the manager who one Scottish sports writer once described as 'the Commandant of Stalag Tannadice'.

McCue, as a gallery officer, held the keys to Ferguson's cell, as well as to his immediate future. Now working as a counsellor, I went to meet him at his home in Fife. Once on the books as a Schoolboy at Clyde Football Club, McCue played on the left of midfield; now, he presented himself as a credible frontline witness to Ferguson's darkest days.

McCue leaves me to read the written statement he has prepared and goes into the kitchen to make coffee. He has clearly taken time to prepare it since I first contacted him, having been given his name as someone to get in touch with while on a visit to Barlinnie.

McCue left the prison service in 2004. He is happy to talk about the Ferguson he got to know during what was a vulnerable time in the footballer's life; few people have probably got as close to Ferguson over such a short, intense period. Indeed, he hands me the copy of *Fever Pitch* that Ferguson signed. Small notelets fall from its pages when I open the book, on which are printed: 'With compliments of the Governor,' along with an address: 'H.M. Prison. Barlinnie. Glasgow'. These are the notelets that McCue asked Ferguson to sign before sending them down to friends and family on Merseyside. 'My wife is from Liverpool and her family are Everton season-ticket holders going back decades,' he explains. 'Before I knew it, I was getting so many requests for his autograph . . . I must have sent down about 40 or 50,' he says. He then points me towards the inside of the front cover of the slightly dog-eared copy. There, too, is Ferguson's signature. And, again in the footballer's handwriting, a 'best wishes' note, dedicated to Cameron, McCue's newly born son. It is a rather strange sensation to hold this artefact in my hands; the yellowing pages help provide a further feel of archival worth. 'You can keep it,' says McCue.

A softly spoken, calming presence, it is hard to picture McCue in the Barlinnie I visited, where the sounds of jangling keys and echoed bangs of slamming doors and shouts provided what felt like a constant soundtrack to the day. Having facilitated Ferguson's promotion to a pass man – 'pass man' being the term for a prisoner trusted to a do a job that rewards that trust – McCue admits to feeling 'embarrassed' when a famous footballer came in to clean the staff office and make cups of tea for him. 'It just didn't seem right. It felt abnormal,' he says. 'But then I didn't want to treat him any differently. So that's what happened – he made my tea and other officers' tea. He was our servant for about a week.'

*

It seems I picked a significant day to make a visit to Barlinnie in order to discover more about the experiences of a high-profile prisoner from the past. Just a few hours after my arrival, a Reliance van deposits Tommy Sheridan, the high-profile former Scottish Socialist Party MSP, inside the gates of the prison, following his conviction for committing perjury during his successful defamation case against the *News of the World* a few years earlier.

'It's a bad day to be a journalist here,' smiles a member of the prison staff, as he checks my driver's licence and processes my identification tag, which must be worn around my neck throughout my visit.

Or perhaps it is a good day. Sheridan's is a different case to Ferguson, even if it feels fateful that my mission to discover how Barlinnie treats well-known inmates has coincided with a one-time politician's arrival. Despite the Sheridan-associated drama, my access is approved.

Sheridan has been incarcerated twice before; Ferguson, however, was not quite so conditioned to spending time behind bars. There was no sign of a smirk as he sat inside the prison van, having been careful to duck his head as he stepped up into the vehicle. Instead, in television footage, he is shown talking anxiously to the police officer responsible for ensuring his safe transportation to prison.

Still in his early 20s, he was less sure of himself and clearly anxious about how he might be treated by fellow inmates. Perhaps Sheridan could be confident of his own 'man of the people' status having been upheld during the course of a trial that he claimed pitched the common man against the establishment. Ferguson, however, feared being 'the man' to only some of the people, since his time with Rangers meant he was indelibly associated with one half of the Old Firm, something you might expect would make things tricky in a Glasgow prison. Even though an Orange Lodge sits on Barlinnie's doorstep, the prison is set deep within Celtic territory; however, McCue points out that among the prisoners there was a 'pretty even split' between Rangers and Celtic supporters at the time.

Even though Ferguson had swapped the blue shirt of the Ibrox club for the blue of another team, in a different country, he was still identified as a 'Rangers man'. According to one prison officer, he was moved from his original cell on his first night after suffering the tyranny of a Celtic supporter in the cell situated directly above. This prisoner's welcome for Ferguson comprised playing what were described as 'Celtic rebel songs' at a high volume. While hardly serious, it was an unsettling welcome and an additional discomfort on top of all else that had to be endured.

'I think he was a bit nervous when he arrived, but I am told he is settling in and that he seemed to be OK after that,' said Paul Burgess, a Prison Service spokesman, after Ferguson's first day.

Of the many problems afflicting Barlinnie, sectarianism, perhaps surprisingly, is far from the most pressing. This is a view endorsed by Dr Andrew McLellan, the former chief inspector of prisons for Scotland. Dr McLellan assured me that a prisoner was more likely to find that he was defined by where he came from, rather than 'what is laughably termed as religion'. This is just as well, because Ferguson's spell coincided with an Old Firm derby – a 3–3 draw – on 19 November 1995.

'The orange/green divide was less prominent that I had expected it to be,' says McLellan, who I first heard speak at a lecture on penal reform, when he had made the startling observation that, in the 1980s, 'only a fool would have felt safe in a Scottish prison'. Not much had changed by the time Ferguson found himself inside one, he concedes. However, while he expected Barlinnie to be a microcosm of 'all that is worst in Glasgow', Dr McLellan was pleasantly surprised to discover that one of the ugliest traits of the city was not so pronounced in its largest jail. However, that is not to say that division and rivalry did not exist; of course they did.

'It tended to be Glasgow versus Edinburgh, Greenock versus Paisley, rather than orange versus green,' says McLellan.

According to McCue, 'If there was sectarianism, then it was most likely to be found within the staff.' Among the wardens, Celtic supporters were relatively thin on the ground. Inevitably, in Scotland a link has always between drawn between the police force and the

British state, which, by extension, can also be taken to mean Protestantism and Rangers, the club seen to represent the Protestant tradition. As Ferguson reportedly turned and said to his lawyer, Blair Morgan, shortly after he was sentenced: 'It's OK, all the wardens are bluenoses [Rangers fans] anyway.'

But that wasn't strictly true. More Celtic-supporting wardens were being bled into the system after what was described as the 'fresh start' programme, implemented in the late '80s. This sought to ensure that prison officers were drawn from a broader cross-section of society. It also aimed to make the staff more academically qualified; previously, there were not too many obstacles to joining up, providing you could 'take care of yourself', as McCue puts it. He adds, 'When I first started, most of the promotions were still going to Protestants, and there were very few Celtic fans on the staff.' McCue, though, was one; Willie McGurk, the long-serving physical-education instructor, was another.

It is ironic that they both played significant roles during Ferguson's time in Barlinnie. In their own way, each helped to make his stay bearable.

*

Each time the phone rings, McGurk answers it in the manner of someone who owns the place: 'McGurk's Gymnasium,' he brusquely informs the caller on the other end of the line. After nearly 40 years of service at Barlinnie, it is understandable that the relationship between McGurk and 'his' gym has become so entrenched. Since the 1970s, he has done as much as anyone to improve not only the physical condition of prisoners, but also their mental well-being, something that is just as critical in an environment such as this.

McGurk's gymnasium dates back to the late 1930s, when it was built by Italian prisoners of war. A volleyball net is slung from one wall to another and there are wooden floorboards. It feels, looks and smells like any school gym might have done in, say, the 1970s. But it is a vital part of the Barlinnie infrastructure. Newer workout areas – where treadmills and weight-lifting machines can be found – have since been added, to the benefit of everyone, wardens as well as prisoners. Abdelbaset Al-Megrahi, the man convicted of planting the bomb that brought down Pan Am Flight 103 over Lockerbie, became an inmate at Barlinnie in 2002. As well as his own specially constructed cell – known as 'Gaddafi's Cafe' – he had access to his own exercise yard. Ferguson's need to keep fit was greater than Al-Megrahi's, yet he was given no such special provision. Ferguson did, though, have a well-meaning physical-training instructor in McGurk, who felt responsible for the footballer's welfare and was conscious of the reputation of the prison. Indeed, both these concerns were interlinked.

McGurk left his staff in no doubt about what was expected of them, even if his first impressions of Ferguson were not favourable: 'I thought he was quite arrogant; I think the fame had gone to his head,' he says. He found Ferguson to be quite bitter, particularly towards one man.

'Oh, he hated Jim Farry,' McGurk says, with reference to the chief executive of the Scottish Football Association, whose efforts to make Ferguson serve a 12-match ban on top of the jail sentence were continuing. 'It came across very much that he blamed Farry for the predicament he was in,' he says. 'I had some sympathy with that. He was hard done by, when you think what other players have done and got away with.'

McGurk also knew he had a duty of care towards the footballer. Everton were understandably concerned about the condition in which their prize asset would be delivered back to them. McGurk sought to assure them on that front. 'Joe Royle, the manager, came up and visited, and I said to him: "If there is anything specific you want done with Duncan, then tell me." Basically, it was a lot of light training. We wanted to keep him ticking over. That was our job. We didn't want him coming out of Barlinnie any less of a £4 million player.'

Of course, the newspapers were desperate to make assumptions about Ferguson's involvement in prison football matches. As *The Herald* noted at the time, Barlinnie has a red blaize football pitch that could be 'very hard on the star's reputedly delicate knees'. Why had they used red blaize? 'So it disnae show up the blood,' one warden informs me.

Barlinnie did have a football XI. McGurk, indeed, had been instrumental in its formation, just the year before Ferguson's arrival. He was granted permission from the then governor to arrange an annual match against the staff team, who, with McGurk adding some ballast to the midfield, were past winners of the British prison championship. His loyalty transferred to the prisoners, as he trained them for a fixture designed to show the importance of teamwork, turning them from a 'bunch of cut-throats' – his phrase – into a well-drilled unit.

Although it ended with defeat for the prisoners, there was no question which team had taken most from the occasion. After the formal presentation of the cup to the winners, McGurk told his players: 'You proved what sport and teamwork and camaraderie can do for you. Not one of you was booked or sent off.'

It is more than could be said for the prison-staff team. Two were red-carded and five others got booked. 'They proved who the thugs were,' says McGurk.

Ferguson, of course, was kept well away from any such danger. In any event, he was still recovering from a hernia operation. He had started only two matches so far that season – both back in August, against Chelsea and Arsenal. Everton failed to score in either game. 'Technically, he was not fully fit when he came to us,' recalls McGurk.

Ferguson did light remedial work initially and then some light circuit training, and was permitted to spend at least four days a week at the gym. He did not take part in the same main PE activities as the other prisoners because of the concerns about his safety. He did, though, play head tennis across the volleyball net. 'Being 6 ft 4, Duncan loved that. The big man was quite good at that; he was good with his head,' says McGurk, before adding with a smile: 'But I took a few games off him, right enough. The gym was a great respite for him. It was as important for his mental well-being as anything else.'

Ferguson also took part in a three-a-side game called skittle-ball, devised by McGurk. The object of the game was to score a goal by kicking the ball at the skittle, which was placed on a mat at either end of the hall. For the goal to be awarded, the skittle had to be knocked over. 'He had quite a powerful shot on him,' recalls Willie McCabe, one of McGurk's PT instructors.

'He came to the gym and he only wanted to play football,' recalls McCabe. 'I asked him what he did in training at Everton. He just said, "I play five-a-side."' McCabe and Ferguson got on well together, though he jokes that Ferguson left prison without returning a pair of trainers he had borrowed from the gym.

He also recalls Ferguson telling him that he had a BMW M3.

McCabe wondered where the fun was in that, since the player was banned from driving at the time. 'He told me he had a driver, and I said: "You don't buy a BMW to sit in the passenger seat, that's crazy." He just laughed. It was just one of the things you would talk about with a professional footballer – cars.'

McCabe was not a football fan, so he had to find other subjects about which to speak to Ferguson – unlike McCue and McGurk, and many others, for that matter. McGurk recalls an incident 'up at the hospital', where Ferguson worked for a spell, dishing out food to patients via trolleys that were known as 'chuck wagons'.

'Nurses were getting his autograph and selling it on', McGurk says. 'I told my staff: if I find out that anyone has so much as asked for his autograph, then I will "code" them, they will be disciplined. Because, technically speaking, he was just a prisoner and he should have been treated that way.'

Blair Morgan, Ferguson's lawyer, had given the player some picture cards during one of his visits; they were of Ferguson himself, in an Everton strip. Since he was being asked so often for his autograph, Morgan thought it would be easier for him to sign these cards and give them out to people. However, Morgan received a phone call from the governor, asking him to desist from bringing in these cards since they were now being used as a form of currency within the prison. A signed picture of Duncan Ferguson, inscribed with 'Barlinnie, 1995' could get you anything from a packet of cigarettes to a phone card.

Indeed, the *Daily Record* reported that a fellow inmate of 'jailed soccer bad boy Duncan Ferguson' was sacked from his prison job for selling signed photos of the footballer. Gary Mery was stripped of his duties after trying to flog one of the photographs to a member of staff for £1. According to the paper, Mery duly lost his 'prestigious' role as a pass man.

Ferguson's links to the outside world were limited. His sister Audrey visited on a regular basis – she was able to take advantage of her Scottish Prison Service special privileges – while Morgan, his lawyer, could also make a request to visit Ferguson as often as required. The footballer, meanwhile, could still access newspapers. It was claimed – by the *Daily Record*, oddly enough – that he was having the *Daily Record* delivered to him each morning from Riddrie newsagents, just yards from the entrance to Barlinnie. The shop, the newspaper informed readers, is 'the main supplier of newspapers for the cons'. To be fair, McCue does confirm that the *Daily Record* was the most popular newspaper among the prisoners.

For more detailed news of the goings-on at Everton, he had to rely on first-hand accounts from manager Joe Royle, chairman Peter Johnson and director Cliff Finch, who, three weeks into Ferguson's sentence, came to Glasgow to visit the player.

At first, says Johnson, Ferguson hadn't wanted them to come. He had indicated that he did not want anyone to see him in those distressing circumstances. 'But we thought, he's our boy, and we better go and see him,' he says. 'And he seemed relatively happy to see us. We just chatted about the conditions, and about how it was. He was quite pragmatic about things. He seemed to accept where he was.'

'But I don't think I would like to commit a custodial offence in Glasgow; it's not the place to be,' adds Johnson of his own experience of Barlinnie. 'It was an awful, awful place. We had to sit in line on wooden benches and wait our turn to see Duncan.'

Perhaps inevitably, given his association with pigeons, Ferguson was given the title of 'Birdman of Barlinnie'. It was one he inherited from Ian Breckenridge, who was one of the original inmates in Barlinnie's Special Unit, an experimental place where particularly violent criminals, including the convicted murderer and now celebrated sculptor Jimmy Boyle, were housed in what was designed to be a responsibly engaging environment. Established in 1972, the scheme has since been discontinued, but, for a spell, it allowed the creative potential of prisoners to be explored. Other prisoners gave Breckenridge the nickname 'Birdman', as he devoted his time to breeding budgerigars.

When Jimmy Anderson, the president of the Barlinnie prison visiting committee, met Ferguson for the first time, he recalls the footballer saying 'only how much he was missing his pigeons'.

As much as such visits nourished Ferguson, there seems little doubt about what truly sustained him. The support of the Everton fans, whose letters and parcels kept coming throughout his stay, was a godsend.

'In those days, you could only write one letter a week, unless you sacrificed a face-to-face visit,' recalls McCue. 'You could get another letter if you bought it. Those were the rules in those days. In Duncan's case, he wanted to respond and acknowledge the senders of all these letters. I was fairly lax about that and gave him extra letters – not hundreds, just a few more.'

I obtained one such reply, sent from Ferguson to Graeme McIver, an Everton fan from Warrington. On a sheet of Everton FC-headed notepaper, Ferguson emphasised just how much such correspondence meant to him, telling McIver that he was grateful 'from the bottom of my heart' for the letter and the photograph also enclosed – 'It certainly helped brighten the walls!' he wrote. He also commented on the 'sheer number of letters and volume of support' he had received from other Everton supporters. 'Words cannot express how much they have meant,' he added, before signing off with his signature, and a kiss.

*

There is a postscript to Ferguson's life in Barlinnie. Indeed, it is still being written. For McCue, however, there was one more meeting with Ferguson, one further crossing of paths. It came some years later at Goodison Park, where McCue and his family were enjoying some corporate hospitality in a marquee that had been erected in a car park outside the ground.

'Myself and my wife are working-class people; it was a once-in-a-lifetime thing when we went to one of these events,' recalls McCue. After the game, they got to meet some of the players, Ferguson among them. It seems extraordinary, but Barlinnie remained an unspoken connection between them. 'We only had about a minute together,' recalls McCue.

They shook hands. If Ferguson recognised McCue, then, remarkably, he wasn't letting on. 'I didn't ask him about the prison, and he didn't ask me. I didn't mention it, but I am sure he recognised me,' continues McCue, adding, 'But I am not his friend. That was a professional relationship. I was a staff member; he was a customer, if you like.'

McCue wasn't on duty when Ferguson was liberated – or 'libbed', as it is known in the language of cons and screws so he never did say a proper goodbye. He remembers watching footage of his early morning departure on television.

Ferguson served exactly half of his three-month sentence: forty-four days. Curiously, it is an evocative time frame in football, corresponding with the length of time Brian Clough was manager at Leeds United, the period on which David Peace's book and its subsequent film adaptation, both called *The Damned United*, are based. Jock Stein, too, managed at Elland Road for 44 days, before leaving to take up the post of Scotland manager. It might seem a short term for a football manager to serve. For a prisoner serving time inside Barlinnie, however, it is enough.

'Six weeks is a bloody long time in prison,' notes McCue. 'Six weeks is horrendous. One night in there is horrendous. I would not wish it on my worst enemy.'

Ferguson's release was designed to be as low-key as possible, although it is true that no one else in the group of 35 prisoners released that morning was picked up by a burgundy, chauffeur-driven Daimler. Due to prison rules, his parents were not allowed to join him in the hired car, which had been parked in the prison overnight. The driver had returned the following morning to collect both it and Ferguson. Four policemen were deployed to keep the photographers and journalists away from the prison entrance when the limousine emerged. Another group, consisting of four Everton fans, had left Liverpool at 2 a.m. to see his release and posed for photographs next to the prison sign.

Ferguson kept his head down as the car drew out of the gate. According to one newspaper, 'It wasn't exactly in the Mike Tyson-class for spectacular fireworks.' Just a few months earlier, radio-station helicopters had buzzed overhead as the boxer emerged with his retinue after serving a three-year jail sentence in Indiana for rape. In contrast to Tyson, there were no Muslim brothers by Ferguson's side in the gloom of a Glasgow morning, no prayer cap on his head to signal a religious conversion.

Instead, as the car slowed briefly to negotiate the speed bumps, the flashes of the photographers' bulbs momentarily lit up a footballer tucked up on the back seat, alone with his thoughts.

CHAPTER 14

Lord of All Hopefulness

Duncan Ferguson had yet to take a step back onto the pitch when he became embroiled in another controversy, little of which was his own doing. On his release from jail, the plan had been to take Ferguson straight to Bellefield, the Everton training ground, where he was to be reunited with his teammates. However, this idea was abandoned due to the number of photographers and journalists who had gathered outside the gates of the facility.

Even the chosen mode of transport between Glasgow and Liverpool proved contentious. Commentators were vexed by the burgundy limousine Everton had hired to collect Ferguson from prison. It wasn't the colour of the car that was the problem in this instance – unlike when Ferguson had turned up to his first Everton press conference wearing a jacket of the same Liverpool red-ish shade. Rather, it was the ostentatious make of the vehicle itself that jarred with many.

The ire of the critics only increased when it became known that the club were planning to parade someone recently convicted of an assault charge on the pitch before the next day's home game with Sheffield Wednesday, as if he were a prodigal son rather than, to the use the phrase employed by the *Mail on Sunday* columnist Patrick Collins, 'a serial thug'.

In the event, he only poked his head out of the players' tunnel and gave the briefest of waves. Nevertheless, the *Liverpool Echo* used the phrase 'Hero returns' in a headline and felt the wrath of critics in the national newspapers – and elsewhere. Many were uncomfortable with the notion that Ferguson was making a triumphant return.

Everton were then accused of going overboard by organising a distastefully exultant reception to mark Ferguson's playing comeback, for the reserves, just days later.

The erudite Collins led the chorus of complaint in a well-argued piece and he hit home with a brutal challenge of his own. He had expected more of Everton, he wrote. After all, 'This is the club of Joe Mercer, Ray Wilson, Alex Young and Howard Kendall.' Now, he lamented, 'the old School of Science' had been 'reduced to a home for celebrity criminals'.

Collins also wrote that we should not be surprised when football chairmen descend to crassly populist gestures, since years of observation have taught us to expect no better. However, he was saddened by manager Joe Royle's involvement in the decision-making process. He is a man, opined Collins, who you would not expect to court popular favour 'with tasteless gimmicks'. This was the mid-'90s, and the rise of lad culture could be discerned almost everywhere, from a musical landscape dominated by Oasis, the rock group led by the irrepressible Gallagher brothers, to the magazine racks in newsagents, where vulgarity was being glorified in the pages of umpteen glossy titles. Collins wondered if this was not yet another illustration of our new boorish culture.

The gimmick referred to was a pipe band, hired to provide the entertainment prior to Ferguson's return in a Central League match for the reserves, against Newcastle United. The chairman accused of making the 'crass populist gesture' was Peter Johnson.

'Looking back, maybe that was not too unfair a comment,' Johnson says now. 'We were really trying to engender some excitement. Maybe, on reflection, the bagpipes were a mistake. But certainly, I felt the carping about the car was unfair criticism.

'How else was he to get out of jail? The only way for his employer to get him out of jail was to send a car for him.

'Does it really matter what size it is?'

Ferguson scored twice on his comeback for the reserves in a 5–0 win. According to witnesses in a crowd of over 10,000 – 9,000 more than would normally have attended such a fixture – he looked remarkably fit, something for which those in the physical education department at Barlinnie, such as Willie McGurk, deserved to take more than a little credit.

With his 12-match ban imposed by the Scottish Football Association still suspended, following another appeal by Everton, Ferguson's first-team return came the following Monday against West Ham United, when he came on as substitute to rousing acclaim in a 3–0 win. Royle, though, was frustrated by the continued focus on Ferguson, as the manager sought to maintain a promising run of form that had coincided with the striker's absence.

Everton's problem was summed up by what Neville Southall had identified in the run-up to the previous season's FA Cup final. 'To the media, we were just Duncan Ferguson and ten other nuggets,' he recalls. And yet Everton lost only one of the six league games that Ferguson missed while in prison. A run of three wins in a row in November included a derby victory over Liverpool. They were, however, knocked out of the European Cup-Winners' Cup by Feyenoord.

Given the successive league wins, it was understandable if some were peeved at the suggestion that Everton were a one-man team, particularly with Andrei Kanchelskis – who had scored both goals in that 2–1 defeat of Liverpool – proving an inspired purchase from Manchester United. And yet, more and more, Ferguson was becoming the focus, for his own teammates as well as for the fans and media. This tendency to rely on the out-ball to Ferguson helped further erode people's impression of Everton as the home for stylish football, although the old School of Science motif, established during the 1920s, had never meant to be quite so literally translated. Of course, Steve Bloomer, the former Derby County and England striker who first employed this term, intended to pay tribute to Everton's precise, attractive play. But the phrase also made reference to that team's pragmatism and ability to play to their strengths. They were scientific, in that they thought about it. Too often when Ferguson played this wasn't the case: they didn't think about it; instead, route-one football became their default option.

There was little concession to style as mere survival became the chief concern; the need to preserve Everton's top-tier status was deemed to be extra crucial since it was something they had cherished since they spent a couple of seasons in the Second Division in the mid-1950s. Pat Nevin was conscious of a gradual change, even when he joined in the late '80s, at a time when Everton were still among the top clubs in the country. 'People talked about the School of Science; I always felt it was a bit overblown,' he says.

'I had to completely change my style to play for Everton Football Club and become a block in a unit,' he adds. 'The very individual stuff I felt did not really fit in with the team. The perfect Everton player was the one I replaced – Trevor Steven. He wouldn't jink past three players. He did everything absolutely right, and did everything well. He was the perfect modern player, really. That was the Everton way.'

Although he had left the club by the time Ferguson arrived, Nevin observed his compatriot's influence. 'Although many fans loved him, they didn't love what he brought,' he says, in reference to the style of football that became an almost subconscious reaction to the presence of a target man with fearsome aerial ability. It often overshadowed what he could do with his feet. Indeed, the first two goals he scored after his release from prison, against Wimbledon at Selhurst Park, were notable in that neither were headers, the first coming via a hooked effort with his right foot, the second from his favoured left. Nine of his next twelve goals, however, were headers.

A late season rally did see Everton finish in a creditable sixth position, although their FA Cup defence ended in rather ignominious fashion at Port Vale. Strangely, on those occasions when wingers Anders Limpar and Kanchelskis and Ferguson all played together – a fearsome front line in anyone's estimation – Everton tasted victory only once, although this tantalising prospect only ever occurred seven times. 'I'd love to have seen him play more with two out-and-out wingers,' says Nevin.

Mostly, it was uninspiring football. The 'Dogs of War' phrase employed by Royle early in his managerial tenure at Goodison took an ever-firmer firm grip. As had been the case in his few appearances for Scotland, Ferguson's mere presence tended to dictate the style of play, even if the intention had been to play in a more fluid, attractive manner.

That had certainly been Mike Walker's wish, though, according to Neville Southall, this desire for the team to play the ball out from the back only meant the strikers were 'starved' of the ball. Southall, on the other hand, was seeing plenty of it while rummaging around in the back of the net. 'Under Walker, we'd play 400 passes in our own half and let goals in,' says Southall. When Royle arrived, the goalkeeper was ordered to kick the ball upfield rather than throw it to either full-back. 'As soon as I got the ball, the players would disappear,' he says. 'They would be on the halfway line as soon as I kicked it. We would squeeze the opposition.

'If you are going to make a mistake, make it in their half, not yours.'

As Royle explained when he described Ferguson as turning into the Incredible Hulk when angry, it had got to the stage where the manager as well as the striker's teammates almost willed defenders to give him a kick in the early stages of a match in order to light that inner fire. The pumped-up version of Ferguson distinguished himself in the run-up to the 1996–97 campaign when, motivated by the thought he would be facing Newcastle United's new £15 million signing Alan Shearer on the opening day of the season, he spent the previous week in training, breathing fire and singing songs about how Shearer was 'going to get it'.

These were no idle boasts. He completely overshadowed the debutant Shearer, earning the penalty from which Everton scored their first goal and then setting up Gary Speed, whose goal sealed the points in a 2–0 victory. In midweek, Ferguson distinguished himself again – at Old Trafford. Two goals in the opening half – the first a raking drive on the turn from the edge of the box, the second a back-post header – put Everton 2–0 in front.

United, as so often is the case, managed to stage a comeback, but Ferguson's double earned Everton a point. It was yet another example of the Scot relishing the opportunity to test himself against the best. According to Southall, Ferguson was like Muhammad Ali in that 'he didn't want to deal with just the crap – he needed the adrenaline of the big clashes to get him going'. Indeed, the goalkeeper wonders whether Ferguson might have benefited from the sophisticated backroom support system that is in place at almost every top club today.

Specifically, he is referring to the contribution a sports psychologist might have made to Ferguson's game, particularly during those first months after he had been released from prison.

'People think he is just a big Scottish fella who goes around and is the life and soul of everything, but he is not really,' says Southall. 'He is quiet and quite shy. Coming out of prison and people looking at him – it would have made his life a misery. There was the shame of it

'He would also have hated people talking about him because he is a private fella. That affected him more than actual prison, in my view. He always put a brave face on it. Deep down, however, that would have crucified him. He takes things to heart.'

The goalkeeper does not recall Ferguson being given any special treatment on his return from Barlinnie. In the unforgiving environment of the dressing-room, the striker was expected to get on with it. Southall suspects that this was something Ferguson himself wished to do.

'I just think, in a different era, we could be talking about someone completely different,' he says. 'Duncan was born with a fantastic talent. In a different age, with psychologists and such around him, I genuinely think he would have been absolutely magnificent.'

I mention Jim McLean's remark that Ferguson could have been as good as Didier Drogba. Southall, who played with the likes of Mark Hughes, Ian Rush and Gary Lineker, three of the finest strikers in modern times, almost splutters. 'Oh no, he was better than him,' he says. 'He could have been the best player in the world.'

It's my turn to splutter. Really?

'He didn't have any flaws,' replies Southall. 'He was good on the floor, he was pretty quick, to be fair to him, and he was great in the air; he could rough people up and he could finish.' He adds that you just needed to find the 'right vehicle' for Ferguson. Were Everton, then, not the right team at the time? Southall pauses, then says, 'I don't think anyone other than Joe Royle would have got more out of him.'

That was the challenge for any manager – coaxing the performance out of Ferguson. More often than not, of course, it was his opposite man who had to be relied upon to do this. 'If someone annoyed him in the first minutes, we used to think "great",' says Southall. 'If someone went through the back of him, that was enough.' There were times, though, when he simply couldn't be roused. In fairness, more industrious players than Ferguson might have struggled to feel motivated during a pre-season testimonial at Aberdeen, in what was a benefit match for the Pittodrie club's midfielder Brian Grant.

'It was not the most demanding of situations, I agree,' writes Royle in his autobiography. 'But Duncan was clearly in one of his not-bothered moods.' At half-time, the manager confronted him. 'Any chance of running about a bit in the second half, Duncan?' he suggested.

'The lads were all tittering in the background,' recounts Royle. 'Duncan looked at me and, though smiling, he said in all seriousness, "But gaffer, their centre-half has been telling me he has been praying for me. He's a born-again Christian who wrote to me when I was in jail. How can I mix it with a lad like that?"'

Brian Irvine, the opposite man in question on that afternoon in July 1996, is amused when I inform him how this tale has made it into print. 'I wasn't praying for him while he was in prison so I could tell him and put him off when I next played against him,' he points out. 'It was out of genuine concern for him.'

Ferguson also felt inclined to take it easy when up against his old friend from Dundee United, Christian Dailly. The pair might have very contrasting personalities – according to Jim McLean, Dailly made the 'very best of himself' – but they got on well together at Tannadice. Post-United, their careers continued to flourish in England. Dailly, who switched from striker to centre-half after leaving United, recalls facing Ferguson for West Ham United and being quite concerned at the prospect.

'He was like: "Don't worry, I am not coming near you,"' recalls Dailly. '"You can win all the headers today. I am not going to contest them." And I was thinking, "Fat chance. He is going to kill me." And the first time I went for a header he was going up to go for it too, then he checked out of the jump. He turned and gave me a little wink, and said: "I'm going to go over there. I will win my headers against the other centre-half." So he ended up battering Tomas Repka instead.'

An angry Ferguson with a point to prove was certainly more desirable than a frustrated, uninterested one. After the strong, Ferguson-inspired start to the 1996–97 season, three successive defeats quickly dampened enthusiasm at Goodison. Suddenly, as the long balls were slung up to him with greater urgency and desperation, the likelihood that Ferguson would succumb to frustration grew more likely. This was when referees could expect some trouble.

An away game at Blackburn Rovers in September saw Ferguson red-carded for the unusual crime of describing the referee as a 'baldie bastard'. Indeed, the striker later claimed he had delivered this message by 'singing a song' to the referee. David Elleray, then also a housemaster at Harrow public school, might well have been follicly challenged, but he took exception to the second part of Ferguson's accusation, and he wasn't thrilled when the Scot repeated it either.

Ferguson was sent off only once at Dundee United and received seven cautions in eighty-eight games, while some would say he barely had the chance to be sent off with Rangers – although, of course, it might have been preferable had he been shown the red card on one particular occasion. In England, his problems with authority began to mount fairly quickly, although Elleray does recall Ferguson displaying a trait that often distinguished Scottish players on their arrival south of the border. Initially, he recalls, Ferguson engaged with referees in a respectful manner.

'He was like many Scottish players, who address the referee as "Mr" in Scotland and then bring this down to the Premier League with them,' says Elleray. Although, he adds, 'this trait tends not to last long'. Elleray soon got used to being met by what he describes as a 'contemptuous' look from Ferguson.

'To me at least, there was no point in trying to "engage" with him,' he says. 'This meant that you could not build any rapport with him, which was generally unusual and unhelpful, as the "banter" between a referee and player could often defuse situations.

'In general, a referee will only send a player off if the player looks at the referee and deliberately swears at him in a personal manner,' notes Elleray. 'In Ferguson's case, what was somewhat "amusing" – if a red card for offensive language can be amusing – was that, having given me the mouthful, I said to him, rhetorically, "What did you say?" at which point he repeated the full abuse! When I sent him off, Craig Short – who I think was Everton captain at the time – said to me, "Well, he gave you no choice, did he?"'

Elleray places Ferguson in the top three of those players he had difficulty in handling, along with England internationalists Teddy Sheringham and Darren Anderton, who, he says, were 'equally remote, disdainful and offensive'.

After the Blackburn incident, Ferguson was handed a two-game ban, and there was further unwanted news when it was revealed that he would miss several other games as well, due to the need for a knee operation.

When he returned, Everton's season was continuing to unravel – Kanchelskis left in February, just after a club record run of six consecutive league losses, amidst which also came a home defeat to Bradford City in the FA Cup. Royle resigned, although it was a more complicated process than him simply telling the board that he was leaving. In actual fact, he had no intention of walking away: instead, he had merely attended a meeting with Johnson to clear the air after he had been overruled in a transfer bid for the tall Norwegian centre-forward Tore André Flo, a move that had placed a question mark over Ferguson's own future at the club. By the time the meeting had ended, Royle detected little or no confidence in his stewardship.

As he relates in his autobiography, the two parties 'drifted' towards 'mutual consent' as a way of explaining the departure to the press. Royle laments the injuries suffered by Ferguson were a major reason for Everton's poor form, although he featured in the last twenty-eight matches of Royle's final season, starting all but two of them.

Andy Gray, on the verge of being installed as Royle's replacement, then elected to stay with Sky, and Howard Kendall returned for a third stint as manager. He had tried to buy Ferguson from Dundee United in his second spell at Goodison, and then tells me he was further impressed with the striker when watching the opening credits to *Match of the Day*, which included a towering header from the Scot against Arsenal, when even Tony Adams, the London side's robust skipper, had been left powerless.

The perception of Ferguson as the conductor unwittingly directing the rhythm of Everton's play persisted, however. 'Other players took advantage of his qualities,' says Kendall. 'They thought: "Well, the big man is up front, and if he's up front then we'll just put the ball up there." He was better than that. We tried to say: "No, don't do it."' Kendall pinpoints Ferguson's ability to head the ball while on the move. First of all, however, you had to get him to move. 'He thought he could just stand and jump,' says Kendall. 'But again, you need quality service. And often at Everton he wasn't getting the service, and he would get frustrated.'

One of Kendall's key decisions in this season-long third spell at the club was to appoint Ferguson captain. 'You had to get him into a situation where he appreciated what the manager was doing,' he says. 'He had to believe in what you were asking him to do.'

The announcement surprised many. After all, only the previous month Ferguson had given the tabloids an excuse to use one of their favourite phrases. With Everton in the midst of a five-game losing run, and the day after a 2–1 defeat to Aston Villa saw them slip to bottom place in the league, Ferguson was reported in the *Sunday Mirror* as having been involved in a 'hotel romp'. The hotel made a complaint to Everton after a suite was trashed – the cleaners had found 'discarded stockings and scattered sheets' as well as a 'shower curtain ripped off its rail' – and Ferguson left the following morning without paying. 'Ferguson's Merseyside Mayhem started when he turned up at the riverside hotel with Everton goalkeeper Neville Southall,' the paper reported, before going on to give details of the incident at Liverpool's 'classy' Atlantic Tower Hotel. Southall and Ferguson had been drinking in the bar before the latter 'disappeared upstairs'.

Perhaps the most significant part of the story is that Southall, who admits he intentionally sought to keep some distance between himself and his teammates, had clearly become someone with whom Ferguson felt comfortable socialising, despite an age difference of almost 15 years.

There was, Southall says, some 'disorder' in Ferguson's life. 'It was like his pigeons – time and effort goes into keeping them, but you also have little control over them.'

However, when Ferguson was given responsibility, he responded in the right manner by scoring a hat-trick against Bolton Wanderers in December 1997 in his first game while wearing the skipper's armband. He was still only in his mid-20s. The 3–2 win over Bolton was vital since it was only Everton's second in 11 league games. 'It was definitely one of my managerial decisions which I can say went right,' says Kendall.

As well as investing Ferguson with a new purpose, there was another positive spin-off from making him skipper. The Everton Clubcall system – a pre-Internet age service offering callers the low-down on latest club news – went into meltdown. The surge in callers to hear Ferguson deliver his captain's message was a welcome further income source for the club. 'We cleaned up that day on Clubcall, so many people wanted to hear what he sounded like,' recalls Alan Myers, who was then in the communications department at Goodison Park and who has since returned to the club as communications director. 'I think I can remember what he said word for word: "I am proud and privileged to be captain of this club and I am looking forward to getting on with the job." That was the interview. That was literally it. It was about 35 seconds long.'

Ferguson's bond with the Everton fans was becoming ever deeper. 'It goes back to the Scottish FA's treatment of him,' says Steve Jones of Everton fans website Blue Kipper. 'They wanted to make an example of him. He had nowhere to go. Everton opened their arms to him, and the fans opened their arms to him. They said, "Come on in, Dunc, you are one of us."'

His popularity with the Everton fans seemed unwavering at the time. While not an island, Liverpool sometimes feels that way: cut off slightly from the prevailing trends, and rightly proud of its reputation for being so welcoming to non-natives. Abandoned by industry and betrayed by governments, it was easy for Liverpudlians, certainly from the blue half of the city, to see Ferguson as just another victim of what the *Sunday Times*, in a profile of the footballer, described as 'a callous and remote authority'. Like other footballing incomers before him, most notably fellow Scots such as Kenny Dalglish and Alan Hansen at Anfield, Ferguson found his own 'Liverpool home' on Merseyside.

Ferguson's links with the area were strengthened in June 1998, when he married a local girl, Janine Tasker. They had met through her sister Karen, who is married to former world champion snooker player and BBC commentator John Parrott. Some unwanted drama was attached to Ferguson's big day. Kendall's latest return to the club had not been deemed to be a success, Everton escaping relegation on the final afternoon of the 1997–98 season, with a 1–1 draw at home against Coventry City. Had Bolton not lost at Chelsea, Everton would have slid into the second tier of English football. Kendall, who had planned to attend Ferguson's wedding, was sacked the day before his captain walked up the aisle of the Liverpool Anglican Cathedral in a kilt.

Whatever Kendall's shortcomings, Peter Johnson (unlike Kendall, the chairman still attended Ferguson's wedding ceremony) was perceived as the villain of the piece. Everton supporters jeered him as he entered the cathedral. Afterwards he was escorted out of a side entrance to his blue Bentley by police officers. In between times, someone described as 'the baddest of football bad boys' in the next day's *Daily Post* announced 'I will' in a 'strong, fiercely Scottish voice', before the congregation stood to sing the hymn 'Lord of all Hopefulness'.

According to the same newspaper, this marriage scene, played out in front of over 500 guests, was 'the least-expected episode of Ferguson's well-publicised life'.

CHAPTER 15

What's Up, Dunc?

While the cult of Duncan Ferguson had grown during his time inside Barlinnie jail, so, too, had his mistrust of the media – although there are contradictions. Ferguson and his fiancée were reportedly in negotiations with *Hello!* magazine prior to the wedding, with the guests having been asked to refrain from taking photographs. According to an article in the *Daily Post* from the eve of the wedding, however, these plans had been quickly abandoned, with a spokesperson for the publishers 'declining to comment on the matter'.

Arrangements were never destined to run smoothly, given Ferguson's recent history with glossy magazines. The journalist Bill Borrows had grappled with difficult subjects before, so the task he was handed by the editor of *Goal* in 1997 did not fill him with too much anxiety. 'Duncan Ferguson? Why not?' he responded. The brief was to go and find out as much as he could from a man who had not granted a major interview since his release from prison.

'Easy,' thought Borrows, who had, he says, been handed tougher assignments than going head to head with a reticent footballer in the company boardroom of a sports equipment firm in Yorkshire. There was, however, only one problem. Ferguson had agreed to speak about just a single topic. And, as topics go, it didn't sound a particularly promising one. Not when there was a proposed six-page feature to fill. Not when he was prepared to discuss only his football boots.

The subject of the footballer's footwear featured near the top of the list of topics Borrows *least* wanted to speak with Ferguson about.

After all, the footballer had a fascinating story to tell. While Borrows did not anticipate that Ferguson would open his heart about his experiences in Barlinnie, he had hoped for something more engaging than a discussion about screw-in studs. But the lot of the journalist is to make something of such inauspicious ingredients. And often the best pieces of writing are born from minimal contact with the subject, and from seemingly banal situations.

In contrast to many who have attempted to write about Ferguson, at least Borrows was permitted to ask him questions, however restricted. At least he could count on a dialogue of sorts. He was also an experienced journalist. Borrows had once worked for the punchy *Loaded* magazine – 'In the days when it had some words in it,' he points out, in reference to the acres of naked female flesh which adorn the pages of the title nowadays – and he knew that not every interview was destined to run smoothly.

'Go to America, get in some trouble,' James Brown, editor during *Loaded*'s heyday of the mid-'90s, ordered him on one occasion. 'And don't come back until you have.'

On his return, he had a feature on Hunter S. Thompson, the godfather of gonzo journalism, to file, complete with the desired amount of trouble, including a bar-room brawl. The visit had ended with Borrows being told by Thompson's attorney to head for the state line as quickly as possible, immortal advice that he wisely followed.

It would be difficult to write a boring word on an encounter with a whisky-fuelled Thompson in a place called the Woody Creek Tavern in Colorado. The story, as the saying goes, writes itself. But Borrows' Ferguson mission was different. For a start, the venue was not some dusty town in the American Midwest. Rather, it was the sterile headquarters of a sports' goods manufacturing firm in mid-west Yorkshire. Borrows made the best of what was, on the face of it, a less-than-encouraging situation.

'There is a limit to the amount of interrogatory dialogue that can be based around a pair of football boots with a player who makes ten minutes with Alan Shearer feel like an audience with Peter Ustinov,' he writes at one point. But he manages to make it work by describing the sheer banality of it all, from the vol-au-vents with 'lacklustre salad garnish' to the Mitre 'goons' who fuss over the required protocol. From this unpromising set of circumstances, he manages to draw some genuine moments of insight from Ferguson.

'I have been around the block, working for *Loaded*,' says Borrows. 'I have been in situations like that before. It was pretty much his first post-prison interview. I knew I was getting great copy.'

The Mitre PR woman who organised the interview did not view what he got as 'great copy', however. She was furious when the piece appeared in the September 1997 edition of *Goal*. Borrows presents a hardly sympathetic portrait of a footballer with 'all the easy charm of a teenager on a two-week family holiday, self-catering, in East Anglia'. This description alone – it featured in the very first line of the piece – was enough to have her stretching for the phone.

Dave Cottrell, the magazine's editor, took the call. 'Bill – and by definition *Goal* – had refused to play the game,' he recalls. 'Mitre's client [Ferguson] had acted like a knob, so Bill quoted him verbatim and took the piss.

'She had hysterics down the phone. I think I just told her we'd reported exactly what happened and it was hardly our responsibility if Duncan was so morose and monosyllabic. Interestingly, to this day people who remember *Goal* tell me that was their favourite-ever feature.'

The experience helped set back relations between Ferguson and the press even further. Strained doesn't even begin to describe it. Borrows simply decided that since his subject had offered so little, he had no option but to use every last cough and splutter. It is an at times excruciating read, entertaining in the way that spoof fly-on-the-wall programmes such as *The Office* are entertaining.

On reading the piece, it is quickly apparent that the subject of the interview would rather have been anywhere else than inside this Mitre complex, talking about his boots. Borrows noted that Ferguson had the body language of a man trying 'too hard to appear relaxed' in what were unfamiliar surroundings.

The interview got off to a bad start. In a bid to make some small talk with the brooding protagonist, Justin Slee, the photographer, pointed out, 'It will be a six-page feature.' Normally, this is guaranteed to appeal to the subject's vanity. As far as Ferguson was concerned, however, this was roughly about five-and-a-half pages too long.

Borrows takes up the story. 'Five or six pages?' repeats Ferguson, who, the writer noted in *Goal*, is 'instantly fearful'. Ferguson looks at the photographers, and then looks at the man liaising between himself and Mitre. 'I thought it was just a small piece to endorse the boots.'

'Oh it is,' the man with the camera says.

'Oh it is,' the liaison says.

'Oh it is,' Borrows says.

'I want to make a phone call,' demands Ferguson. The boardroom is quickly cleared while Ferguson calls his lawyer, Blair Morgan.

And so begins – or very nearly didn't begin – the footballer's first major one-on-one interview since 1995.

Ferguson comes across as almost heroically determined to stick to his script. 'Do you have any set ambitions?' an increasingly desperate Borrows asks at one point.

'Just to wear Mitre,' replies Ferguson.

But there is the odd off-guard moment when the footballer, possibly inadvertently, opens up. Despite the pathological insistence that he won't speak about prison – 'we are told this six or seven times by various agitated employees at Mitre Headquarters,' notes Borrows – Ferguson brings the subject up himself.

Following a brief conversation with his lawyer, Ferguson agreed to have his picture taken. 'Last time I had this done I had a number around my neck,' he tells the photographer.

The reader is surprised by an unexpected moment of poignancy in what is clearly a tense situation. 'Perhaps the attitude is just a self-defence mechanism,' ponders Borrows. 'Perhaps.'

Slee was simply relieved he had not contrived to scupper the interview before it had started and he'd got the pictures he needed. He admits to having treated Ferguson quite 'gingerly' when taking the photographs prior to the interview. He had learned that this was the best order in which to do things when it came to footballers. He was only just recovering from another brush with a Scot. Gary McAllister, then a player with Leeds United, refused point-blank to be photographed when he saw Slee setting up a lighting system that he felt was too elaborate. 'I'm a footballer, not a fucking model,' he growled, and walked out.

Ferguson, for all his wariness, at least remained in the same room – most of the time. 'Although he clearly wanted to be elsewhere, he wasn't obstructive,' Slee tells me, with the memory of the day still fresh in his mind. 'He wasn't going to do anything adventurous for me, but at the time he had that hard-man image, so I was happy just to have him looking stern. In the end that more than fitted with the piece.'

It is worthwhile simply recording every word of what was said during the interview, since that is what Borrows did, to good effect. Words from Ferguson's mouth intended for the public domain were too rare to waste.

Goal: Why Mitre?

Ferguson: Because when they first approached me with their boots I liked the product, and they were comfortable. That's why I chose Mitre.

Goal: Were you wearing Mitre before the company approached you?

Ferguson: Er, no, but when they asked me to try them I was only too willing because I hadn't signed a boot deal with anybody else. So when Mitre approached me to wear their boots, I said, 'Yeah, I'll give them a go,' and I've liked them ever since.

Goal: What do you like about them?

Ferguson: They're comfy enough. That's the main thing. As long as the boots are comfortable and you're comfortable with them. I've only ever worn a couple of brands of boot and ever since I've been at Everton I've been more or less wearing Mitre.

Goal: What were you wearing when you were a kid? Was it Adidas Beckenbauer and the like?

Ferguson: Yeah, you know, Puma and Patricks, like every kid had. I went through the card, really.

Borrows then senses that, with boots fully endorsed, the time has come to broaden the area for discussion. He is quickly disabused of this notion, however.

Here, Borrows takes a well-earned breather and provides a quick glance back at Ferguson's career to date. He makes mention of Ferguson's 'off-duty discipline problems' and notes the tendency for the cream of Scottish footballing talent to self-destruct, citing Jim Baxter as a reference point. He includes a comment from Maurice Malpas, a former teammate of Ferguson's at Dundee United. 'You've got to be firm, but occasionally he needs an arm around him,' the left-back said of Ferguson. 'If he gets the feeling he's not wanted, he'll play havoc.'

The redoubtable Borrows ploughs on. He informs Ferguson he just wants 'a bit extra to fill round the boots'. He asks: 'What are you looking to do?' Borrows then informs the readers that this is the tipping point, 'the question which did it'. Ferguson's mood changes from one of 'forced surface civility to irritable impatience'. The interview is all but over.

Borrows cannot resist signing off with a flourish. 'And with that,' he writes, 'Duncan Ferguson gets up and walks out the door: Duncan Ferguson wears Mitre boots. Get hold of a pair before they sell out.'

The headline seeks to reflect the level of agitation the writer detected in the subject: 'What's up, Dunc?' There is no doubt that Borrows had succeeded to some extent in getting past Ferguson's defences. He'd managed to draw from the player some notably contemplative answers; in fact, he sounded almost meditative at times. Now and then a sentence would be let slip that ruined his apparent pledge of non-cooperation. Asked whether he considers he has 'made' it or not, he replies: 'I don't think anybody knows when they're going to make it.'

Ferguson is clearly not stupid; he is intelligent enough to play a game – just not the one Borrows had originally wanted – although it turned out well in the end for the writer, who went on to employ his skills at dealing with prickly sportsmen in his award-winning book on Alex Higgins.

The next issue of *Goal* contained a letter that took the writer – and magazine – to task. 'I am writing in reference to your recent article on Duncan Ferguson,' the correspondence – from a Gary Ashdown of St Helens – begins, continuing, 'Duncan is one of the few players at Everton who has genuine class and talent – a talent appreciated by most at Goodison. It is not his job to entertain us with his wit and wisdom off the field, a point your reporter seems to have missed.

'As far as I can tell, Duncan agreed to talk about football boots – a subject he was paid to talk about. What more can you expect from a man who, as your reporter told us, has been stitched up by the press in the past?'

The letters' page editor offers the magazine's viewpoint, and in it can be found no trace of contrition. 'When football manufacturers pay players to endorse their products, they generally expect them to give interviews with the press,' goes the *Goal* argument. 'This was one such interview. Surely, as a Ferguson fan, you would want to read about the man and not just his choice of footwear.'

Reading about his choice of footwear was about as in-depth as it got, however. Borrows was simply reaping the harvest from seeds planted years earlier, from the moment the then 18-year-old Ferguson sat down with *Scottish Football Today*'s Keith Jackson and gave his first major interview.

Having helped break the news of Mo Johnston signing for Rangers, Jackson was already beginning to make a name for himself in football journalism, just as Ferguson was starting to cause a stir in Scottish football. They had something else in common. A few years earlier, the pair had formed the strike force for the same football team. 'I only got the interview because I used to play up front with him in the Central Region Schools' Select,' recalls Jackson, who struck five goals – 'Dunc just got two,' he tells me – in the team's run to the semi-final of the Scottish Cup, where they were beaten by a Dundee select, whose match-winner was a certain Christian Dailly.

The goodwill engendered by their past experience on a football pitch together did not survive the publication of the article, however. The feature in question was an enjoyable enough romp through Ferguson's eventful formative years as a professional footballer, although the inclusion of the phrase 'Duncan Disorderly' did help lodge the nickname that dogged Ferguson forever in people's minds. 'Don't call me Duncan Disorderly!' the headline urged. 'Home Loving Fergie just wants his folks, his pigeons – and a little peace.'

The picture painted by Jackson is of someone coming to terms with his newfound fame and yet who was already having to deny talk of notoriety. 'As he sits among the clutter of his bedroom at his parents' neat home, Duncan Ferguson looks nothing like the beast of Scottish football,' writes Jackson. Save for some details of Ferguson's recent brushes with the law, there seems little to cause offence, although Jackson's attempt to set the scene does offer a glimpse of the footballer's lad-about-town credentials. 'He's dressed in a polo neck – "to hide the love bites" – and tracksuits pants,' reveals Jackson, who is now chief football writer with the *Daily Record*.

A photograph of a grinning, happy-looking Ferguson illustrates the piece, while a smaller photo is also included, showing Duncan senior with his son, who is cradling a pigeon. The choice of an image depicting such domestic bliss didn't serve to placate the elder Ferguson. 'I don't think his old man much liked the piece,' recalls Jackson. 'Suffice to say, the blossoming relationship between me and Dunc pretty much ended there and then.'

Jackson might have been among the first, but he was not the last to suffer the cold-shoulder treatment from Ferguson. However, as is often the case with the striker, there are contradictions.

Paul Joyce, who was once a football reporter for the *Daily Post*, recalls the player turning up for training at Everton with most of the national tabloids tucked under his arm. 'He used to stop and stock up on the way,' Joyce says. So he wasn't completely uninterested in the press.

Phil McNulty, now chief sports writer with the BBC but who once wrote a trenchant Friday column for the *Liverpool Echo*, confirms this. 'Yes, I saw the same thing,' he says. 'He would wander into Bellefield with all the tabloids. That was fair enough – we didn't ban him from reading us!'

Ferguson's eye could not fail to be drawn to headlines such as: 'Braveheart – or is that Faintheart?' This question appeared in bold above an opinion piece from McNulty, who was billed in the newspaper as 'controversial, outspoken, giving it to you straight from the hip'. The writer christened Ferguson as the 'Totemic Tartan Talismanic Trappist', on account of his reputation as a hero to the blue half of Merseyside, though one who had evidently lost his tongue.

One Liverpool-based sports writer told me that he knew – via a friend of Ferguson – that the footballer hated this name, which began as the 'Tartan Totem' and was later amended to the 'Tartan Trappist', when it became clear that the Scot would not deviate from his policy of non-cooperation with the media. 'McNulty was Ferguson's bête noire,' he says.

McNulty was often left unimpressed by Ferguson. The journalist certainly did not miss with his assessment of Ferguson's role – or non-role – in Everton's penalty shoot-out defeat to Sunderland in the fourth round of the League Cup in November 1998. He launched a withering attack on the player for the dereliction of duty that saw him elect not to take one of the kicks from the spot, with Everton eliminated 5–4 on penalties following the 1–1 draw at Goodison Park. 'Duncan Ferguson's status as an Everton legend – largely mythical and much of his own making – took a bit of a battering this week,' wrote McNulty.

It was only Everton's third-ever competitive penalty shoot-out. Nerves were jangling, with Sunderland leaders of the First Division at the time. The situation required a strong leader, someone prepared to grab the ball and make a statement, by taking either the first or a decisive kick. Ferguson took neither. He didn't put himself in the firing line at all.

Instead, defenders Michael Ball – then only a teenager – and Marco Materazzi took two of the first three attempts, with John Collins, under pressure himself at the time due to perceived poor form, also stepping up to the mark. The Scottish midfielder scored from the spot, just as he had done for Scotland against Brazil in the opening game of the World Cup finals in France six months earlier, when Ferguson was again posted missing. John Oster, another teenager, was next up, and missed, which meant Tony Grant had to score to ensure the tie went to sudden death. He did, and still there was no sign of Ferguson. Instead, Ibrahima Bakayoko – who by now was wearing a tracksuit, and looked for all the word like a man who had clocked off for the night – was nudged towards the penalty spot. Unsurprisingly, he missed, and Everton were out.

McNulty later expressed his view that Ferguson had let down his teammates and the fans by not taking one of the kicks. After all, he was not only captain but also the club's principal striker. Yet, wrote McNulty, there he was, 'effectively pushing the most reluctant penalty-taker in recent history, a freezing and tracksuit-clad Bakayoko, to be cast as the villain of the piece'. Bakayoko had recently missed another penalty at Middlesbrough. But 'at least he stepped forward and had a go', McNulty pointed out.

Ferguson, on the other hand, 'ignored his responsibilities' and 'shrank away'. The defeat deprived Everton of a winnable home tie against Luton Town in the next round.

'It may just have been the moment when the Everton fans, who fill the mail bags with vitriol at the very hint of criticism of their hero, may have finally seen the woods from the trees,' proposed McNulty. As promised at the top of his column, he was giving it to his readers straight.

'Duncan Ferguson, whether he liked it or not, had a duty as Everton captain to step forward and take a penalty against

Sunderland,' he added. 'We will never know why he refused, of course, because his thoughts and words are not to be shared with the club's supporters. We will just assume he did not have it in him to do it, and that is condemnation enough for a man who likes to paint himself as being afraid of nothing.'

This was a far from isolated example of McNulty setting his sights on Ferguson, although he admits he has 'contrasting' feelings about the footballer. 'You saw games when he looked so good and then watched so many others where he was just ordinary,' he says. 'We also used to hear stories from fans about acts of generosity that were in contrast to the hard-man image. I am sure Duncan Ferguson loved Everton and Everton fans – I am just not sure he actually loved football, although only he could tell us that.'

Even the most rabidly pro-Ferguson fan will have been alert to the sound sense in which many of the points and complaints raised in McNulty's columns were rooted. Although the highest-paid player at the club, he was afforded the further luxury of avoiding even the most basic media duties, such as post-match press conferences. This would have been fine had he been just another member of the squad. But he was the fans' hero, their talisman. And he was also their captain. The high-wages/low-profile equation didn't sit well with some, including his own teammates. 'A few I am sure were quite jealous of him,' smiles David Weir.

Still, it was Ferguson's own idea to ask the Everton fans, through the *Evertonian* magazine, to come up with ideas for a tattoo to further mark his devotion to the club, having signed a new five-year contract with the club in 1997. He then picked the design he wanted and went to a tattoo parlour – called Sailor Jack's in Liverpool, he later revealed – to have it inked onto his skin. The results were displayed on the front page of the January 1998 edition of the *Evertonian* magazine. Ferguson is pictured tugging up the sleeve of his shirt to reveal a number 9 positioned in the middle of the distinctive outline of the club's crest.

Below this arresting photograph is the headline: 'World Exclusive – Duncan Signs Up for Life'.

Except, of course, he hadn't.

CHAPTER 16

That's Just the Way It Is

It is supposed to be what dreams are made of if you are a Scot, particularly one hailing from the old warrior turfland of Bannockburn. A first goal at the national stadium, scored in a blue shirt.

It isn't just any goal. It is one he creates for himself. Seeing his teenage strike partner unmarked, he slips the ball through to him and then keeps on running in anticipation of the return ball, the way Jim McLean had once urged him to do.

The teenager beats a couple of men and then serves the ball back at the feet of his teammate. And then, at the end known to some as the Rangers end, the more experienced striker rifles a sweet shot low into the net. *Pick that one out, pick that one out.*

But just as there was no roar of the crowd in that prison cell, there is no roar here. Only 1,588 spectators witness the goal. It receives scant mention in the next morning's papers. And unless the scorer had fantasised about one day grabbing the second goal for Everton in a 6–0 pre-season friendly win over Queen's Park, the Scottish amateur side, then no childhood dream had been realised.

Duncan Ferguson had finally scored a goal at Hampden Park. But Scotland didn't care.

And neither did he.

*

As with the case of those who wrongly remember Duncan Ferguson's overhead kick against Germany causing a crossbar to shudder, there are two versions of the story of when his stop-start Scotland career finally ended. There is the factual version, then there is the fictional one.

The received view is that Ferguson, consumed with bitterness, didn't play for his country again after he'd been released from Barlinnie prison. In reality, he played a further two times and even attended a two-day get-together at Troon ahead of the European Championship finals in 1996, a full sixteen months after his previous Scotland outing. Significantly, it was also three months after his release from prison.

His most recent appearance for Scotland, against Greece in Athens, had come more than a year after his last cap, against Germany. In the interim there had been a record-breaking move to Rangers, as well as injury after injury, and several court appearances. Andy Roxburgh had also been replaced as Scotland manager by Craig Brown, who had already proven himself to be a sympathetic influence in Ferguson's life.

Ferguson was granted permission by Brown to arrive late ahead of the trip to Greece for a Euro '96 qualifier because he was tying up his permanent move to Everton. The assault charge after the clash with Jock McStay was still to make it to court. As well as being sorely aware that his liberty remained in peril, something else hung over Ferguson: the prospect of a 12-match ban from the Scottish Football Association, imposed following the same incident, which the player's lawyers were vigorously contesting, on the basis that it pre-empted the footballer's criminal court hearing.

So there was much to occupy his mind as he drove up to Glasgow from Merseyside ahead of the trip to Greece, where he would win his fifth cap. Perhaps at the forefront of his thoughts was the realisation that he was about to step on a plane to Athens with many of the blazered officials who he felt were going out of their way to obstruct his career; and worse, who were at risk of prejudicing his then forthcoming trial. At the head of this group, and the focus for much of Ferguson's ire, was Jim Farry, the chief executive of the SFA and someone not known for calling a spade a spade. Indeed, his convoluted-style of communication even spawned a noun: Farryspeak

A career administrator, he had begun immersing himself in the rules and regulations of Scottish football on being appointed secretary of the Scottish Football League at the age of just 25, later becoming the youngest secretary of the SFA, then its chief executive. Curiously, his downfall was instigated by a failure to implement the rules on one significant occasion. Fergus McCann, the wily Scots-Canadian tycoon credited with reviving Celtic, pursued Jim Farry after the SFA's failure to register the Portuguese striker Jorge Cadete in time for a cup fixture against Rangers, something that eventually led to the chief executive being forced out in disgrace.

The Ferguson case also caused some embarrassment for Farry. According to international midfielder Jim McInally, the SFA chief executive had always been 'wary' of the striker. McInally had become fond of Ferguson at Dundee United and had viewed with some concern his younger teammate's efforts to be 'one of the boys' with Scotland. 'He was like a child, in that he didn't know when to stop,' says McInally. 'He was the guy who carried the can for everyone.

'I remember on the North American tour of '92, having to go around his room packing his bags for him, because he'd been out with McCoist and Gough and hadn't come back in time. Of course, McCoist and Gough would be in the bus on time; he wouldn't be. He was a fall guy.

'People like Farry had made up their mind about him there and then,' he adds. 'They had him down as a headcase. But he was led astray a bit.'

Brown, though, was supportive of Ferguson. He indulged him more than others might have done in the same circumstances. He argued back when it was put to him that Ferguson should be left in international exile until there was a verdict in the assault case. Although he says he was never 'leaned on' to exclude Ferguson, there is enough evidence to suggest that there would have been few complaints had the player been left out. Brown recalls Farry treating Ferguson as a 'non-person'. Brown, however, stood firm. Why should he be prevented from picking Ferguson because of such off-field issues? Tony Adams, after all, continued to be selected by England despite a drink-driving charge that had seen him spend eight weeks in prison in 1991. Adams resumed his England career shortly after his release, winning more than 40 further caps.

Ferguson, however, hadn't done much to endear himself to Farry in the weeks leading up to the Greece game. The player's impending court appearance for a fourth assault charge had not made him think twice about driving through a Liverpool bus station while over the permitted alcohol limit. Brown, meanwhile, still regularly inserts an anecdote about Ferguson's trip to Athens in his after-dinner speech routines, one relating to the player's apparent surprise when a pre-match visit to the Acropolis is mooted. 'What a place!' Ferguson cooed. 'The nightclubs are open in the afternoons!'

While probably apocryphal, the tale firms up the image of a daft laddie on tour; it certainly wouldn't have helped improve Farry's opinion of Ferguson. The player didn't do a lot to further his international ambitions in the Olympic Stadium either. Scotland fell to a 1–0 defeat in a vast ground that was barely a quarter full and Ferguson's personal performance came in for criticism. Even the previously supportive *Courier* raised a doubt about his attitude. 'On a night when all-out effort was called for, £4.26-million-man Ferguson did not look particularly willing to roll his sleeves up and muck in,' its report of the game stated.

Looking back, and with the benefit of considerable hindsight, it is now easy to see how Ferguson's performance might have been understandably compromised by the tumult in his head. Up in the stand sat people like Farry who were, he felt, intent on persecuting him, and had been since the SFA's announcement, just days after the clash with McStay, that they were imposing a ban on the player; one they intended to see served whatever the outcome of the court case. It prompted protest from Rangers, whose complaints grew louder still when it was revealed that Celtic chairman Kevin Kelly had sat on the six-man committee that had decided the length of the ban.

At Rangers' annual meeting in October 1995, Findlay, the Ibrox club's vice-chairman, was asked whether he felt there was 'a Scottish establishment vendetta' against Rangers, something that jarred with the long-held perception by many football supporters in Scotland that the Ibrox side *were* the establishment club in the country. Findlay replied that he could understand why people might feel there was one set of rules for Rangers players and another for others, given Ferguson's fate, and with the memories of the numerous battles between then Rangers player-manager Graeme Souness and the SFA still fresh in people's minds. At one point, Souness was handed a touch-line ban totalling two years. When he was charged with breaching this ban after encroaching onto the pitch to celebrate a League Cup victory over Celtic, Souness bitterly noted that 'on matters of discipline, we [Rangers] have come to accept that we are treated differently. There is nothing more that we would accept from the SFA.'

Findlay explored this theme as well. 'It's easy to be paranoid about this sort of thing,' he told the gathering of shareholders, before adding: 'We are Rangers, no one likes us. We don't care.'

Ferguson, meanwhile, viewed the two-pronged attack, from the Scottish football authorities as well as the courts, as a personal witch-hunt. He was particularly dismayed by the SFA's determination to punish him with what was apparent cavalier disregard for the law of the land. With this in mind, perhaps it is surprising that he remained 'available' for Scotland for as long as he did.

The 12-match ban handed out to Ferguson was then unprecedented in the British game; it eclipsed the five-week suspension served by Kevin Keegan and Billy Bremner after a punch-up during a Charity Shield encounter between Liverpool and Leeds United twenty years earlier. Findlay was not permitted by SFA legislation to represent Ferguson due to his position as an office-bearer at Rangers. Instead, Ferguson was accompanied by the former Hibernian player Tony Higgins, the secretary of the Scottish Professional Footballers' Association. This in itself got Findlay's back up.

He had no problem with Higgins' involvement – 'He did a good job,' says Findlay – he just could not accept why he should be unable to represent him. 'It was ridiculous and antiquated,' says Findlay. 'They were living in the dim and dark days of the past, when organisations like the SFA thought they could do what they wanted.'

The SFA had been keen to appear on top of the situation; hence, what had been, by their standards, an unusually quick response to an incident that hadn't even been seen by the match referee. Within a month, the matter of Ferguson's 'head-butt' had been dealt with – or so they thought.

On hearing of the decision, Findlay quickly expressed the hope that the SFA were 'cognisant' of the implications of arriving at a conclusion before the sheriff had disposed of the impending court case. The Ibrox club appealed on the grounds that criminal proceedings arising from the same incident had still to be processed by the courts. This meant Ferguson, they argued, was at risk from suffering double jeopardy, meaning he was being 'tried' twice for the same crime.

Not that Farry appeared too concerned about this when I contacted him, in 2009. He died just over a year later, following a massive heart attack at the age of only 56. 'I think we both know it does happen,' he said, when we discussed this issue of double jeopardy in relation to Ferguson's case. 'There are many examples in any walk of life where such a thing can occur. An individual can lose his job but yet still be subject to some form of court action – that is double jeopardy in that sense. It is not to be regarded as unique; it just so happens that football captures a lot of airtime and column inches.'

Farry acknowledged that there had been pressure exerted on football to get its house in order at the time. However, he strenuously denied that there had been any desire on his – or the SFA's – part to make an example of Ferguson. Indeed, he argued that their efforts to be seen to treat him severely were in the hope that this would ward off the threat of a criminal trial.

Farry recalled the threat of interference from non-footballing authorities becoming more pronounced after the breach of the peace charges levelled at Celtic's Frank McAvennie and the Rangers trio of Graham Roberts, Terry Butcher and Chris Woods. Their spat, during an Old Firm match in 1987, has been referred to as the case of 'Goldilocks and the three bears' in Glasgow, on account of McAvennie's blond hair. Rangers, meanwhile, are sometimes known as 'the Bears'. The semi-comedic context didn't stop Butcher and Woods being fined, after they were found guilty of conducting themselves in a disorderly manner and committing a breach of the peace. McAvennie, meanwhile, was cleared and Roberts' charge was deemed not proven.

Seven years later, the sense of Scottish football being on trial remained. 'It was an intense atmosphere, a febrile atmosphere, and I was aware of that at the time,' said Farry. He remembered a lot of pressure 'from the very highest level in Scottish government' being brought to bear on the game.

'We dealt with a lot of conversations privately,' added Farry. 'It was quite clear, throughout all the disciplinary matters that cropped up over a number of years, that all the relevant authorities were looking to football to keep its house in order.'

He very firmly resented the idea that the SFA were somehow to blame for the matter escalating to the extent that Ferguson served time in jail: 'There was a suggestion at the time that the football authorities had hung him out to dry,' said Farry. 'Not at all. In fact, quite the reverse was the case. Stringent efforts were made that it was retained within football.'

Of course, it is impossible to believe the SFA, or Farry, had willed an international player to be sent to prison. Still, these 'efforts' to hand Ferguson a punishment that could be interpreted as 'fitting the crime' did not help forestall a criminal charge. When the Ibrox club appealed the suspension, the SFA appeals committee, on legal advice, decided to postpone the hearing 'pending the outcome of criminal proceedings'.

By the time Ferguson's court case took place, Everton were the ones fighting the campaign to have his suspension overturned, or at least reduced from the eleven games that he had left to serve – Ferguson had sat out one Rangers game in the week after the sentence was originally imposed, in April 1994. Everton's actions dismayed Farry. According to him, the English club had guaranteed they would respect the outcome of the disciplinary appeals tribunal. In November 1995, while Ferguson was still in prison, his lawyers again failed to have the ban overturned. However, rather than accept the decision, the Goodison Park club took the matter to the Court of Session in Edinburgh, where Ferguson's appeal against a three-month jail sentence had failed three months earlier. On this occasion, there was better news for Ferguson. In February 1996, he won a landmark judgment. Lord MacFadyen decreed that because Ferguson had not been punished during the game itself, the appeals committee could not impose an additional ban.

Had he lost this legal battle, then it was reported that the player would have walked away from Scotland there and then. But he came back, perhaps surprisingly. 'If the truth be known, Farry would probably be delighted if he never saw or heard of Ferguson again,' wrote Hugh Keevins in *The Scotsman*. The feeling was definitely mutual. Nevertheless, Ferguson returned to the Scotland scene, although it never looked as though he did so with much enthusiasm – or at least the enthusiasm expected from someone representing his country at its national game.

Although he had turned up for the pre-Euro '96 get-together, along with 31 other players, in March of that year, any chance that Ferguson might appear in the finals in England was extinguished when Joe Royle announced that he was ordering the striker to rest his troublesome groin complaint over the summer.

Still Scotland, who only scored once in three games in Euro '96, returned to his door and still Ferguson answered it – on occasion. As Kevin McCarra put it in *The Times*, 'Scotland have never been able to resist the lure of his potential.' Ferguson, however, did not always accept the invitation. Indeed, more often than not he declined it. When he failed to make the World Cup '98 qualifier with Sweden at Ibrox on account of a calf strain, it was, one newspaper calculated, the 15th time in 17 international call-ups that he had pulled out. In the opening game of the same campaign, Ferguson started – and finished – the clash with Austria in Vienna. It was, however, the same old story. For the fourth successive game in which he had played, in a period stretching over four years, Scotland failed to find the net in a 0–0 draw.

Even when the opposition didn't turn up, Scotland couldn't win. The away fixture in Estonia is memorable because the home team refused to accept Fifa's decision to bring the kick-off forward by four hours due to inadequate floodlighting. In surreal scenes, Scotland kicked off against phantom opposition at the rescheduled time, but rather than award the visitors the 3–0 win, as expected, Fifa ordered the match to be re-played at a neutral venue. An injured Ferguson had also not turned up in Tallinn, but he returned for the re-match, with the principality of Monaco selected to host the game. Once more, Ferguson might well have wished he hadn't bothered. Again, Scotland were uninspired in the 0–0 draw.

Brown was sympathetic. 'Subconsciously, his presence affected our style of play,' he says. 'There was a tendency to thump the ball up to him. It wasn't deliberate, it wasn't planned. It was a case of "There's big Duncan, let's send it high."'

'It was a disappointing night in Monaco. And then the crowd turned on the players, and that rarely happens with the Tartan Army.'

Ferguson's namesake Ian, his old teammate at Rangers, whipped up controversy as he walked off at the end by appearing to swear at fans in an outburst that was picked up by a nearby television microphone. It took some of the heat off Duncan, whose performance was described as 'lackadaisical' in at least one report the following morning. As with Ian, he might have responded with something quite trenchant. Something like: 'Stop playing the ball to my fucking head all the time.'

While much of the post-match fall-out concentrated on the question of whether Ian Ferguson would play for Scotland again – he didn't in the end, although Brown forgave him for his outburst – the Scotland career of the other Ferguson also ended that same evening. It would, however, take another seven months for this to become official and then years would need to pass before it was accepted, finally, that he was not coming back to the fold, no matter what happened or who it was doing the asking.

Ferguson withdrew due to injury from the squad to play Estonia in the return game at Kilmarnock the following month, which the home side won. However, with Scotland in sight of the finals, Ferguson sent what was described as a 'two paragraph letter' to the SFA, confirming he did not wish to be selected for the foreseeable future. The news emerged shortly after a 4–1 victory over Belarus, for which he had been overlooked. He had also missed the four previous qualifiers. His decision to end his international career was not made in the heat of the moment. Indeed, it didn't even sound unequivocal; he appeared to leave some room for manoeuvre.

'Does anyone care anyway?' asked an article in the Scottish football fanzine *The Absolute Game*.

'At least Mo Johnston and Richard Gough made contributions to the international cause before taking the huff.' Scotland certainly wouldn't miss his goals. Remarkably, in the four games Ferguson played under Brown, not only did he not score, neither did Scotland. 'It was a horrendous record,' says Brown. 'Maybe I shouldn't be flagging it up, actually.'

'I really admired him,' says Everton teammate David Weir, someone else who walked away from international duty, but for different reasons – and only for a spell. 'He stuck to his guns. He has his faults, but he is very principled in what he believes in. Typically Scottish, I always thought.'

Still, when Jim Farry was dismissed for gross misconduct in 1999, it was natural to wonder whether the development might pave the way for a return for Ferguson, who was by now at Newcastle. Indeed, Graeme Bryce, a football reporter at what was then the *News of the World*, was sent down to Tyneside to visit Ferguson and test the water, with a mutual friend in John Clark, Ferguson's former United teammate, for company. They thought they might entice some promising noises from Ferguson.

'I mentioned the fact that now Farry had left the SFA in disgrace, would he consider doing a U-turn?' recalls Bryce, whose hoped-for exclusive, facilitated by Clark's involvement, perished after Ferguson became angered by the photographer, who persistently asked him to strike a series of ridiculous poses with a glass and a bottle of champagne. 'He did tell me that he was sick of being slaughtered about Scotland,' says Bryce.

He insisted there would be no U-turn, something Ferguson spelled out in an extremely rare and surprisingly candid interview with the Newcastle United club magazine *scene@stjames'*.

'The Scotland thing is over for me,' he told the magazine for its December 1999 edition, although it was published in November – the same month Scotland played England in the play-offs for the Euro 2000 finals. 'It's in the past, finished. That's the way it is. It's passed me by.'

He even suggested he had made the decision 'three years ago', which suggested that it pre-dated his last appearance for his country, in 1997. 'It goes back a long, long way,' he added. 'That's just the way it is.'

But, with Farry gone, there was a new man at the top of the SFA: David Taylor, a likeable lawyer from Forfar – someone deemed to be not nearly as fractious as his predecessor. There would soon be a new manager, too. Berti Vogts, who had led Germany to the Euro '96 title six years earlier, replaced Brown. Vogts, of course, knew Ferguson from that game at Ibrox, when the German manager had looked on from the dugout as the striker announced himself in a Scotland shirt. With Scotland having been drawn in Germany's group for the qualifiers for Euro 2004, he hoped he might strike a psychological blow, by having someone who had created so many problems for the Germans, albeit nine years earlier, lining up alongside them.

Vogts liked his teams to operate with a tall target man, but Scotland were lacking in that department. Only the raw and rather agricultural Kevin Kyle had the physical attributes, but, there was no getting away from it, he was a very poor man's Duncan Ferguson. Vogts quickly resolved to visit Ferguson – who had by now returned to Everton from Newcastle – and ask him to reconsider his decision. This was at the start of Vogts's reign as manager, before the headlines about 'Blundering Berti' had begun to accumulate. As a former

World Cup winner with West Germany, he had enviable credentials.

And yet, you can also imagine some sniggering when he left the SFA's office, which had now been moved to the fifth floor at Hampden Park from the long-time dwelling at the association's Park Gardens address, nearer the Glasgow city centre.

'*Where are you off to Berti?*'

'*Oh, I am off to Liverpool to ask Duncan to play for Scotland again.*'

It was a fool's errand, if ever there was one. In March 2002, Vogts turned up at Goodison Park to watch Everton take on Fulham.

'What's he here for?' Weir recalls Ferguson saying when alerted to the Scotland manager's presence. It didn't sound promising.

In the Everton boardroom, Vogts made a beeline for David Harrison, the Everton secretary. 'Do you think I could speak with Duncan?' Harrison recalls the German asking him, to which he replied: 'You are brave, aren't you?'

Harrison told Vogts not to take it personally, but, while he would certainly go and ask the player, he expected Ferguson to refuse to see him. 'I actually thought he was either going to piss himself laughing, or he was going to go ballistic,' says Harrison, who did indeed search out Ferguson after the 2–1 win, in which the Scot had scored the winner.

'I went down to the dressing-room to get Duncan,' continues Harrison. 'I couldn't keep a straight face, to be honest.'

Harrison told Ferguson that Vogts was waiting upstairs. 'He wants to have a word with you,' the secretary said. 'Duncan had this big smile on his face,' he recalls. 'And Dunc said: "Tell him to get lost."'

But Harrison convinced Ferguson to at least do Vogts the courtesy of speaking to him. 'So I brought Berti down,' he says. 'They went into the medical room together, where they could get a bit of privacy.

'Thirty seconds later, Berti was back out again.'

In Vogts's version of events, the conversation is not remembered as being so brief. He timed it as 'three or four minutes'. There is no confusion about the contents of the message, however. 'I spoke to him and asked him why he did not want to play for Scotland,' says Vogts. 'He told me he had a lot of problems with the SFA. The SFA, he said, did nothing for him.

'I told him: "We can change that." He said: "It is too late, I am not a young boy any more."'

Even those closer to him could not influence his decision. A family friend told me that even Ferguson's father tried hard to persuade him. 'He said: "You can't take on an institution. The older men will go, the new men will come in. Play for yourself, for your fans and for your family. Play for your country."

'I have known Duncan for a lot of years,' the source adds. 'Boy, is he stubborn.'

Those who worked closely with Ferguson on a day-to-day basis soon learned not to broach the subject. 'I don't consider myself an expert on the man, but I once joined the extensive list of people who have asked him to reconsider his decision to quit international football,' said David Moyes in 2002, shortly after he arrived at Everton as manager. 'The answer he gave was so emphatically negative that I promised myself there and then I would never ask the same question a second time.'

When Vogts was sacked after just over two years in the post of Scotland manager, the identity of his successor was viewed as a possible game-changer in the Ferguson situation. Walter Smith's appointment prompted speculation that Ferguson might think again. 'I thought [Smith] might have had a chance of convincing him,' says Weir. 'He was the only one.'

Smith did, in fact, approach Ferguson, although it was not made public at the time. This was in 2005 – 13 years after he made his debut. Few players have international careers stretching so long. Few players are still wanted by their country at the age of 33, as Ferguson then was. It is another teasing glimpse of what might have been. And yet still the answer was no. Or, more accurately, it was: 'Let me think about it.' This was an improvement on the time it took to reject Vogts's invitation. 'We asked him,' says Smith. 'I have never said that before. But we asked him. He said that if he was going to come back, then I was the one person he would come back for at that stage.

'They were his words, not mine.'

Smith left the task of sounding out Ferguson to his assistant, Ally McCoist. He knew that they, too, had a good relationship, stretching all the way back to their days together in the international team, in the early 1990s. 'I said to Walter: "I'll phone the big yin,"' recalls McCoist. 'He listened to what I had to say, and he did not say "No" immediately.

'But I knew him well enough,' adds McCoist. 'I picked up the phone to Walter and said: "No chance."'

In the end, Ferguson never set foot on Hampden Park as a Scotland player, as much because of circumstances as anything. Renovation work, which included the building of a new south stand, meant the ground was out of action for long periods in the 1990s. Indeed, of 17 competitive internationals hosted by Scotland between 1993 and 1999, only six were played at the national stadium. In any case, only one of Ferguson's seven international appearances was a 'home' game. Rather than the Hampden Roar, it was the shrill scream of Ibrox he heard – several thousand £1 tickets were distributed to schoolchildren when he made his home debut against Germany.

Much less gifted players from this era managed to live the dream of stepping out for Scotland at Hampden; much less gifted players felt the thrill of scoring for their country. But Ferguson scored only once while wearing a Scotland shirt, and in crushingly downbeat circumstances compared to what might have been, and really should have been. In February 1993, just a month before he lined up for the full team against Germany at Ibrox, Ferguson powered a header past goalkeeper Tony Malia as Scotland Under-21s defeated Malta 3–0 in a European Championship fixture, watched by just over 4,000 people. The venue? Tannadice Park, of all places.

Before taking the field for Everton in a pre-season friendly against stadium tenants Queen's Park in the summer of 2002, Ferguson had appeared only twice at Hampden Park. They were both Scottish Cup finals. On both occasions he finished on the losing side, having only played a portion of the match – it was not a place he associated with happy memories.

His next – and last – appearance came on a July evening when he led his Everton side out and was roundly booed by the few hundred Queen's Park fans present. In this reaction could be traced the difficult relationship that had developed between Ferguson and his own country; if, indeed, there was any relationship left by then. Ferguson and Scotland were by this time estranged. Many viewed him as football's equivalent of a deserter.

There was more interest in the squat teenager who partnered Ferguson that night, just weeks after Real Madrid had again found Hampden to their liking when lifting the European Cup against

Bayer Leverkusen, courtesy of a wonder goal from Zinedine Zidane.

Merseyside had already started to buzz in recognition of a very special talent on the verge of breaking through into the Everton first team; now it was Scotland's turn to get a look at the 16-year-old Wayne Rooney. He didn't disappoint, scoring a hat-trick in the 6–0 victory. Ferguson again failed to last longer than a half at Hampden. He was replaced at half-time, but not before remedying a glaring omission from his career. Remarkably Ferguson, at the age of 30, had still not scored a goal at the national stadium, for either club or country. He had his young accomplice to thank for helping put this right. After 25 minutes Rooney squared a ball across the penalty area for Ferguson, who slid a shot past goalkeeper Tony Mitchell. The *Daily Record* noted, 'There was hardly anybody there to see his side-footed shot hit the net, which lends it a kind of mythical status to fit with Ferguson's troubled image.'

The goal is not why the Queen's Park fans jeered him, however. Rather, the feeling that Ferguson had spurned Scotland coloured their view, while another outrage, that of failing to make the most of such obvious talent, perhaps also prejudiced them against him. Here was another Scottish story of unfulfilled potential writ large.

It is fascinating to now speak to four former Scotland managers and hear their views on Ferguson. Not one of them expresses dismay at the decision he made, although they all admit to a sense of disappointment that he did not develop into the Scotland player he briefly promised he might become. As far as Andy Roxburgh is concerned, 'frustration' is the one word that comes to mind when the subject of Ferguson comes up. 'At the time, we really could have done with him,' he says.

'There is no doubt that he had the potential to make the difference. So there's frustration when I look back at this young guy who could have been the answer. But it's all water under the bridge now.'

Smith, too, is wistful. He felt the SFA let the player down. 'Let's be honest, the reason I asked him to come back was from a selfish point of view,' he says. 'I needed him for footballing reasons. But I also thought it might have been nice for him, in an Indian summer sort of way.

'At the end of the day, I appreciated his reasons. What I appreciated more than anything was his depth of feeling. He didn't think he got the backing from the SFA, and I don't think he did either. They just sat on their hands and waited for something to happen.'

Even Brown, who worked at the SFA for 16 years in total, can understand why Ferguson believes he was abandoned by Scottish football's governing body, while he also regrets not making a request to visit the player in prison – not that it is likely Ferguson would have agreed to see him. 'Maybe it's something I should have at least tried,' he says, a good man momentarily burdened by guilt.

'He emphasised that not playing for Scotland was a point of principle; a stance taken against the establishment,' continues Brown. 'And while I couldn't say it in the media at the time, I have to tell you now, I had a lot of sympathy with him.'

Even when he left the Scotland scene for the last time, he did so in an undeniably Duncan Ferguson-esque manner. His last international squad involvement had been six months earlier and he was clearly out of the habit of packing for trips with the Scotland team, who had gathered at Gleddoch House in west Renfrewshire ahead of the Estonia re-match in Monaco.

'The players all had blazers, trousers, shirts – we got them fixed up with everything,' recalls David Findlay, the then head of media relations at the SFA. 'All they had to bring was their own shoes.

'But Duncan turned up and he only had a pair of trainers on. He hadn't brought any other shoes. I think it was a genuine oversight on his part. He hadn't read the squad letter properly and he was genuinely apologetic – he liked to look the part.'

It had been so long since he had last played, he thought the squad still travelled in tracksuits. It presented Craig Brown with a problem; as we know, the Scotland manager was a stickler for ensuring that everyone was dressed uniformly, off the pitch as well as on it.

Findlay recalls fielding a call from an exasperated Brown. 'You are about the same height as Duncan, what size are your shoes?' he asked.

'So Duncan ended up getting a pair of my shoes to go to Monte Carlo, so he could be photographed with the rest of the squad in the proper rig-out. Before they got on the flight I had to meet the team bus at Glasgow airport with a bag and a pair of shoes in it.'

Findlay never saw them again. On his return to Glasgow, Ferguson picked up his luggage from the carousel, and kept on walking. 'Somewhere in the bottom of the Ferguson wardrobe, there is a pair of my shoes,' he says.

CHAPTER 17

Flogged Like a Hamper

In the midst of another slow start to a season for Everton, rumours started to circulate about Duncan Ferguson's future.

'Cash-strapped Everton are heading for a winter of discontent,' reported a piece in the *Liverpool Echo* in the middle of November 1998, following a 3–0 defeat to Coventry City that left them sitting 17th in the Premier League. The scrapping to avoid relegation was in danger of becoming habitual. They had won only two league games since the start of the season, something that was not felt acceptable after the signing splurge undertaken during the summer, when Walter Smith, Howard Kendall's successor, was permitted by chairman Peter Johnson to spend £20 million on new players, pushing Everton further into the red.

Smith had been looking forward to working with Ferguson again, for the third time, and the striker quickly helped out his manager by making his start seem not so bad as it might otherwise have been. In the first thirteen league games of the 1998–99 season, Everton scored only seven times; four of these goals were provided by Ferguson, including a match-winning double against Nottingham Forest (when it was noted that the player seemed to have made farewell gestures to the fans after the game). 'He was captain when I went down and, I must admit, I was pleased to be involved with him again,' Smith says. 'And in the first three months, he was fantastic for me; he never missed a game.'

On the morning of 23 November – it was another Monday, Everton were being shown live on Sky again – the return to

Merseyside of Paul Dalglish, the former Liverpool player and son of Anfield scion Kenny, was the main talking point in the local sports pages, as Newcastle United prepared for their trip to Goodison Park. Ferguson was suspended and so the captaincy duties were transferred to Collins. 'New Tartan Leader', ran a headline in the *Echo*. Elsewhere in its pages, a smaller story mentioned apparent interest from Sunderland in Ferguson. Something was clearly afoot on Merseyside.

When we meet in his office on the Wirral, Peter Johnson is surrounded by decorative boxes of microwaveable pies and photographs of himself, including one where he is posing with Bill Clinton. Welcome to what is known as the 'Hamper Shed', the headquarters of Park Foods Ltd. It also served as the Everton nerve centre for much of the time he was Everton chairman, between 1994 and 1998. Christmas hampers, for which customers would save throughout the year, earned Johnson his fortune and propelled him onto the rich lists, hence the access to the former President of the United States. However, the business also brought him a degree of ridicule within the football community. Newspaper reports would often include references to the wicker baskets stuffed with food items from which he had made his fortune. Indeed, when Duncan Ferguson was so controversially sold, he was described as having been flogged, 'like one of Johnson's hampers'.

The negotiations for the controversial deal would almost certainly have taken place in this room; Johnson sitting on his side of the desk, Clinton in a picture frame peering over from a sideboard, and Newcastle chairman Freddie Fletcher in the chair where I am seated, going through the dizzying figures that comprised a deal set to earn Everton £8 million. Unlike those Christmas hampers, the fee would be paid in one significant portion rather than in instalments – £7 million there and then, and another £1 million after 30 first-team appearances (Newcastle clearly had not learned from Dundee United's experience).

More than five years on from the beginning of Sky's investment in the English game, money was being flushed out as well as through the system. Some might say common sense simply evaporated. It was the third multimillion-pound move of Ferguson's career. He hadn't scored more than 11 league goals in a season since his days with Dundee United, although he had finished as Everton's highest scorer in each of the previous two seasons, which said everything about the club's struggles. The amount of games he had played was a perhaps more significant issue. Yet Newcastle were prepared to hand such an injury-prone player a five-year contract that was set to earn the player £38,000 a week, until his early 30s.

The money-up-front detail seduced Johnson, whose own business had suffered a terrible trauma, with the failure of the DJ Puddles 'potato gourmet snack' – a type of flavoured chip – that was launched in the mid-'90s. It was designed to be a healthier alternative to the humble chip, but when taste buds remained resolutely untickled, the venture ended up costing Johnson over £10 million.

As can be imagined, Everton supporters were less than thrilled to learn that the desperation to sell their star striker might well be linked to the commercial failure of a brand of frozen chip.

We sit overlooking the gates that were locked when transfer negotiations were in progress. 'To keep away reporters and snappers,' explains Johnson.

It is an impressive set-up, and Johnson still looks an impressive man. His cut-glass accent means you would not automatically place him as a native of Merseyside. However, he is undoubtedly one, with an association to all three senior football clubs in the area. He first supported Tranmere Rovers before switching to Liverpool and becoming a season-ticket holder at Anfield, something that, of course, didn't help his cause when news of Ferguson's sale rippled through the crowd at Goodison Park before and then during the game against Newcastle. But Johnson was never involved in an official capacity at Liverpool. As his business interests flourished, he took over at Tranmere Rovers and then moved on to Everton, before returning as owner of Tranmere. He has since retired to the rather more tranquil shores of Lake Geneva.

It was another home, on the Channel Isles, to which he fled in the days following Ferguson's departure, the news officially breaking shortly after Everton's 1–0 victory over Newcastle. Indeed, legend has it that Ferguson's own father went into the Winslow, a pub situated just outside Goodison Park, to tell the fans the news that his son had been sold before the game.

Walter Smith, meanwhile, claims to have been informed of the development by Ferguson himself, *after* the match. Even his wife, Ethel, had known before he did. This is exceptionally strange, given that Dennis Roach, Ferguson's agent, of course, was also Smith's.

'We don't want to rake over old embers,' says Johnson.

However, raking over old embers is exactly what I am here to do.

*

'I didn't decide who we buy or sell, I just facilitated it,' explains Johnson. 'It's no good me saying Walter knew this, Walter knew that, in the same way as I don't think he should say it either.'

'Whatever he has said you should just reflect on what I have said. I don't want to go into that one. I have made my point. The amount of money that was offered by Freddie Shepherd was an incredible sum. And well, I don't know how long Walter lasted after that.'

Smith remained *in situ* for another three years – a lot longer, certainly, than Johnson, who by contrast made a rapid disappearance act. Indeed, on the morning after the night before, the chairman – who Smith referred to as 'Jinky' Johnson, in impish reference to Jimmy Johnstone, the tricky and often elusive Celtic winger – was already proving hard to pin down. The *Liverpool Echo*'s David Prentice was despatched to the manager's office by the paper's news editor, who was struggling to believe Smith's contention that he had not known about the transfer. It was an unenviable task. In short, he was handed the task of going in and accusing Smith of being a liar.

'He was incandescent,' recalls Prentice. 'If he was lying, then he's a great actor.

'You fucking listen, you listen while I get in touch with Jinky myself,' Smith told Prentice.

'Predictably enough, Johnson could not be contacted,' recalls the reporter. 'But from Smith's reaction, I just knew he was telling the truth.'

To be fair to Johnson, arranging to see him to discuss Ferguson has been fairly straightforward. The details are efficiently organised by his secretary. On my return home, and having transcribed the interview tape, I wanted to establish something that I hadn't quite been able to glean from our initial conversation. 'Did you feel that, in the final analysis, the sale of Duncan was the ultimate catalyst for your own departure, or at least hastened it?' I asked, via email.

'No,' he replied, minutes later. 'I hope that helps.'

While he can be blunt, Johnson is undeniably entertaining – and informative. He knows he had fought a losing battle to be accepted from the start. 'One of my problems there, when things are going well, you are all right,' he says. 'Of course, you have to remember that I was a Red for 25 years.' And now, nearly a decade after his association with Everton ended, he is happy to confirm that Liverpool can still count on his support. 'Certainly in Europe', he says. 'Of course I want Everton to do well, but they are not in the Champions League.

'And while I believe I can move my allegiance to wherever I want to be, I remain proud of the fact that I am the only Everton chairman never to have lost a derby. I think we were unbeaten in nine.'

At the time, Ferguson could make a similar boast. He had not tasted defeat in the eight derbies he had appeared in to date; a remarkable record given Everton's struggles. This helped establish his reputation among the fans as a talisman. Understandably, supporters preferred to trace a link to the striker who had scored three times in these meetings than to an unpopular chairman when it came to identifying lucky charms. Indeed, Liverpool fans were more likely to praise Johnson, who they still viewed as one of them. They used to sell T-shirts outside Anfield with his caricature on the front, above which was written: 'Come home Agent Johnson, mission accomplished'.

'I would go through Speke airport, as it was then, and I would get taxi drivers, most of whom are Reds, coming up to me and saying: "C'mon, Pete, you have nearly got them down,"' Johnson recalls. 'I'd reply, "I am not trying to get them down, I am trying to get them *up*."

'And then one day one guy collared me; they were all sitting outside waiting for their fares to disembark from planes. He said: "Hey, Pete. Will you give me your autograph?" Who to? He said, "To Dave." So I wrote, "To Dave, with best wishes." He showed it to his mates and said, "I have got the whole fucking set now – Hitler, Saddam Hussein and him." This one was an Evertonian who didn't seem too pleased with my efforts.'

Johnson knows that top of the perceived crime sheet was the decision to sell Ferguson. Flogging the fans' favourite was inadvisable. However, the manner of the transfer was simply unforgivable in the eyes of Everton supporters. Their fury meant Johnson had little option but to make his shares available to buy, although it would be another 13 months before he finally severed ties with the club, leaving him free to return to the helm at Tranmere shortly afterwards.

As far as his Everton association was concerned, and despite his comment that indicated otherwise, it proved impossible for him to recover from the events that saw Ferguson depart. If the Everton fans were being honest with themselves, however, they could not deny there was some method in what the majority perceived as madness.

Smith refers to the episode as 'that famous scenario when the chairman sold him without telling me' when we meet. It's clear where he still stands on the matter.

'I never thought it could happen,' he says. 'And because I never thought it could happen, I never thought that much about it. There were a lot of circumstances leading up to it. Everton had a real financial problem.'

This, Smith says, he had gleaned from Cliff Finch, Johnson's deputy, rather than from Johnson himself. Finch has since referred to the Ferguson transfer as 'the deal of the season'.

Smith continues: 'We came to the evening in question, Newcastle United at home, and strangely enough, the chairman did not appear as normal for a cup of tea before the game.' After the game, Smith went for a drink with Ruud Gullit, the opposition's manager, as again was the routine. Remarkably, it seems nothing about Ferguson was mentioned. He then did a TV interview where the interviewer asked about a story that Ferguson was heading to the north-east, although this time Middlesbrough were the club mentioned.

'I said: "No, that's not true,"' recalls Smith. 'He was one player I wanted to keep, even though I had brought in a lot of players and I knew that because of the financial situation we would need to move quite a few others on.

'But he was obviously one of those who I did not want to leave. So I said on television: "He is not going anywhere, I do not know where you have got this from."'

Smith returned to his office before heading to the boardroom with assistant manager Archie Knox in order to collect their wives. 'I was going upstairs with Archie and we were talking about this rumour going about regarding Duncan, when who should come down the stairs but Duncan,' he recalls.

'I remember saying to him, in a joking way: "After that result you will struggle to get back into the team."'

Smith says he will never forget Ferguson's reply: 'You are fucking right about that, you have just sold me to Newcastle.'

'I was taken aback. I replied: "What?"'

'He repeated it. "You have sold me to Newcastle," he said. "I have just signed for Newcastle United."'

'So I went away up to the boardroom. I met my wife coming down. She said, "You have just sold Duncan to Newcastle." She had known before me. And Archie's wife Janice was there, and we met her down the stairs. She said, "Where are you going?" and I said I am off to see the chairman. She said, "You've sold Duncan Ferguson, haven't you?"'

The repercussions were mostly significant and varied. Johnson immediately became a lame-duck chairman, while Smith, having briefly wavered, decided to stay on, persuaded to do so by Johnson's swift disappearing act. Bill Kenwright, meanwhile, glimpsed his opportunity and headed a consortium that saw the club eventually passed into their hands from Johnson.

'If ever the sale of a footballer finished a chairman, that was it,' says Kenwright. 'We all went the next day to Park Foods for a board meeting. I am not even sure Peter turned up. The last time he ever appeared at Goodison, I think, was that night.'

Among the other, more trivial consequences of this episode was that I was asked to point my car in the direction of Newcastle and head to St James' Park for Ferguson's unveiling as a Newcastle United player. Although the controversy's epicentre was Merseyside, the ripples were felt in other places, including Scotland, where the escalating worth of someone who was still refusing to play for the international side was being viewed with a sense of dismay. It proved a worthwhile expedition. For a start, Ferguson spoke.

'I've always been a bit uncomfortable in front of the cameras,' he said at the press conference, held in a suite at St James' Park. 'I just carried that on from Scotland. Maybe now it is about time that I started speaking to some of the press people.' It was a memorable press conference, far removed from the ones I had already known in the brief time I had spent working at *The Scotsman*.

There was a definite sense of it being an event. Gullit was next to Ferguson, beaming away and explaining how he had tried to first sign the striker when he had been manager at Chelsea. Fletcher was asked whether the signing would impact on Ferguson's future at the club. 'It is Duncan Ferguson's day,' he stressed. Ferguson was even asked about his tattoo. He confirmed that it was still there, on his shoulder. He didn't regret it. 'I think everyone knew the loyalty I showed to Everton, and the fans' loyalty to me,' he said. 'I can't just switch on and switch off like that.'

He was luring reporters in. Many wondered whether this portrayal of Ferguson as truculent and stand-offish, almost charmless, had been a figment of the imagination of their colleagues on Merseyside and sought to prepare the way for a good working relationship between them and the new star signing. 'We are a lot friendlier here in the north-east,' one local journalist assured him.

Another reporter, whose beat was Liverpool, resented this sudden burst of charm. When contrasted with his previous reticence, this outbreak of fairly congenial dialogue was the equivalent of someone singing like a canary.

'Bastard – that's more than he's said to us in three years,' hissed a Scouse voice from the floor of the room in which the press conference was being held.

For some in the trade, it was hard to take. Since he almost never spoke to them, the Merseyside-based reporters took umbrage at this new side to Ferguson. They were quite offended. And it annoyed them more because it proved that he *could* speak engagingly about the game, and his own ambitions. Among those in the Merseyside press corps, Paul Joyce could perhaps claim to have come nearest to forming a relationship with the player. However, he is careful to point out that it was still a long way from being what most would classify as a 'relationship', in the normal sense of the word. He did, after all, have only three sustained bursts of 'on the record' dialogue with Ferguson. It was, though, still three more conversations than almost all of his peers.

The reporter started his career at the *Evertonian*, the monthly magazine that came out with the *Liverpool Echo* but which sought to retain its independence from the newspaper. This was not always possible, however. Joyce's dealings with Ferguson got off to a shaky start when he was held responsible by the player for a photograph that had been intended for publication in the *Evertonian* being purloined by the *Echo*. Slightly comically, and illustrating just how acute had become the thirst for 'news' about Ferguson, the row erupted over what had supposed to be exclusive use of an image of the player sporting a new haircut.

'It was just after the Cup final in '95,' recalls Joyce, who now works for the *Daily Express*. 'Everyone was Duncan mad. He was the big hero. He did a picture with us after he got a new haircut that was just for the front cover of the *Evertonian* magazine. But because the *Echo* produce the *Evertonian*, they used it in the *Echo*.

'The next time I went down to the training ground there was a bit of "Why did that picture go on the back of the *Echo*?" from Duncan. The gateman at Bellefield was a chap called Harry Scott, who died a few years ago. Duncan was very close to him. Harry actually saved the day. He said: "Listen, Duncan, it was not his fault. It was out of his hands."

'Duncan calmed down,' adds Joyce. 'He had this thing where he was close to older people.'

Despite this inauspicious start, things improved for Joyce. He even managed to avoid swerving off the M6, having answered a call on his mobile phone. A Scottish voice informed him that it was Duncan Ferguson on the other end of the line. And he wanted to talk.

Joyce was on his way back from Newcastle to Liverpool following Ferguson's unveiling and was approaching the Killington Lake service station, near Kendal. It had been a long, strange day. Joyce was exhausted after a hectic period at the frontline of sports journalism on Merseyside. Just the previous night he had been in Galicia, reporting on Liverpool's 3–1 defeat to Celta Vigo in the UEFA Cup.

In southern Spain, news had filtered through to Joyce from Merseyside: Duncan Ferguson had been sold to Newcastle. Liverpool's slump in Spain that night was a major story. However, it paled into insignificance next to the sale of Everton's folk hero. It was a major story, not least because Ferguson would now be paired with Alan Shearer in a fearsome-sounding strike partnership, valued at over £20 million. There was also talk of Ferguson's Scotland ambitions being re-awakened, although like so many other things he said that day while turning on the charm for the cameras, it was proved to be exactly that.

He did, however, keep one promise. Joyce had all but given up on Ferguson phoning him back, as he had pledged to do at the end of the press conference which, unsatisfyingly for reporters, had taken on an 'all in' format. By this, it is meant that journalists – from the broadcast media and from print; from daily/Sunday newspapers, and from evening ones – had to make do with the same material gleaned from the half an hour or so Ferguson spent at the top table, flanked by Gullit, Newcastle United chairman Shepherd and Roach. With the Sky Sports News channel having started transmission only the previous month, it meant reporters were forced to recycle information that had already been relayed.

As it stood, Joyce had nothing fresh to file for the *Daily Post*, and nothing particularly Everton-centric. Unhelpfully, Ferguson's responses to the questions he did ask from the floor were snaffled up by the *Echo*, rivals as well as stablemates of the *Post* and, being an evening paper, the first out onto the streets of Liverpool later that day. Decisive action had been called for.

'At the end, as the top table left, Duncan began to walk out of the room, and I just went over to him and said, "Will you do a piece with me?"' recalls Joyce. 'He said, "What's your phone number?" So I scribbled it down on a bit of paper. He said, "I will call you later." I couldn't believe my luck. I hung around for a bit and then started to drive back to Liverpool. I was thinking, "Oh well, he's changed his mind, he's not going to call."'

Then his phone rang. It was Ferguson.

'I still have the tape of the interview now, one I consider the best I have ever done, given the circumstances,' he says.

These circumstances involved Joyce steering into the service station while frantically gathering his thoughts and searching around for a pen. 'I felt excitement, mixed with terror,' says Joyce.

This, he knew, was his one chance to get Ferguson's account of why he left Everton. He was alert to the need to ask the questions the Everton supporters wanted answered. But in the end it was more a case of simply chronicling what Ferguson wanted to say.

'He was clever that way,' says Joyce. 'He's quite savvy. He just wanted to get his point across.'

Joyce listened, and scribbled, and then agreed to phone Ferguson back later that evening to read back the piece he had composed for the following day's edition. Ferguson, having inserted some further paragraphs of quotes, declared that he was happy with the article, in which he insisted he had been 'forced out' against his will.

'The move was forced on me,' he told Joyce. 'Everton simply didn't want my services any longer. I knew on Monday morning that Everton were inviting offers for me. I knew by Monday afternoon that it was Newcastle, and the deal was done after the match that night.

'The manager had told me on Monday morning the club was looking to sell me if the money was right, but I don't think he knew a move was actually on later that day. He brought me into his office and just said I was being put up for sale. He said it wasn't his idea to sell me and that it was for financial reasons.

'I was numb with shock really. It sickened me. I couldn't believe it. I am absolutely heartbroken to leave the club.'

Ferguson then turned his thoughts to the Everton fans, asking Joyce to 'send them my love' as he embarked on a new stage in his career. 'I will never, ever forget the Everton fans and I mean that,' he added. 'They will be with me forever.

'When I was in jail it was a very difficult time in my career and my life and they stuck by me. All the letters I got then I appreciated so much; they made a hell of a difference. Everything they were saying to me I will remember. They were encouraging me and saying "keep your chin up". It did help.'

Any journalist worth his salt would have done what Joyce did and carefully squirrelled away Ferguson's number for future reference. Emboldened by Ferguson's decision to use him as the messenger, Joyce made quick use of Ferguson's contact details and rang the number the following month. The hook was Ferguson's scheduled first return to Liverpool with Newcastle, who were due to visit Anfield shortly after Christmas. Ferguson was not in the habit of taking calls from journalists. At first he was far from delighted to hear from Joyce.

'Since we got on so well in that interview, I thought, I will try him again,' says Joyce, reasonably. When Ferguson answered, he was initially frosty. 'How did you get this number?' he asked Joyce, who reminded Ferguson that he himself had provided it. 'Well, you know you should not be ringing this number,' replied Ferguson. 'But he gave me a few lines of quotes anyway, and we spoke briefly about how he had always done so well against Liverpool in the past,' recalls Joyce.

The redoubtable Joyce chanced his arm once more, again with surprisingly productive results. 'The third time and final time was before the first time he was due to face Everton,' he recounts. 'I went up to the Newcastle training ground by Durham cathedral. I waited by one entrance, and he had gone out of another entrance.

'Luckily, there was a kit launch for Newcastle that same day, so I bombed up to St James' Park and walked in and saw him. I asked him if he would do a piece about him facing Everton again. He said, "No." And I said, "Look, I have driven up here and the fans are all still interested." He said, "No, no." So he went off to do the photographs, and he came back out and I said, "Look, please, it will be a positive piece." And he said, "OK, then." So we went and sat in my car just round the corner from St James' Park, and he was good once more.'

In the event, Ferguson sustained a groin injury in the game the article was previewing and he didn't play again until April. The injury curse had struck again and would bedevil his time at Newcastle United.

It had all started so promisingly, as well. He scored twice on his debut for Newcastle against Wimbledon. The win lifted Newcastle to 11th in the league, a point above Everton. Afterwards, Ferguson was the only story in town. Reporters waited, and waited, for him to appear after the match. Ferguson's apparent resolve to be more cooperative had melted within days of him arriving in the northeast. Eventually, Russell Cushing, the club's chief operating officer, was sent to find him. He finally showed an hour and a half after the game had finished – usually players are offering their thoughts on the 90 minutes within half an hour of the final whistle, at the latest. 'And he had to be forced out,' recalls Alan Oliver, a reporter with the *Evening Chronicle* for 30 years.

Oliver has had run-ins with many a player. These include being punched by Laurent Robert in the press room after giving the Frenchman a four out of ten rating and having asked, in print, whether he knew 'what it meant to wear the black-and-white shirt'. This question might also have been better directed at Ferguson, since it simply did not happen enough.

This was mostly down to injury, though Oliver also suspects his heart simply wasn't in it from the start. Inactivity on Ferguson's part meant Oliver did not have too much contact with him. 'But when I did, I found that his bark was worse than his bite,' he says.

'I've known some guys who have been horrors with the press up here. Duncan would not be in the top five.'

Ferguson reserved much of his ire for Gullit, whose treatment of some of his bigger-name players left something to be desired. His pigeons might not have followed him to Newcastle – 'They are not that good,' Ferguson, charm personified, smiled, when asked about them at his first press conference. Unhappily, however, his injuries did pursue him all the way there. It cannot have helped the relationship between manager and player, particularly since the Dutchman had expected the Scot to re-pay his faith in him on the pitch, not unreasonably. Instead, Ferguson – owner of 'the most troubled groin this side of John Wayne Bobbitt's', as Tom Lappin put it in *The Scotsman*, referencing the infamous American who had recently had his penis sliced off by his wife – took up residency of the treatment table almost immediately, and, after his two-goal debut, he made only six more league appearances that season, failing to add to his tally of goals.

His contribution to Newcastle's second successive FA Cup final appearance was limited to a second-half stint as substitute. On his fourth appearance in a national cup final in eight years – two in Scotland, and now two in England – he maintained his record of failing to complete 90 minutes. Manchester United barely had to break sweat to win 2–0, on their way to the treble. On the following Monday, Ferguson underwent more surgery on his groin.

The then Newcastle physio Paul Ferris came up with an ingenious solution to Ferguson's problems; if the footballer can't leave the treatment room to play football, then simply bring the football to the treatment room. 'Actually, come to think of it, it was more Duncan's idea,' says Ferris, whose career since tending to the ailments of Newcastle players has included writing a romantic novel. 'You wouldn't normally have a football in the treatment room. But Duncan, when he was injured, would bring in a football and we devised this competition where we would play two-touch with each other. You'd have one touch to control the ball and then you'd smash the ball at the other person, who would have to try and control it. Duncan became a bit of a master at it.'

According to Ferris, it was the player's calf muscles that bothered him most while he was at Newcastle, although the physio suspects this might have been associated with his back and groin problems. Whatever was the reason for his absence from the first team, it was clear Gullit had not spent £8 million so Ferguson could belt the ball around a treatment room. With all the egos at Newcastle United at the time, things could be equally turbulent inside the dressing-room. Gullit had been hired due to a reputation that meant he was expected to command respect. Before long, however, the Dutchman was engaged in a long, brooding war with Shearer, the scion of Newcastle and occupier of the famed No. 9 shirt. Accordingly, Ferguson's respect for Gullit the player, the one he briefly shared a pitch with at Euro '92, began to be polluted by his view of him as a manager who appeared to relish picking the wrong fights.

Shearer, the golden boy of the Gallowgate, challenged the contention that no man is bigger than the club. Newcastle finished in an underwhelming 13th place in the league at the end of Gullit's first season in charge, and the following campaign had not begun well, with Newcastle without a win in the opening four games, their worst start for forty years. Shearer had scored just once, from the penalty spot. Ferguson, meanwhile, was inching his way back to full fitness after a spell, at Gullit's insistence, in the Netherlands, where he received treatment for a strain behind his right knee. 'I came back worse than when I went to Holland,' he later grumbled in an interview with the club magazine, offering an insight into how his relations with the manager had worsened since that day when they sat together at St James' Park, beaming from ear to ear.

Gullit then compounded matters by compiling his 'suicide note' – since it did not contain Shearer's name, this is how several reporters described the team-sheet he pinned to the wall before a derby with Sunderland. The England striker was dropped to the bench, alongside Ferguson. The 20-year-old Sunderland-supporting Paul Robinson, who had only made his first-team debut in a friendly against Dundee United in the summer, had been chosen to start instead.

Even the Geordie skies seemed to spit in elemental fury. Something was happening here. Something significant. The rain lashed down, and when Robinson was replaced by Ferguson after 57 minutes, Newcastle were leading 1–0. There seemed to be some method in Gullit's madness. Seven minutes after Ferguson's introduction, however, Sunderland drew level through Niall Quinn.

Gullit finally turned to Shearer with 18 minutes left and, shortly afterwards, Sunderland's Kevin Phillips put his side 2–1 up, which is how the game finished. Not surprisingly, the post-match focus centred on the dropping of Shearer and, to a lesser extent, the decision to have Ferguson seated on the bench next to him. Possibly unwisely, Gullit later pointed out in his post-match press conference that his side had been winning prior to Ferguson and Shearer being sent on, a comment that more than hinted at where he thought the blame for the defeat should lie.

It wasn't what the Newcastle fans, particularly those who had chanted Shearer's name throughout, wanted to hear. It wasn't what Shearer wanted to hear, either. However, when Gullit arrived at work the next morning, it wasn't Shearer who he found waiting for him outside his office. Or, at least, Shearer wasn't his first unscheduled appointment.

'The door was still just about on its hinges when I came out again,' recalled Ferguson, rather proudly, in an interview with *scene@ stjames*', the club's official magazine. He was now free to be so indiscreet. Ferguson was the first visitor to Gullit's door on the Dutchman's penultimate day as manager of Newcastle United. Gullit left the position without a request for compensation, acknowledging that he had 'lost' the dressing-room and, specifically, the battle of wills with Shearer, whose exile from the side seemed to cause Ferguson as much pain as his own absence. Indeed, there was a feeling that Ferguson, who had grown close to his strike partner, had gone into Gullit's office on that morning to fight Shearer's corner rather than his own. Not that he needed to. Shearer was next man in. 'I think Ruud got the message,' Ferguson noted.

In the same interview with the club magazine, Ferguson railed against Shearer's critics, who numbered not only Gullit. 'I couldn't believe how much people were queuing up to have a go at him,' he said. 'If there was any justice in this world, those people who wrote all that rubbish about a great, great player who since rammed every word down their daft throats should have been thrown out of their jobs on newspapers, radio and television.'

As for Gullit, the player he had once so admired as he looked on from the substitutes' bench for Scotland against the Netherlands in Euro '92, it was 'crazy, just stupid' to drop Shearer, Ferguson said. '[Gullit] didn't win the game, and then he had the cheek to tell the media that Newcastle were winning the match until he sent me and Alan on, the inference being that if he hadn't made the substitutions Newcastle might have won.'

It was with some trepidation that I later broached the subject of Ferguson with Gullit, who was competing in the Alfred Dunhill Links golf championship in Carnoustie, one of the courses in north-east Scotland used to stage the annual event. He took me aback slightly when he told me how much he had 'loved' Ferguson, how much he had 'believed in him'.

'He was a target man, and he could hold the ball up,' he said. 'And Shearer was a finisher. I was hoping they would make the ideal partnership. But, for many reasons, it did not happen.'

Gullit seemed to sound a lament for Ferguson's career. Ferguson, he said, 'got into situations he could not control. If he could have avoided that, then who knows?'

Ferguson's fierce defence of Shearer is a mark of the man. Perhaps because of his own past, he didn't like to see someone persecuted, although sympathy for Shearer had to be tempered by the fact that he was patently off-form. I saw it with my own eyes in the first game after Gullit's sacking, when, with Shearer and Ferguson restored to the attack, Newcastle went down 5–1 at Manchester United. In the next day's *Scotsman*, I wrote that Shearer 'skulked around the Old Trafford pitch, as if the match owed him a goal'. Ferguson was replaced by Robinson in the second half and only played another ten games for Newcastle, all under Bobby Robson, the popular successor to Gullit.

Injury again claimed him, courtesy of a hamstring strain picked up in a UEFA Cup second-round tie against CSKA Sofia, Robson's second game in charge. Ferguson was back in time for the next round, against FC Zurich. 'A funny thing happened here last night,' began the match report in the *Evening Chronicle*. 'For the first time in 49 weeks, Duncan Ferguson scored a goal for Newcastle.' Three weeks later, on the first anniversary of his signing, I headed down to Newcastle to research an article, one designed to reflect on the player's seriously stalled career. A year had passed since my first trip down on Ferguson business, when everything had seemed so upbeat and promising, when he'd teased reporters with talk of a Scotland return and the possibility that he might – gasp – even speak to them.

It hadn't quite worked out that way. With little hope of catching a word with Ferguson, I made my way to Bobby Robson's pre-match press briefing, with Newcastle due to face Tottenham Hotspur the next day. There I learned that the player's most recent injury – a calf strain – was 'progressing'. I can still picture the look of genuine shock on Robson's face when I informed him that Ferguson had been at the club a year, with so little effect to date. Once he had recovered his composure, he said, 'I wouldn't say it is make or break, but it is obviously essential that we get him psychologically, physically and clinically fit. And that he stays with it and doesn't break down.

'He is searching his own soul about that. Every time a new injury comes up, he says, "Oh no, not again," because he knows what the media will do with it.'

Robson added that, in four years' time, when the player's contract was due to end, he truly believed Ferguson would have proved 'value for money'. As wise as Robson was, it didn't quite work out like that.

CHAPTER 18

Like a Scottish Dirty Harry

Bill Kenwright remembers a conversation he was having with Walter Smith as they plotted the way ahead at a breakfast meeting in the summer of 2000. Signing targets were being discussed. One of the two names at the top of the list was Eidur Gudjohnsen, then at Bolton Wanderers. The other was Duncan Ferguson.

Kenwright knew only too well the players that he wanted to see back at the club. 'The big fellow,' he says. He was also aware that Ferguson was not having the best of times at Newcastle. 'He was in a bit of a state,' Kenwright recalls. The owner hoped Smith might suggest Ferguson. Eventually, he did. 'He was talking about all these other players and I was thinking, "There's only one guy who can save this football club."'

It sounds slightly melodramatic. Everton, however, had endured a dismal end to the previous season. They scored only once in their last four matches. Nick Barmby, the scorer of that solitary goal, was sold to Liverpool, of all places, while John Collins and Don Hutchison had also left. Following a period of bright form at the beginning of 2000, the team fell away at the end of the campaign and finished in 13th place.

Paul Gascoigne's arrival at Goodison Park from Middlesbrough was greeted with some apprehension as well as excitement. However, it was Smith's decision to try and re-sign another of his former players that caused the biggest stir.

As with Gascoigne, news of Ferguson's capture wasn't met with an overwhelmingly positive reaction. Kenwright was aware there were some supporters who would oppose the player's return. Many had viewed him as an unaffordable luxury during his first spell at the club, while the fans also feared the long ball game that Ferguson's presence encouraged, often unwittingly.

Everton club secretary David Harrison remembers sensing 'quite a lot of cynicism' from those who viewed it as simply one last pay day for Ferguson. And yet, even now, Kenwright says he has 'no regrets' about sanctioning the move. Encouraged by the owner's enthusiasm, Smith made contact with Ferguson. 'Walter had given him a ring, then I'd spoken to him,' recalls Kenwright. 'Duncan and I talked for about 40 minutes. I said, "Listen, if you want to show them how great you are, then come home and wear that blue jersey."

'I put the phone down and an hour later it rang. It was Duncan. He said: "I am in a car, I am coming home."'

As much as Everton fans might wish it was simply a case of jumping into the car and 'coming back home', as Ferguson put it, there was more to it than that. This being the Premier League, there were money-related obstacles to be overcome. As was his right, Ferguson wanted to ensure that his exit from Newcastle was worth his while financially, something that jars with Kenwright's slightly sentimentalised version of the events.

Before he could 'come home', there was, then, much work to be done. Indeed, Ferguson had managed to do the impossible and make even the avuncular Robson sound exasperated – or at least his agent had. After the deal had been completed, Robson vowed that he would never deal with Dennis Roach again.

Ferguson was clearly tempted by the move back to Goodison Park but wanted some form of compensation for the lower wages he would be paid by Everton, who could not hope to match the player's £38,000-a-week contract at Newcastle, nor wanted to. In addition, reported the *Evening Chronicle*, Ferguson had just bought a plot of land 'next door to Alan Shearer' on which to build a new house. 'He was more than happy to stay at the club,' stressed Roach.

It looked like he would be remaining in the north-east. Newcastle stuck to their guns and refused to 'settle up'. In their eyes, Ferguson had proved a very costly mistake and agreeing to give him money to leave was a difficult concept to accept. Indeed, 'expensive failure' is how former Newcastle director Denis Cassidy describes Ferguson in *Newcastle United – The Day the Promises Had to Stop*, a book that shone a light on the St James' Park club's financial largesse in the transfer market during the 1990s; Ferguson's arrival had taken the club's spending over the £100 million mark since 1992. Bobby Robson had not proved shy in the transfer market either, spending £16 million in his first 12 months in charge.

An unfit Ferguson was clearly a drain on resources, though he can hardly be blamed for the details of the lucrative contract he had signed in good faith only 18 months earlier. Having thought they had identified a buyer, Newcastle were described by the *Evening Chronicle* as being left 'dumbfounded' when the proposed deal to Everton collapsed, with the player unable to agree the terms of his release from Newcastle. Roach complained that they had 'only' wanted £250,000 to leave. '*Only* £250,000?' wrote Alan Oliver in the *Evening Chronicle*. 'Does Roach not realise that it takes United fans ten years of hard graft to earn that sort of money?'

In the event, Ferguson and Roach relented, having reached the conclusion that the player's position at Newcastle was now no longer tenable. There was no point in him staying if he wasn't going to be selected. 'Once Newcastle had decided they no longer required my services, there was never any doubt in my mind about returning,' said Ferguson at a press conference at Goodison Park. Everton got their man for a relatively knock-down price of £4 million and Ferguson reached an 'agreement' regarding his personal demands. 'Duncan is a very proud man. Maybe he felt there was unfinished business at Everton,' says Kenwright now.

'What is extraordinary with Everton is the love affair the club has for centre-forwards,' he adds. In his office, there is a large photograph of Dixie Dean. There is also a picture of Alex Young, the Scot who captured Evertonian hearts, and one of Dave Hickson, the fearless striker who died in 2012. Hickson will always remain Kenwright's hero. 'He would have gone through a wall for Everton,' he says.

Ferguson would do the same, believes Kenwright. 'And let me tell you, Duncan engendered that same kind of belief with Evertonians. They'd have gone through a wall for him,' he adds.

Ferguson also occupies a spot on Kenwright's office wall. It is a photograph from when he arrived back to sign for Everton for a second time. His fists are clenched in the air outside Goodison Park, as he salutes the fans that have gathered to welcome him back. Aged 28, there was still time for him to flesh out the legend, to be the player Joe Royle once challenged him to become.

It wasn't long before frustration set in, however. Although he had passed his medical examination and had, in a slightly irritated manner, stressed he was '100 per cent fit' when asked about his fitness at his unveiling, Ferguson was cruelly cut down as he sought to gain some momentum back at Everton.

Injury, says Walter Smith, was the 'strand that ran through' his second spell at the club. 'He hadn't played the way he might have wanted at Newcastle – because of injury, not because of form,' says Smith. 'I had still been keen to take him back. I felt that he could still give us the lift that we needed. He was just so popular in the area.

'But he was affected terribly by injury. Usually with footballers who play the way Duncan did, it is a specific injury that causes bother. That wasn't the case with Duncan. When he came back, he showed good enough form – when fit. It was just the sheer number of injuries he had. He fell into an advertising board and damaged his shoulder. It was things like that.'

In only his second appearance after his return, and having again come on from the bench, Ferguson fell victim to a nasty challenge from behind by Charlton Athletic's Richard Rufus. Nevertheless, Ferguson recovered to score twice in a 3–0 victory.

However, the next day it was reported that his calf had quickly stiffened up afterwards and he was already a doubt for that weekend's fixture. In actual fact, he did not play again for another four months, making another return in a substitute's appearance, again against Charlton, in December. It was, the cynics suggested, as if he had never been away. When he was named in the team for the next game, against Coventry City on Boxing Day, it was the first time he had started a game for Everton since November 1998, during his first spell at the club. According to *The Guardian*, Ferguson looked 'about as mobile as a lighthouse'. He was, however, described as 'crudely effective' in a 3–1 win.

Two successive starts followed this milestone before the first in a pair of incidents that defined Ferguson's later career – in the way that Barlinnie has to dominate discussion of his early years – occurred. When discussing this book with others, one of the most frequent comments I heard, over and above what he did in his football career, was simply: So, what about those burglars, then?

The idea of Ferguson as vigilante certainly appeals to the public's imagination. Unluckily for him, it was a case of burglaries plural; the first in the very early hours of 7 January 2001, after Ferguson had contributed to a last-gasp FA Cup victory over Watford, and the second, two years later. You would have thought that the news that one of the first two intruders had been hospitalised might have acted as a deterrent to any others who might be considering such a cavalier raid. Simon Barnes, writing in *The Times*, referenced the BBC comedy series *Dad's Army*, describing the first break-in as rating 'very highly on the Sergeant Wilson Scale'.

Wilson, of course, was the one who always asked Captain Mainwaring: 'Do you think that's quite wise, sir?'

The very notion that someone might consider breaking into a 6 ft 4 in. Scotsman's house certainly seems like lunacy, particularly when the homeowner is not known for a softly-softly approach in physical situations. Although it won't have crossed his mind as he fought to defend his wife and six-month-old daughter, Evie, who were also in the house, anyone with four previous convictions for assault and a prison sentence to their name had to fear the somewhat ambivalently worded self-defence laws in place at the time, which had become the subject of national debate after an incident involving the Norfolk farmer Tony Martin two years earlier. Martin, having shot and killed a teenage intruder who had broken into his remote farmhouse, was initially convicted of murder, though on appeal this was reduced to manslaughter on grounds of diminished responsibility. The episode ignited a debate about how much force is reasonable when protecting one's own property and family members.

Ferguson did not resort to quite such extreme measures when dealing with Barry Dawson, after the footballer caught him trying to steal bottles of champagne, CDs and pictures. Michael Pratt, who had broken in with Dawson, managed to flee but gave himself up the next day.

Pratt, his lawyer later argued, had only been meaning to show Dawson where Ferguson lived. They then 'found' themselves in the footballer's conservatory. It was, she argued, a 'compulsive, foolish' act, one that had been committed 'in drink'.

Both were sentenced to 15 months in jail, though Dawson came off worse at the time, having been forcibly restrained by Ferguson until police had arrived. Dawson's lawyer, Gerald Jones, later told Preston Crown Court that he could have little complaint about the 'vigour in which Mr Ferguson apprehended him'. The unexpected physical confrontation saw Ferguson sustain a broken bone in his hand; he missed the next three Everton games, before making only sporadic appearances during what was left of the season.

Ewing Grahame, a Scottish sports journalist who had travelled south to interview Walter Smith shortly after the break-in, recalls being met by the sight of Ferguson 'bouncing around' Bellefield, wondering whether then Home Secretary Jack Straw had been on the phone yet. 'He was all but demanding an MBE for his have-a-go success,' adds Grahame.

Incredibly, two years and one day later, it happened again, though by this time Ferguson had moved to Formby, to a property where there was a gatehouse fitted out with a storage room and a gymnasium. His wife was now pregnant with their second child, Cameron. There is never a good time to break into Duncan Ferguson's house, but this was undoubtedly a very badly timed piece of misadventure by a heroin addict and Everton supporter called Carl Bishop, who later claimed Ferguson was his 'hero'. He was left counting the physical cost upon meeting the footballer in the flesh for the first time. Ferguson had been roused by noises emanating from the storage area, where Bishop was busily helping himself to bottles of champagne, whisky and other spirits, ready to steal. According to local legend, when confronted by Ferguson, he quickly set the items back on the floor in front of him, as if giving them back would make everything all right.

'It disnae work like that,' he was informed by the owner of the house. Or so the story that circulated Merseyside rather entertainingly goes.

Ferguson used a variety of methods, including hitting Bishop with a vodka bottle, to restrain the unwelcome guest, who spent a few days in hospital with a broken jaw before being sentenced to a five-year prison sentence, since it emerged that he should already have been in jail when the offence occurred after he had failed a drugs test while out on licence.

For a few days, there was some concern that Bishop, who pressed for Ferguson to be charged with assault, might create some problems for the striker, who of course had his own criminal record. However, Merseyside Police later ruled that again Ferguson had been put in a position where he felt the need to protect his family, and there was no evidence to suggest he acted 'unreasonably'.

Still, the incidents helped firm up the impression of Ferguson as someone it would be unwise to cross, although few could criticise him for defending his own property and those loved ones therein. One newspaper ran a poll that wanted to know who it was possible to feel most sorry for: Ferguson, or the 'unfortunate' burglars? Ferguson won only 28 per cent of the sympathy vote.

Perhaps, Barnes reflected in *The Times* following the first of the pair of incidents, the burglars had quickly realised, after seeing pictures on the wall of a 'surly-looking bastard' heading the ball into the net, that they'd hit upon the house of a footballer, before reassuring themselves: 'Aren't all footballers clever little foreigners who fanny about with the ball and do shampoo adverts?'

Slowly, however, the penny drops, as Ferguson descends the stairs to investigate. 'Like a Scottish Dirty Harry' was the memorable phrase employed by sports writer Paul Hayward.

Everton teammate David Weir argues that the media portrayal is far different to the Ferguson he encountered. According to Weir, he was far more sensitive than people imagined. He took the matter of the Christmas night out very seriously, for example, carefully banking the money paid into the 'account' in instalments throughout the year, and counting and then re-counting the wedge of notes that he kept in his steel locker. Weir recalls him being crestfallen when one year the party was cancelled after a particularly dismaying 5–0 defeat against Manchester City in December 2000, a few months after Ferguson had returned to the club.

He was also deeply hurt when, after sending out invitations to a christening, some Everton teammates did not turn up, leaving empty seats in a well-appointed marquee that had been erected in his garden. Scottish midfielder Stephen Glass, who Ferguson had befriended at Newcastle United, recalls Ferguson trying to persuade him to stay longer. Glass had mentioned the need to return to his house in the north-east to let out his dog. 'We were leaving about mid-afternoon and he was like, "No, stay. I'll send someone to collect your dog for you,"' recalls Glass. 'That was Dunc to a tee. Nothing was impossible, or too much trouble.'

He could, however, be violently dismissive of those who thought they had established a bond with him. Steven Caldwell recalls playing a reserve game for Newcastle shortly after Ferguson had re-joined Everton. Despite being one of his former teammates, and despite also being from Stirling, he finished the game with a broken nose after being caught by a flying Ferguson elbow. 'The red mist came down, and it was just some silly reserve game,' recalls the centre-half. 'I don't hold a grudge about it. But despite always looking after me at Newcastle, all that was forgotten on the park. He couldn't care less.

'He was probably a bit peeved at playing for the reserves, and of course I was trying my very best because I wanted to get in the first team and probably being a bit annoying.'

Weir arrived at Everton during Ferguson's short stay in Newcastle. Indeed, he joined the club just weeks after Ferguson departed for the north-east. Because he is roughly the same height as Ferguson, Weir was handed the club suit that had been measured up for Ferguson. 'I wore it the rest of that season. It must have been lying in a room somewhere, and it was like, "You can have that," recalls Weir.

As a rule, Ferguson always liked to look sharp-suited. 'He would always come in smartly dressed,' recalls Weir. 'The rest of the lads were in jeans, but he was always well dressed.'

He took care of himself as well. 'He was always in the gym and working hard. And he worked on his football as well, which a lot of people don't realise. He was a perfectionist about his football. He was very proud of it and thought he was good. He wanted everyone to see that.

'People had this perception of not being that interested, but that was not the case. People like Jim McLean might have said that, but I would say they were not really pressing the right buttons. He definitely wanted to be the best. But he also just wanted to be appreciated.'

Weir was thrilled to be reunited with Ferguson, the player he had marked on his first senior appearance back in Scotland. 'Football is like that. Your paths diverge and then they cross again,' says Weir. 'There is value in not making enemies.' In his own autobiography, Weir includes a comical passage highlighting Ferguson's fierce pride. It harks back to McLean's comment about

Ferguson sharing Richard Gough's trait of looking in the mirror after a victory and seeing only himself, and then after a defeat seeing only his other teammates.

James McFadden and Weir used to delight in impishly playing on this streak of vanity in Ferguson's make-up. 'He used to buzz if one of the boys said, "You were good today, big man,"' Weir recalls. 'Gary, Faddy and I used to love saying that to him. He would say, "Thanks, I thought I was brilliant today."'

Occasionally, things hadn't gone so well. 'You weren't the best today,' McFadden would say, to which Ferguson would reply: 'Aye, but I wasn't the worst.'

Sometimes it felt as if Ferguson was more concerned about his own performance than that of the team. Everton supporters, meanwhile, began to wonder whether the club had re-signed the same player. Although the dismaying injury lay-offs were familiar, it seems Ferguson's style of play had changed; or perhaps, more accurately, Everton's had. Remarkably, of Ferguson's first 17 goals after his return, none were scored with his head. This is in contrast to the start of his first spell at the club, when 15 of his first 25 goals were headers.

It showed that he was as versatile as his supporters claimed, that his game wasn't solely about flinging himself through the air to get on the end of crosses and long punts up the field. It also illustrated the stark absence of wingers in Smith's side of the time. When once Ferguson could expect reliable service from the by-line from Anders Limpar and Andrei Kanchelskis, and, most productively of all, from set-piece expert Andy Hinchcliffe, now it was all about filling up the midfield area. Balls that were flung at him in the air were more likely to be long clearances from left-back David Unsworth rather than tempting crosses for him to attack.

'People say never go back,' notes Graeme Sharp. 'Howard Kendall came back three times, but he was never the same after his first time. It was difficult, the game was changing. I just think the team over-relied on him. And it became very "route one". We were just hoofing the ball up to him. It was a difficult time.'

Ferguson might well argue that he never got quite the same quality of service on his return as he'd once had from the likes of Limpar and Hinchcliffe. 'We probably didn't see the best of him,' says Sharp, although Ferguson did have his moments.

Perhaps the remarkable drop in the number of headed goals also points to a body that was beginning to lose its flexibility. Rather than Ferguson being more unwilling to put his body on the line for the cause, it was more a case of simply being unable to do so.

According to Weir, Ferguson was a different animal to the one that had frustrated Jim McLean all those years ago. He yearned to be the best player on the pitch, to be the one to whom all eyes were drawn. Frustratingly, however, these occasions were becoming less frequent. If he was the centre of attention, it was often because of unedifying reasons.

Weir wonders whether the outbursts and violent acts that saw Ferguson sent off so often for Everton stemmed from his annoyance that his body 'wouldn't let him do what he wanted to do'.

It is a plausible theory – and is one that Mick Rathbone subscribes to. Rathbone was club physiotherapist at Goodison Park for nearly eight years, and he reflects that 'the years took their toll' on Ferguson. 'He felt he wasn't the almighty player he had been in the past,' adds Rathbone, who notes that Ferguson had 13 surgeries. 'You can't be the same player after that,' he says. 'No one can be.'

Ferguson sometimes went to extreme measures to pep himself up. In his autobiography *How Football Saved My Life*, Alan Stubbs mentions how his teammate and friend grabbed a whole handful of caffeine pills and threw them down his throat before one particular game, then, when their effects wore off, he spent the entire second half 'coming down'.

'I don't think he knew what the consequences would be,' writes Stubbs. 'He came in at half-time on a right downer – the caffeine, which had got him buzzing during the first half, had all but worn off and now he was on the flip side of it.'

Rathbone soon hit it off with Ferguson, which is just as well since they spent so much time together. On Rathbone's arrival at Everton, Ferguson joked that he'd already seen several physios off the premises, thanks to his complicated medical history, and he was just the next one to be despatched.

In fact, Rathbone is credited with prolonging Ferguson's playing career. One of the first decisions he was asked to make proved a major one; Ferguson's immediate future hinged on it. A muscle problem had left him unable to play for several months and Rathbone suspected the cause of the discomfort was a nerve running beneath the muscle rather than the muscle itself. One surgeon, in Manchester, was prepared to operate but spelled out the dangers in frank detail. If it wasn't a success, then Ferguson's career could be over.

With the footballer leaving it up to Rathbone to make the call, the physio weighed up the options, concluding that there was only one choice: Ferguson would have to go under the knife – again. Fortunately for Ferguson (and Rathbone), the operation proved a success.

Perhaps as a thank you, Ferguson was persuaded to make a contribution to the physio's autobiography, *The Smell of Football*, published in 2011. It was a tribute of the backhanded, jokey variety that is so common in the Jack-the-lad environment of a dressing-room. Ferguson recalls the first day Rathbone arrived at the club, dressed head-to-toe in denim. 'Oi, pal, this is Everton Football Club,' he told him. 'Not a building site.'

According to Rathbone, Ferguson was a proud man. He was certainly no malingerer, even if some fans quickly grew tired of his prolonged absences from the team. 'He would sniff at players getting treatment on the pitch,' says Rathbone. And it's true; while the time he spent on the sidelines provoked critical comment, it was rare to see Ferguson writhing on the turf. 'Before every game, he'd say to me: "Baz, if I go down and stay down, I am telling you, bring everything you have got, 'cos I am fucking dead,"' recalls Rathbone.

Even though his body betrayed him at times, Ferguson was still a handful. You only need to ask Paul Ince, dismissively tossed to the ground like a rag doll during a Merseyside derby. The self-styled Guv'nor then got up again and patted Ferguson on the back of the head, as if to say he understood who was in charge on this particular afternoon. Footage of the incident has since been watched over one million times on YouTube.

Ferguson relished playing against Liverpool and Manchester United since these clashes guaranteed high stakes and large crowds, and he tended to raise his game accordingly. As discussed, he had never finished on the losing side against Liverpool during his first spell with Everton. With Ferguson spearheading the attack, Everton had beaten their rivals twice and drawn on six occasions. The striker had contributed three goals. But he scored only once in the eight derbies in which he featured on his return. Indeed, his 'lucky charm' status in these fixtures seemed to desert him, with Everton losing six of these eight clashes. Five of Ferguson's appearances came as substitute.

Even then, Everton's city rivals felt they had reason to fear him. There is the story of the Liverpool management team spending an entire half-time talk on how to handle the aerial threat of Ferguson, who was preparing to come on as a substitute for the second half.

The likes of Stéphane Henchoz and Sami Hyypia, both imposing Liverpool centre-halves, brought out the best in the player. Ferguson later nominated Henchoz as one of the most difficult defenders he had faced, while Hyypia, in his autobiography, identifies Ferguson as one of his toughest opponents. He recalls spending New Year with a black eye after facing Ferguson when he played for Newcastle. 'Nothing has really changed between us since then,' he wrote in a book about his career, *From Voikkaa to the Premiership*, which was published while he was still playing, in 2003. 'The battle is fierce every time we play against each other.'

In a phone call from France, Gerard Houllier, the former Liverpool manager, emphasises to me how much he had admired Ferguson. However, he stops short of confirming Liverpool had been interested in buying him, a wild rumour that circulated in the city on occasion.

Of course, signing someone with an Everton tattoo on his upper arm was always likely to prove problematic.

And yet Houllier was undoubtedly a fan. 'On his day, he could be a match decider, it was as simple as that,' he tells me. 'As an opponent, we feared his aerial ability, no question.' As for attempting – or wanting to – to sign him, he adds: 'Ah, that would have been controversial. We saw what happened when Nicky Barmby came to us. But I do like to have a target man.' That, he explains, is why he bought Emile Heskey.

Houllier recalls Ferguson 'greeting' him when they saw each other. 'He is a nice character, but a fighter.' Because he was quiet, the perception was that he was aggressive and not someone to cross. People felt he carried an air of menace.

'He was just a nice lad, but in the dressing-room he would turn into a different animal,' says Weir. 'He got closer to what people's perceptions of him were. He motivated people, and raised the profile of the game – made them realise how important it was. He never frightened people or bullied people, not at all.

'But he could definitely turn it on when he wanted to.'

CHAPTER 19

The Man

David Moyes walked into Goodison Park and declared that Everton were 'the people's club' in the city of Liverpool, almost immediately winning approval. He was only 38 when he took over in March 2002 from Walter Smith, who left following a dispiriting 3–0 defeat to Middlesbrough in the FA Cup. Although he made his managerial name with Preston North End, Moyes would be the first to admit that his 'moderate' career as a player meant he could expect to find some resistance in a dressing-room packed full of fully fledged internationals, even if several of them were not playing like they were international footballers.

A centre-half, Moyes played for Cambridge United, Bristol City and Shrewsbury Town after leaving Celtic, where, contrary to popular belief, he fared well enough, playing a sufficient number of games to win a Scottish championship medal in 1981–82. However, there's no question he felt slightly apprehensive about entering an environment where the likes of Paul Gascoigne, David Ginola and, of course, Duncan Ferguson ruled the roost.

Mick Rathbone, who was recruited by Moyes a few months later, describes Everton as an 'injured club'. 'There were too many older players clogging up the medical room,' says the former physio. Moyes, he adds, wanted players to train hard and play hard. If they didn't train on the Friday, then they wouldn't play on the Saturday, the manager told them. With Ferguson, he had to compromise these principles slightly. 'Duncan was such a special player, he had to handle him differently,' he says.

According to Keith Wyness, the former Everton chief executive, Ferguson's influence at the club was often overpowering. 'His personality went into the administration staff, into everyone – he pervaded the club in many ways.' Into this difficult situation had walked Moyes, who was, even at this point, he has since conceded, still learning as a manager. 'One of the biggest challenges he ever had was Duncan Ferguson,' says Wyness. 'And how he dealt with it is what made him what he is now, one of the best managers in Europe.'

Both of them, he recalls, left an impression in whatever room into which they walked. And there was something else that Ferguson shared with Moyes. 'Look at those eyes, they both had eyes of steel,' says Wyness, who was alert to the potential for conflict. 'I had information coming in from the playing side, and there was always an issue. It seemed to be a constant concern at the club: "So how are David and Duncan getting on?"'

Like Kendall and Smith before him, Moyes quickly discerned leadership qualities in Ferguson. He also quickly recognised that having Ferguson on side was preferable to having him brooding on the sidelines; Duncan Discontented was no use to anyone. However, as much as Moyes did seek to keep Ferguson near at first, he came to view the Scot as a principal agitator, particularly when it came to the case of a certain teenage prodigy with the world at his feet.

Nevertheless, he made Ferguson skipper for his first game, handing him back the No. 9 shirt after he had missed the last seven games of Smith's reign. In an interview with Jonathan Northcroft in the *Sunday Times* in March 2012, ahead of his tenth anniversary as manager, Moyes recalled the effect this had on Ferguson. At twenty to three, after Moyes had completed his match preparations, the dressing-room fell quiet.

And then from nowhere came a shout of: 'Yooouu fucking bluuue boyyys! Yooouu better get IN THERE!'

Ferguson had stirred.

'Big Dunc was on his feet, getting in every single player's face, screaming in the roughest Scottish accent,' recalls Moyes. 'And I thought I'd been a good captain.'

He described the players walking out as if they were the Scotland rugby team coming out against England at Murrayfield. Everton, through David Unsworth, scored after 31 seconds, and then Ferguson himself, in front of the watching Scotland manager Berti Vogts, added a second after 13 minutes, his first goal from open play in the league that season. Despite also having Thomas Graveson sent off in the first half, Everton held on for a 2–1 victory.

David Weir describes Ferguson as the best captain he ever had. 'Without a shadow of a doubt,' he adds. 'I played with Richard Gough, and Dave Watson, people perceived to be great captains, but Duncan was the best I had in regards to motivating the dressing-room.'

He had also been given some incentive of his own. Ferguson was aware that he now had a genuine rival for the fans' affections. Wayne Rooney had broken into the first team at the start of the 2002–03 season. However, if some might have expected some jealousy to creep in on Ferguson's part, it was certainly not evident. Ferguson mentored Rooney, whom he had first met when Rooney and his two brothers, Peter and Graeme, were photographed with him as young boys in a picture since widely used. Ferguson is crouching down, arms slung around the brothers' shoulders and is looking intently at the camera. Wayne not only looks like a child, he *is* a child next to him, one who later admitted he grew up with pictures of Ferguson on his bedroom wall. It is hard to believe that only a few years later they would be leading the Everton line together.

'Wayne Rooney saw Dunc as a hero, and Duncan liked that,' smiles Weir. Moyes, meanwhile, was not so thrilled about the relationship that had developed between the pair, while his own bond with Rooney was breaking down. Rooney revealed some of the details in his book, *My Story So Far*, published shortly after he joined Manchester United. Moyes promptly sued over a specific claim made by Rooney. There was something in the book which Moyes could not deny, however, and that was advising Rooney to 'stay away from Ferguson'. Rooney reveals that Ferguson had 'burst out laughing' when the manager's warning had been relayed to him. 'I think the background to all this was that Moysey was having his own battle with Fergie,' adds Rooney, through the medium of his ghostwriter, Hunter Davies (note the reference to 'Moysey', who was to become, of course, very much his manager again at Manchester United).

Kevin Kilbane, a midfielder who joined the club in 2003, the year after Rooney made his first-team debut as a 16-year-old, describes

Ferguson as emerging as 'a father figure' for Rooney. 'Wayne liked the fact that Duncan did not want anything in return. It was refreshing for him, at a time when everyone was wanting a bit of him.' Rooney remembers being a little fazed by Ferguson at first. 'It was strange, having idolised him for all those years when I was at primary school,' he says in *My Story So Far*.

It wasn't just Rooney. Phil Jevons, who went on to play for Grimsby Town and Yeovil Town amongst several other clubs, was a graduate of the Everton academy and once had some very important tasks to complete. 'Every morning I'd get in early before the rest, run Duncan Ferguson's bath and get him his cuppa and copy of the *Daily Star*,' he recalled later. 'He was hard, but he always treated me with great kindness, and you remember things like that.'

'Duncan was brilliant with all the young boys,' recalls Weir. 'With any young boy that came to train in the first team, most of the lads would just act normal with them, but he would be the opposite. He would make them welcome, and try and help them – almost overdo it. It was especially the case with the local lads, Liverpool lads.

'I think he wanted to help them because he felt he had been treated badly when coming through at Dundee United, so was very aware of the struggle.'

Ferguson clearly enjoyed this connection with the younger players, many of whom had grown up hero-worshipping him, but he was careful not to give too much of himself away. 'There was a mystique about Duncan', says Ian Ross, the club's former director of communications. 'Every dressing-room has 'the Man'. He was 'the Man' at Everton.

'At least until Rooney came along.'

One source recalls Ferguson's waning influence on the pitch as having a detrimental effect on his demeanour. Although he liked Rooney and wanted to help him, it must have been difficult to take to be superseded in the affections of the supporters by a teenager. It was noted by a least one reporter that when Ferguson scored his aforementioned first-ever goal at Hampden Park in a friendly against Queen's Park, having been set up by Rooney, he barely acknowledged the part the teenager had played in what should have been a significant goal for the Scot. Ferguson made only eight appearances in Rooney's first full season, each of them from the substitutes' bench. Weir also recalls Ferguson becoming a more detached and aloof presence. 'He was being very quiet, he wasn't getting involved,' he says.

His relationship with Moyes was becoming almost unworkably strained, with the new manager's style perhaps reminding him too much of Jim McLean's harsh, disciplinarian ways.

One falling-out between the pair was described as 'spectacular' by David Prentice, whose informant – a player – had been sitting on the toilet downstairs, reading a newspaper, when all hell broke loose in Moyes's office. 'He heard Duncan go in, and it was a major slanging match,' says the journalist. 'He couldn't hear the exact words, but it was definitely a case of raised voices. Anyway, the player came out and Duncan by this time was downstairs, swaggering about: "I have just told the gaffer a few home truths – I don't think he liked what I had to say." And the next thing, Moyes comes down the stairs after him: "Duncan, get back here!"'

Moyes admits that his style was necessarily authoritarian; he was trying to impose himself, make the players realise that they might not respect what he did as a player, but they were to damn well respect him now. Possibly wisely, he brought some of his own men in. Rathbone had been part of his back-room team at Preston North End. Kilbane, meanwhile, had played with Moyes at Preston and was given a peg next to Ferguson's in the dressing-room when he arrived, after transferring from Sunderland.

'What I noticed about Duncan first and foremost was his ability,' says Kilbane now. 'And secondly, I was surprised at how quiet he was. Considering that he had a reputation for being this hard man, he was not loud and boisterous every day. He would say his piece, if necessary.

'I used to sit beside him when I first signed and I was probably intimidated by him when I signed, not because of him as a person but more because of the "Big Dunc" persona that went along with him. I sat beside him and we hardly spoke for the first month. I think Dunc was weighing me up to make sure I was all right.'

According to Rathbone, Ferguson had been 'the head boy, the prefect, call it what you want' at the club. He wanted to maintain high standards and commented archly when Rathbone turned up looking less than smart on his first day at the club. Keith Wyness, meanwhile, compares Ferguson's status at the club at the time to the one enjoyed at Aberdeen by Willie Miller, the Pittodrie club's legendary captain. 'Except even he was not quite at the same level as Duncan,' says Wyness, which is interesting; at Aberdeen, Miller is referred to as 'God' for what he did for the club as a player.

Indeed, perhaps because of the developing power struggle, the relationship with Moyes grew to become as fascinating as the one Ferguson shared with McLean. Like the former United manager, Moyes was well aware that Ferguson had a footballing talent that he could only have dreamt of during his playing career, but the flip side of this was Ferguson's combustible personality. He was sent off four times under Moyes – five, if you count the retrospective three-match ban for jabbing an elbow into Thomas Hitzlsperger, the Aston Villa player, in 2003. His first red card under the new manager ruined an impressive start to their time together, when, after scoring in Moyes's first three games, Ferguson was sent off after just twenty minutes of a relegation crunch match with Bolton Wanderers, having punched the German midfielder Fredi Bobic in his midriff. It meant he was suspended for the last three games of the season, when Everton completed their latest survival mission.

As frustrating as his actions could be for the Everton supporters, Ferguson wasn't always prepared to offer contrition. After one red-card episode, Ian Ross recalls being summoned to Moyes's office. The manager asked him, 'What do we do with Duncan? He needs to apologise to the fans. He is letting people down.'

Ross was instructed to write a few paragraphs – 'just the usual crap', he says – designed to articulate Ferguson's remorse and intended for publication on the club's website. The press officer returned to Moyes's office to show him what he had come up with. Moyes read it, then told him, 'Aye, that looks all right,' then called Ferguson into the room.

According to Ross, Ferguson had a habit of going around the training ground with a just a small towel wrapped around himself, to preserve his modesty. 'Although he was slim, he was like Charles Atlas – it was just pure muscle,' says Ross. 'He had just come out the shower and was dripping wet.'

Moyes said, 'Rossy's done this for you.'

Ferguson looked down at Moyes, clutching the piece of paper in his hand, and replied, 'What is it?'

'It's an apology for you,' said Moyes.

Ferguson took the sheet of paper, read it and then went, 'Nah, I don't think so.'

Ross recalls him throwing it back down on the table. 'Then he just walked out of the room, leaving a trail of droplets of water behind him,' he says.

*

I spent a revealing couple of days in Liverpool at the time, having been sent down to research an article detailing the latest crossroads at which Ferguson's career had reached. In May 2004, he was at the end of the penultimate year in his contract. He wasn't playing much and his prospects looked bleak.

It was becoming clearer that Moyes wanted him out of the club in order to free up some more of the budget. They had also recently clashed on the training pitch. As well as being sent home, Ferguson had been told to stay away from Bellefield for a week.

'Duncan is not the kind of person who would come in and make a scene of it, try to tell his side of the story,' says Weir. 'Something would just happen [between Moyes and Ferguson] and he would be gone the next day. That's how it worked. It wouldn't be in the press because Duncan didn't talk to the press. I wouldn't claim to know what it was about, but obviously I saw it happen.'

Ferguson was becoming an outcast, it seemed. As well as club skipper and principal wage earner, he had, in a surprising number of fans' eyes, become the chief waster; fans were queuing up to have a go at him in the pub I visited.

'He is called an imposter by most in here,' one drinker in the Stanley Park bar told me. The well of pity and sympathy that was so apparent following his prison sentence had long run dry. 'If the club could get shot of him tomorrow, they would,' a local sports writer said. 'He is on £30,000 a week, plays one game in five and lasts for three-quarters of it. And he hasn't reached double figures in goals since God knows when. Apart from that, he is doing fine.'

When I drove down to Bellefield to attend a Moyes press conference, I had an unexpected close encounter with Ferguson: he was leaving just as I arrived. I noted that he was conspicuous for driving the biggest car, and for being amongst the first to depart following training. A poignant theme ran throughout the story I later filed for *The Scotsman*, which was given the headline: 'Precious few returns from prodigal son'.

Of course, having not featured in the previous seven games, Ferguson returned that very afternoon and scored Everton's goal in the 2–1 defeat by Bolton. Still, it is easy to understand why he might have felt paranoid, and perhaps fearful, that his powers were waning. In his book, Rooney recalls Ferguson telling him that Moyes had taken him aside and told him he was now 'the sixth-choice striker' at the club. In the club shop at Goodison, shirts with 'Rooney' stretched across the back were selling the way the ones with 'Ferguson' arced across the shoulders once did, although it wouldn't be long before Rooney would manage to erode most of this goodwill in an instant, by signing for Manchester United.

And yet Moyes remained aware that Ferguson could still bring something to the team that no one else could. Weir's observation about Ferguson being able to turn it 'on' in an instant is no better illustrated than when, in the midst of this cold war between Moyes and his fellow Scot, the manager handed him the captain's armband back just prior to a match.

The player initially declined it, perhaps because, as Weir states, he and Moyes were experiencing difficulties in their relationship, and perhaps also because Alan Stubbs, one of his closest friends in football, was skipper at the time.

'He didn't want to be captain because he had fallen out with Moyes,' recalls Weir. 'But he made him. He came and told him in the dressing-room, "You are going to be captain today," and Duncan was like, "I don't want to be captain – I don't want to be captain."'

It is a remarkable glimpse into dressing-room life, and the rutting between two strong, proud characters. According to Weir, you could cut the tension with a knife. 'The manager did not know what to do,' he says. 'And then suddenly Duncan said, "Right, I will be captain."'

'It was the stage when he was being very quiet, he wasn't getting involved,' Weir continues. 'But he got the whole dressing-room going on that occasion. I wasn't playing that day, but I was conscious of it happening. It was amazing. Not many people are able to do that – at least, not from what I have seen.'

With the teenage Rooney by his side and the captain's armband on his arm, one might have expected Ferguson to be conscious of creating the right impression. This wasn't so on 20 March 2004, when he was sent off against Leicester City in memorable style. In truth, he was harshly treated. Two bookings for separate tangles saw him pick up another red card; it is what happened after referee Barry Knight sent him off that remains ingrained in the memory of not only Evertonians.

Ferguson searched out Steffen Freund, whom he had wrestled with when picking up the second booking, and placed both his hands around his throat, in what seemed an ill-disguised attempt to throttle him. Ferguson then marches off the park, although not before directing an 'up yours' gesture in the direction of the baying Leicester City fans. He then ripped off his shirt, flexed his muscles and, according to the *Daily Mail*'s John Edwards, 'dared anyone in the dugout area to return his stare'. It was a masterpiece of delinquent behaviour, made all the more eye-opening because footage of the incident confirms the then 32-year-old is wearing the captain's armband, which he handed to Rooney as he walked off, much to Moyes's consternation.

'Get that fucking thing off,' the manager roared at Rooney at half-time.

David Harrison, the Everton club secretary, accompanied Ferguson to the inevitable disciplinary hearing, after the English FA charged the striker for violent conduct and also for making gestures to the Walkers Stadium crowd. The hearing took place at Birmingham City's St Andrews ground. Ferguson declined Harrison's offer to pick him up.

'I was thinking: "You better turn up,"' says Harrison. 'Sure enough, he arrived, and we sat at the reception.

'He said to me: "Go on, then, what's the defence?"

'And I said, "Well, there isn't really one, to be honest."

'He thought for a moment, then replied, "I've got one for you. He's a German."

'I don't think that's much of an excuse, Duncan,' said Harrison, to which Ferguson answered: 'Hang on, it's a bit of a trait. Remember the last time I got sent off, it was that lad Bobic from Bolton. He was German, too. I just have this thing about Germans.'

'He was kind of laughing about it,' recalls Harrison. 'I said, "I can see where you are going, Duncan, but I really don't think it is going to stick."'

Harrison always wondered about the state of Moyes's relationship with Ferguson, since he could sense a distance between them at times. 'Usually David would have pulled the player in and said, "I am fining you this amount for this or that offence," but I was always quite conscious that that conversation might not have gone on with Duncan.

'I would always try and see him at the training ground or call him – he would not give his mobile number out to anyone. But I had one, and I would tell him there was a letter coming in the post, that David wants to fine you. And he would say, "OK thanks." Little things like that he might respect you for.

'Under the rules, he had the opportunity to appeal. But he never appealed.'

On my trip to Liverpool, it had seemed hard to credit Ferguson had a future at Everton beyond the end of the season, let alone one that saw him recapture some of the old glory, the old possibilities, and which helped him earn one more contract extension, for twelve months. Credit has to go to Moyes, who began to employ Ferguson as an effective substitute; indeed, he still holds the club record for the number of appearances from the bench. Sent off on eight (official) occasions, he was sent *on* to the park an incredible eighty-two times.

It was hard to reconcile the more established image of Ferguson, as a proud, some would say arrogant, individual who clearly wanted to believe he was still 'the Man', with the one where he is sitting on a bench, biting on the zip of his Puffa warm-up jacket, patiently waiting to be unleashed; a last, desperate gamble when he was once the totem figure. However, he seemed to settle into the role.

And even though he was handed briefer spells on the pitch, it was often still time enough to land himself in trouble. On for only the last 13 minutes of a derby victory versus Liverpool in December 2004, he was booked after a ragged tussle with Sami Hyypia. It is during this cameo appearance that the endlessly engaging photograph of Ferguson towering over referee Steve Bennett, the one featured on the cover of this book, was taken. Ferguson is bending forward as he seeks to make a point to Bennett; the referee, meanwhile, looks as though in the process of taking a step back, and is very obviously taking precautionary measures as the striker thrusts his head towards him.

Rarely can a player have made a referee almost cower in that manner. It is Big Dunc summed up in a three-hundredth of a second: intimidating, frustrated, passionate, gigantic. Look at his face. His eyes. The veins in his neck. His hands. His fingers. Where are they going next? Look at the referee's hands. One is thrust deep in his pocket. Is there a card coming out? What colour? Will he get it out without losing his balance? It is an arresting, enduring image.

Ferguson was still capable of breathing fire. However, Wyness does recall one incident – anecdotal, of course – when Ferguson informed Moyes that he would be remaining on the substitutes' bench because, as he told the manager, 'I'm no' up for it today.'

Nevertheless, Moyes warmed to the idea of Ferguson as super-sub, just as the player seemed to. But the manager also knew there were times when it was worthwhile playing him from the start, when it was guaranteed that he would, in the player's own words, be 'up for it'.

CHAPTER 20

Encore

By what he describes as a 'trans-cultural trick of the football gods', the composer Osmo Tapio Everton Raihala was born an Everton supporter in a small town in north-east Finland – though the addition to his name was made some years later. It is, he suggests, the equivalent of having a tattoo of the club crest on his shoulder. He now wonders whether his devotion to the club might have something to do with the fact that Everton were still the reigning Football League champions at the time of his birth, in January 1964.

A Finnish composer is not, on the face of it, the most obvious candidate to appear in a book about Duncan Ferguson, while Helsinki is not the most likely destination for the author of a book about Duncan Ferguson to visit. But Helsinki is where I am; sitting in the Musiikkitalo, the recently opened music space planted in the centre of the Finnish capital, between the modern art museum and the austere, Soviet-style parliament building.

On my right sits Raihala, whose past, I am discovering, is a constant source of intrigue; he formed Neuroosi – or, in English, Neurosis – one of the first punk bands in the country, whose self-published first single is now widely sought after around the world.

He does not much look like a young punk now. At a well-preserved 49 years old, he is wearing a smart pair of jeans, a blue suit jacket and a turquoise-coloured shirt when we meet. With the pair of Woody Allen-esque specs that he places on the bridge of his nose from time to time, he emits an air of academia, just as you might hope for from someone who has made his name as a serious composer.

He once harboured ambitions of becoming an opera singer. However, he realised that only by writing music could he soothe his thirst for making a career from music. In composing a 12-minute-long orchestral piece about Duncan Ferguson, he managed to combine two of his passions: music and Everton. But it was Ferguson who acted as his specific muse – if it isn't too difficult to picture an attritional Scottish centre-forward in a role traditionally played by goddesses or water nymphs.

'I sensed there was a lyrical element to him,' Raihala explains, when attempting to answer my obvious question: what possessed him to write a symphonic poem about Duncan Ferguson, which he titled – rather mysteriously, at least so far as his compatriots were concerned – *Barlinnie Nine*? Less cryptic is the subtitle: *A Tribute to Duncan Ferguson*.

Raihala was still a young man – only in his early 30s – when he began work on this project. However, he was already well established, having composed several well-received pieces. He had also earned a reputation as a music reviewer for *Helsingin Sanomat*, still the largest-selling daily newspaper in the Nordic countries. He was well enough known to want to avoid the ridicule of his peers.

Ferguson, it is true, inspired a number of songs, but mostly they were chants from the terraces, some cruel – and crude – in nature. One, conjured up by Liverpool fans, was a jaunty ditty comparing him to a tampon – 'in for a weekend and out for a month'. Others, however, were slightly more flattering and celebrated his status at Everton: 'To Duncan, our king, our king, our king, he's the leader of the team/He's the greatest centre-forward the world has ever seen,' the club's supporters sang.

There is also a studio-recorded song, though one that again played it for comic effect; or at least it was comical for the Celtic supporters who make up the majority of Charlie and the Bhoys' audience. This still active band wrote a song entitled 'Drunken Duncan', an up-tempo folk stomp that 'celebrated' Ferguson's problems with the law during his time in Scotland.

'The young men from Kirkcaldy they came to Govan Town/And Duncan's big bad temper was sure to let him down', is a sample lyric. When I contacted the band, I learned that the song has since slipped from the set list, but it proved one of their most requested songs when Ferguson was still playing.

As he came to the end of his Everton career, it emerged that Ferguson was the inspiration for yet another, somewhat more epic musical work. This was rather different in tone, literally. It had also taken rather longer to be conceived. Only in early 2014 was *Barlinnie Nine* finally officially released on CD in Finland. Raihala began writing the piece in the summer of 1995; Ferguson had recently played in an FA Cup final but had also just been convicted of assault. The composer would include a swift reference to the win over Manchester United at Wembley, courtesy of a burst of the cup final hymn 'Abide with Me', by the time the piece was completed, while a snippet of the theme from the BBC drama police series *Z Cars*, the Everton club anthem, is also audible for those with keen ears. 'When Duncan was facing his jail sentence, I somehow got the feeling that I should let this enigmatic person play a role in my music,' explains Raihala.

So he started sketching out the Ferguson piece – and sketching is the right word. First of all he began by drawing on pages of blank paper. He takes my pad from me and he illustrates how he 'saw' the music. 'These were the shapes, surfaces and lines, the ups and downs of Duncan's career, the ebbs and flows,' he says, as he scribbles on the sheet on the table in front of us. 'I already knew it would be a shortish orchestra piece, and that it would describe him and things around him in some way – that it would, I suppose, be a musical portrait,' he says.

Raihala did not have a commission to write the piece when he began his sketches, and neither did he have a firm idea about where and by whom it might be performed. He just felt that it had to be written. Another ten years would pass before it was premiered by the Finnish Radio Symphony Orchestra in the Finlandia Hall, the principal music venue for orchestras in the Finnish capital, before the Musiikkitalo was opened in 2011.

As luck might have it, my visit to interview Raihala coincides with a concert being given by the FRSO at the latter venue, one in which Raihala's wife, Maria, a second violinist in said orchestra, is performing. 'You are not lucky in one way,' smiles Raihala, before we head in, with reference to the British-born composer Gustav Holst's *The Planets*, which is on the programme. 'For a Briton must be the same as for a Finn going abroad and hearing Sibelius's *Finlandia!*' The bourgeoise, middle-class audience listen intently to the music – a piano concerto by Brahms forms the first half of the concert – that sweeps around an auditorium that has been designed to resemble a vineyard.

Outside in the foyer, red and white wine is being poured into bulbous glasses in preparation for the interval, during which the well-dressed concert-goers mill about discussing the merits of the first half of a concert conducted by Vasily Petrenko, who, in another coincidence, is chief conductor of the Liverpool Philharmonic Orchestra – and a keen Liverpool FC supporter.

Meanwhile, in a corner amidst the babble of chatter, two figures resume their discussion of Duncan Ferguson. It was much the same scene, Raihala assures me, several years earlier, when he was a nervous composer watching a capacity audience file in next door, at the Findlandia Hall. He was invited to take the stage by conductor Sakari Oramo to explain the background to the work that the FRSO were premiering that night. Specifically, he wanted to know the reason for the title. Who – or what – is Barlinnie Nine?

'There were a few blank looks,' admits Raihala, as he recalls telling the 1,700-strong audience the genesis of the piece. He explained to the audience the story of a young Scottish footballer sent to jail for a crime he committed on the football pitch when he was only 22 years old.

'I've described the work as a musical portrait,' he continues. 'In the music, there are several phases that bring the different natures of Duncan Ferguson into the picture – remember that I don't know Duncan personally, and I was always aware that my portrait would be based on the picture the media had painted of him. He might really be a nice man and a grown-up person, but he will always remain the hard man: Duncan Disorderly. That is the reputation he will bear all his life.'

In answer to my request, Raihala gamely attempts to describe the music, something musicians and composers are often reluctant to do. 'It is impossible to describe music with words, otherwise there would be no need for the music,' he says.

To my uncultured and musically limited ears, it is a haunting melding of contemporary and classical sounds; an at times sweeping work, containing powerful passages that stop abruptly, as if a door has shut suddenly. 'There are very powerful starts that stop abruptly, short victorious passages, the feeling of promises that are suddenly broken,' agrees Raihala, politely. 'And, then, of course, there is a most gloomy phase. After all, Duncan had to do his time among hard-boiled criminals.'

He adds that he felt Ferguson deserved something more powerful than chamber music, which is normally more intimate in sound. So he decided to sketch an orchestral piece. He came up with a title almost immediately.

'I very often get inspiration for a work when a title pops up in my head, when I hear a word or a couple of words that turn themselves into music,' he continues. 'Barlinnie Nine – it sounded good. I know Barlinnie for a lot of people is a horrible place, but the name looks good on paper. It has a ring to it.

'And the number nine does not reveal what it is about, it is quite cryptic.

'*Barlinnie Nine* – nine what?

'Of course it was nine, the shirt,' he continues. 'It could have been cell number nine. All traditional forwards at Everton have been number nine since the days of Dixie Dean. In almost all teams there is something magical about the number nine jersey.'

'Just as Ferguson's career had stops and starts, I'm well aware that there are projects that seem to die, only to surface after a long while,' he adds, with reference to the delay in completing the work. 'And, as so often happens, the idea was buried under other projects for a long time, mainly because I was a young composer and would have difficulties to get an orchestral work premiered.'

In late 1998, and in the same week that Ferguson was sold to Newcastle United, Raihala noticed that the Norwegian Stavanger Symphony Orchestra had announced an orchestra workshop. Young Nordic composers were urged to apply and send in sketches. So Raihala returned to his old idea, penned out some of the early minutes of the work and, to his delight, was chosen for the workshop, along with three others.

'But nobody had told me that it was at the same time a competition, and not all four works would be performed,' he continues. 'For this reason, *Barlinnie Nine* wasn't completed when the workshop was finished.

'So the work went back in my drawer,' says Raihala. 'In any case, Duncan was no longer with Everton. Nothing pointed to it ever seeing the light of day, although I sometimes mentioned the work to colleagues in music circles.'

A stroke of luck arrived in 2003, when Sakari Oramo, someone known for eagerly looking for unknown or forgotten repertoires, became the artistic director of the Finnish Radio Symphony Orchestra. In the meantime, Raihala had continued building his reputation as a composer, and when he received a phone call from the FRSO's manager, who asked whether he had a yet-to-be premiered orchestra piece to hand, he knew instantly that this was the moment to return to something that was lying dormant – perhaps a little like Ferguson's career, at the time. 'They didn't have the time to commission a new work, so would premier an existing one,' explains Raihala. 'Without further thinking, I mumbled, "Yes, I do", although I knew I would have to re-work the one that I had in mind.'

It was, of course, *Barlinnie Nine*.

After he re-worked the piece, a concert date was set for 20 April 2005 – the same night as Everton were due to play Manchester United in a game that was critical to their Champions League qualification hopes, although Raihala was not to know this.

My meeting with the composer in Helsinki hinged on one novel and very strict condition: that I reveal no clue as to how Everton are currently performing. A clearly passionate character, Raihala had worked himself up into such a frenzy because of Everton results that, in 2004, he made the decision to stop following them during the season. An active member of various Everton website chat rooms, this means he logs off in August and returns in May, at the end of a season he has gone to extraordinary trouble to avoid hearing about.

It is eccentric behaviour, he accepts. 'I was sick,' he says. 'I began to realise I was getting more pleasure from Liverpool losing than Everton winning.'

It is nearly five years since I first made contact with the composer via email, having read about *Barlinnie Nine*. Naturally, it had intrigued me. We continue talking over dinner, during which Raihala stresses to me that he had never idolised Ferguson. 'I only ever had one idol and that was when I was 12 or 13, that was Bob Latchford,' he says, of the much-loved striker who played for Everton between 1974 and 1981.

As has been the case for so many, Raihala admits that Ferguson has proved an elusive figure. Although he has visited Goodison Park to watch a game on four occasions, he has never seen Ferguson play live. The first time was on Boxing Day in 1990, just weeks after Ferguson made his senior debut for Dundee United. Raihala's second

Everton match was in early 1994, several months before Ferguson joined the club. When Raihala returned again, for a match against Southampton in December 1998, Ferguson had left just weeks earlier for Newcastle United. And on his most recent visit in 2002 to see Everton play Middlesbrough, the Finn was again left frustrated – Ferguson was injured.

However, the striker was fit to start against Manchester United in a midweek fixture that pitted fourth-placed Everton against the side lying in third position.

Ferguson had started the previous match against Crystal Palace, but that had been his first full appearance of the year. If used at all by David Moyes, it was normally as a substitute. However, this particular fixture seemed to provide the optimal conditions for Ferguson to excel, and Moyes was alert to this.

While his temperament was clearly suspect, it is worth pointing out that, for all his red cards, he was never sent off against Manchester United or Liverpool; mostly, his ill-discipline reared its head against lowlier teams. Ferguson didn't want to miss a minute of the more high-octane occasions. And if the floodlights were on, then so much the better.

Unbeknown to Raihala, who was still observing his self-imposed ban on Everton-related news, the team were enjoying a fine season, despite the loss of Wayne Rooney, who was sold to Manchester United in August for a fee between £25 million and £30 million. Yet, from September, Everton were never out of the top four. Because it offered the potential of Champions League qualification, finishing in at least fourth place was the main objective.

A win against United would mean Everton taking a major step towards securing a place in the Champions League qualification rounds – and would help shake rivals Liverpool off their tail. An extra ingredient had been added to the pot, that of Wayne Rooney's return to Goodison Park. The former Everton striker was wearing the red of Manchester United for the second time at his former ground, having appeared in an FA Cup clash earlier in the year, which had garnered the expected rancorous reaction.

This helped ensure that the Grand Old Lady, as Goodison Park is affectionately known, conjured up one of its most potent atmospheres. And in a delicious, almost unbelievable, coincidental collision of events, a re-born Ferguson was the inspiration behind one of the great Everton performances of recent times.

He had already announced himself on United goalkeeper Tim Howard, barging him to the ground in classic Ferguson style before scoring what proved to be the match winner. Ten minutes after half-time, he stooped to head a free-kick from Mikel Arteta into the net after stealing space on the edge of the six-yard box. It was Everton's first win over United since Ferguson's header had secured the 1–0 victory ten years earlier. The shirt stayed on this time. Sky commentator Martin Tyler referenced the afternoon in 1995 when the striker had scored at the same Gwladys Street End of the ground against the same opponents, to secure the same result.

'It's Duncan Ferguson, ten years later!' screamed Tyler into his microphone. The striker had succeeded in doing what Moyes hoped he might; he had reconnected with the Ferguson of old, the one who had given the striker's namesake in the dugout at Manchester United such terrors over the years, to the extent that Sir Alex Ferguson was reported to have complained to Moyes: 'Och, not Duncan Ferguson again.'

The comment said it all. United were the most successful club during Duncan Ferguson's career in England, and he had certainly left an impression when playing against them, scoring seven times in total. 'Sir Alex dreaded the thought of playing Everton with Duncan Ferguson in the team,' says Ian Ross. 'Phil Neville, who obviously came to play for Everton after so long at United, used to say that he hated coming to Everton. He remembered Sir Alex saying that it was "Chaos, bedlam, like the Alamo – then they would throw Duncan Ferguson on!"'

On this occasion, Ferguson was taken off rather than sent on, his work done. When the final whistle sounded ten minutes later, Ferguson rose from his seat on the bench with little emotion; it was as if he knew he had already made his point. Ferguson's critics in the press-box were forced to tip their hats to this unlikely re-emergence as a serious operator. On an explosive night (United finished the match with only nine men), Ferguson came out on top against Rio Ferdinand, who had been in the news for haggling over improved terms on a new contract at United, with his agent reportedly demanding £120,000 a week. Ferguson ended up embarrassing him. Indeed, it was Ferdinand whose attentions Ferguson had easily shrugged off to score.

This was noted in the press-box. According to David Prentice in the *Liverpool Echo*, he had made Ferdinand 'look like a journeyman centre-half'. Ferguson's old friend Philip McNulty conceded that this had been a very special performance.

'Duncan Ferguson has been the subject of more critical words in this column than any other player,' he wrote, again in the *Liverpool Echo*. 'And it would be wrong of me not to give glowing credit.' Even Jim McLean had his say, although he could not resist some implied criticism: 'The last time I saw Duncan Ferguson play the way he did against Manchester United was for the Dundee United youth team many moons ago,' he noted, in his column in the *Daily Record*.

Because of the two-hour time difference between Finland and Britain, Raihala did not hear of it until later that evening, when he was in a bar celebrating his own Ferguson-inspired triumph in Helsinki. 'It had been a great personal success to me, lots of bowing and generous clapping,' he says. With the applause of the audience still ringing in his ears, he had no thoughts about what Ferguson might or might not have achieved that very same evening. After all, he did not know Everton were even playing such an important fixture.

A friend had imparted the news after travelling back home to see the end of the game on television. He had been hesitant about phoning Raihala at first, conscious of the composer's wish to remain oblivious to Everton's progress – or lack of it – during the season. However, he felt this was something his friend simply had to know.

'He said to me: "I am terribly sorry, but I have to break your silence. The final whistle has just gone 20 seconds ago and Everton have beaten Manchester United. Duncan Ferguson has scored the winning goal."

'He has done what?' replied Raihala.

'Yes, Ferguson has scored the winner,' his friend confirmed.

'My friend screamed how unbelievable this was, and it was true,' continues Raihala. 'Duncan was now a bit-part player at Everton, mostly used as a late sub, and from all possible dates he had chosen this one to rise from the ashes and head home the winner in front of a packed Goodison Park. At this time I had already celebrated with a few Ardbegs, and you can imagine the scene.'

'It felt unreal,' he adds. 'Over 1,000 miles from Liverpool, my work has just been premiered at long last. And of course, Duncan just has to return to Olympus that same night to humiliate the Red Devils.

The coincidence was not lost on people. For a short while, I replaced Sibelius as the most talked about Finnish composer in Britain.

'But only a very short while – and rightly so,' he adds.

Raihala, of course, also sensed the irony. There he was, receiving all the plaudits for a work that was inspired by someone considered to have failed to realise his potential. But this timely reminder of what Ferguson could be, of what he might have been on a more regular basis were it not for the combination of injury and his own lack of application, also underlined why Raihala had already chosen to give *Barlinnie Nine* an alternative title: *The Apotheosis of Underachievement*.

If Ferguson's life were a musical score, then this should have been the crescendo. Perhaps it would have been better had he retired there and then; the cheers still ringing in his ears, the words of his critics rammed back down their throats. Bravo, maestro!

He didn't, however. Ferguson carried on. According to Raihala, *Barlinnie Nine* ends with an intense final rise and then what the composer described as an 'enigmatic' final passage. It can be viewed as more than a little appropriate. Largely on the evidence of his performance against Manchester United, Moyes was encouraged to hand Ferguson another contract, one based on appearances and involving a significant pay cut. Even after a winning goal against Manchester United, his bargaining position had lessened somewhat.

It would have taken an extremely harsh man to deny Ferguson the chance to play Champions League football, with the player having been instrumental in helping Everton qualify for the competition for the first time since it had been given its 'makeover' in the early 1990s. Not only had he scored the decisive goal against United at such a significant stage of the season, but he also followed this up by coming off the bench to secure an invaluable point against Birmingham City just three days later, with what proved the penultimate goal of his career. Everton secured fourth place just over a fortnight later, following a Liverpool defeat at Arsenal.

The much-anticipated return to Europe was not, however, the experience everyone was hoping for. David Harrison, the club secretary, recalls feeling a rising sense of dread at the draw, which saw Everton paired with Villarreal. 'Hmm, they are pretty good, aren't they?' he remembers chairman Bill Kenwright whispering into his ear as the teams were paired together.

'We came away quite deflated,' adds Harrison. To simply get into the Champions League group stage, Everton needed to beat the team that had finished third, behind Barcelona and Real Madrid, in La Liga the previous season.

When Everton lost 2–1 at home in the first leg (Ferguson came on as a second-half substitute), few gave them a chance of progressing. However, they almost did.

Indeed, perhaps they should have done; or, more accurately, at least they should have had another 30 minutes in which to try. It is one of football's great travesties that the tie did not go into extra time, and at the heart of the controversy was Duncan Ferguson, whose first goal for the club in European competition, with the score at 1–1 in Spain, was ruled out by referee Pierluigi Collina, who claimed that he had blown his whistle for a foul before Ferguson's header had crossed the line.

But a foul by whom? It wasn't Ferguson, this much was clear. He had jumped with his customary determination, rising well clear of any defender, with marginal, if any, physical contact, to meet Mikel Arteta's corner. The referee later gave an unconvincing explanation that he had, in fact, penalised Ferguson's teammate Marcus Bent for committing a foul on the fringes of the six-yard box.

However, no one will persuade Everton fans that there was not some prejudice at work, with conspiracy theorists pointing to the saga that developed when it became clear Liverpool could win the Champions League, which they duly did. Although Everton had pipped their rivals to the Champions League qualifying spot, it was agreed by UEFA that Liverpool must defend the trophy, and they were given a spot in the third qualifying round – where Everton were also scheduled to come in. It meant that UEFA were left with the prospect of an unprecedented five teams from the same country competing in the group stages. Or at least this would have happened, had Everton not been the victims of a decision that mystifies to this day.

When Collina suddenly announced his retirement just six days later, the news failed to placate the Everton fans. Indeed, the surprise move simply helped harden their belief that something was not quite right. Why would a referee considered to be the best in the world – several Everton players later complained that Collina had asked them not to question his decision because he was just that, 'the best referee in the world' – retire only a few weeks into a season that would end with the 2006 World Cup in Germany?

Although Duncan Ferguson carried on, he might as well have called it a day then, too. There was another, final red card of his career to come. It was all rather wearingly familiar: an off-the-ball punch aimed at Wigan defender Paul Scharner (an Austrian, this time), for which he was red-carded, and then a further spat with Pascal Chimbonda as he left the field, which earned him a separate suspension of four matches, on top of an initial three-match ban for the first red card.

It meant he was sidelined until the penultimate month of the season. 'Duncan Doughnut has to call it a day,' the sports writer Brian Woolnough reflected in the *Daily Star*. 'The former Scotland centre-forward has to be the biggest waste of money in the Premiership. What he needs to do is take a long, hard look in the mirror and ask himself if he deserves to pick up his £40,000 a week at Goodison Park.'

In fact, he was on a lot less than this in his final season, his contract having reportedly been plied with incentive-based clauses, such as an appearance bonus and goal bonuses – although this was beginning to look a rather hopeful insertion. As the season neared its end, Ferguson had still to score, the Villarreal 'goal' notwithstanding. There were no positive noises coming from the manager about whether he was going to be retained. Indeed, much to Ferguson's displeasure, there were no noises at all.

He complained of being left in the dark about whether he would be given a new contract or not, although seven-match bans at the age of 34, at a time when Ferguson should have been doing his utmost to prove he could still be a worthwhile addition to the squad, were hardly helpful.

The silence from Moyes was simply his way of doing things at the time. He wanted to ensure that players gave their all until the very last game and were not encouraged to ease off because they were either already assured of a new contract or knew that their displays didn't matter since they were considered surplus to requirements in any case.

I wrote a piece on David Weir, another player due to be out of contract that same summer, for an article that was published in *The Scotsman* on the morning of the final match of the season, against

West Bromwich Albion. He, too, did not know whether he was in Moyes's plans or not, even at such a late stage. 'It's just the manager's way of doing things,' he said. Ferguson wasn't the only one to be given no clear indication of the manager's future plans, yet he considered it to be a grave personal insult.

Although it had not been made explicitly clear, it was generally accepted that this was likely to be Ferguson's final appearance, certainly in an Everton shirt. He started his first game since January and found the going tough. Everton trailed 2–1 to the already relegated West Bromwich Albion, when, in injury time, they were awarded a penalty. Mikel Arteta, the regular taker, prepared to step up, but James McFadden quickly reminded him that it was likely to be Ferguson's last game.

Ferguson had emerged as a fairly successful penalty taker in his second spell, having already scored eight times from the spot when Arteta handed him the ball. With Everton lying in mid-table, little rested on the outcome. However, the kick was invested in meaning for Ferguson, and for the fans, who could not bear the possibility that he might miss a penalty with his last kick of the game – and probably his career.

Ferguson placed the ball, and then, with his left foot, scuffed it towards the goal. Fortunately for Ferguson, the save made by Tomasz Kuszczak was not as effective as the West Bromwich goalkeeper would have hoped and the ball bobbled back up in the six-yard box. Ferguson followed up. With cramp having taken hold in both his calf muscles, he later admitted he had worried whether he would even be able to reach the rebound. Though the second effort, this time with his less-favoured right foot, seemed to be mis-hit too, the gods were on his side. The ball made it into the net, just. The final whistle blew just seconds later. It was probably the scruffiest of the 72 goals he had scored for Everton and, perhaps, in his entire career.

However, it at least meant he was not finishing a season goal-less for the first-ever time. Ferguson, though, was angered at being denied a proper opportunity to say farewell to the fans, although, in the end, it turned into a perhaps more fitting last lap of honour. It was how farewells should be conducted – emotional, un-choreographed and heartfelt. Tears flowed as Ferguson, joined on the pitch by his children, saluted the supporters, who must have felt wrung-out by the end. The afternoon had begun with a minute's silence for the legendary Everton defender Brian Labone, who had died suddenly earlier in the week.

'I just think the supporters didn't know what to do at first,' says Harrison. 'Is he going, or not? In the end, it was a walk around the pitch. And then he just disappeared down the tunnel, and we all thought: "That's the last we'll see of Duncan Ferguson. He's not the kind of person who is going to come back."'

He could not avoid making one last return visit, however. In David Moyes's office, he was given the news that would end his career. As expected, there was no new contract on the table. In the *Liverpool Echo*, the decision merited only a single sentence, and even then it was a 'meanwhile' mention, in a story about goalkeeper Nigel Martyn being handed a new one-year deal. Perhaps because he had given them so little cooperation over the years, this could be seen as a subtle form of 'payback' from the newspaper. However, it also illustrates just how far his star had faded. Duncan Ferguson's Everton career should never have ended with just a 'meanwhile' in the local paper.

Keith Wyness, the club's chief executive at the time, knew that Moyes had been mulling over the decision of whether to give Ferguson a new contract or not. Wyness suspected there might be a 'volcanic' explosion if the player was given news he didn't want to hear; even if, like everyone else, the striker surely knew it was coming. 'I was aware of the decision having to be made,' says Wyness. 'Everyone was waiting anxiously to hear the outcome.'

It would have been understandable had certain Everton officials felt a measure of relief that it was not they who had to tell Ferguson that it was over, that the love affair was finished. But perhaps it was better this way. Ferguson was battle-scarred and wounded. He would turn 35 during the coming season. Other clubs were reported to be watching the situation, with Bradford City one of those credited with interest in signing Ferguson. 'With all due respect, Duncan just isn't a Bradford player,' noted Graeme Sharp, the former Everton striker, in his autobiography.

In his office, after informing Ferguson of his decision to release him, Moyes went to shake his hand. Hurt, offended and, he later admitted, completely bereft of ideas about what to do next, Ferguson rejected the gesture. Rather than shake his manager's hand, he simply turned around and walked back out of the door. Not for the first time, Duncan Ferguson had been freed. Unlike the last occasion, there was no limousine waiting for him at the gate.

CHAPTER 21

You Forget the Rest

Liverpool, March 2009

It is almost three years since Duncan Ferguson made his low-key exit from Everton, and from Merseyside. His disappearance seems total; he is said to be living in Majorca, but doing what, nobody knows. Living quietly seems to be the consensus, which is what one tends to do on an island popular with Britons and Germans, in particular retirees and hedonists. Perhaps surprisingly, it is as a member of the first group that Ferguson left Merseyside, bound for the Balearics. But then he never seemed like somebody who would remain in the game, as a coach, manager or agent, or even, God forbid, as a media pundit.

There have been sightings. In *OK!* magazine, incongruously enough, he could be seen looming in the background of one of the photos at Wayne Rooney and Coleen McLoughlin's wedding in Portofino. He has been spotted at Real Mallorca games, so clearly isn't taking a complete break from football. Tam McMillan, an old friend and teammate from Dundee United days, also bumped into him at Palma airport. 'He was dressed like the Mayor of Majorca and looked like a million dollars,' he says.

Whatever he was doing in the Balearics, there was little debate about one thing: he hadn't been seen at Goodison Park. It seems they were right: he wasn't the type who was going to come back.

*

But then, abruptly, I hear that Ferguson has agreed to return to Liverpool for his first public appearance since his last game for Everton. He is being inducted into the Gwladys Street Hall of Fame and, surprisingly, has agreed to attend the ceremony. It seems almost as unlikely as an appearance in the Sky Sports studios.

I drive to Liverpool, check into a hotel and head to the designated venue: the Adelphi Hotel. The sense of anticipation hits me hard as I climb the steps and enter through its rather grand front door, passing a gaggle of young autograph hunters on the way. Finally, I am going to come face-to-face with Ferguson.

Well, maybe. I'm taking nothing for granted.

I had taken a pragmatic approach to writing a book about Ferguson right from the beginning. When I mentioned the project to people, the stock response was: 'Big Dunc? Good luck la, you'll need it!' One Everton fan informed me, 'He wouldn't even agree to be interviewed for his own DVD!'

It is true, he didn't.

Big Dunc: The Story of a Goodison Hero was released just before Christmas in 2008 – more than two years since Ferguson had last been seen at the club, following that emotional last appearance – and goal – against West Bromwich Albion. The film contains an impressive cast list of interviewees, including Wayne Rooney, Alan Shearer and the late Gary Speed. There is, of course, someone missing. While Ferguson seemed happy enough to see it released, he declined to make any active contribution to its making.

Simply having Ferguson associated with the project helped persuade others to say nice things about him. His reputation meant the talking-head recruitment process was a lot easier than it might have been. 'A lot of people were frightened to say no because they thought that Duncan was involved!' Darren Griffiths, the media and publications manager at the club, laughs. 'I didn't tell them that Duncan refused to cooperate. I could imagine the press boy at Newcastle saying to Alan Shearer: "You better do it, you never know when you might bump into him again!"

'Thankfully, word came that Duncan had no problem with me putting it together, because he knew I would do a good job. I used to write his captain's programme notes, a task he took seriously. Before each home fixture I would speak to Duncan at the training ground and he would tell me the topics he wanted to include in his notes. I would then go away and write the pages for him to have a look at.'

As for the DVD, Griffiths knows that Ferguson has a copy of it. He just didn't want to be involved in something that, on top of featuring every goal he scored for Everton, explores some less orthodox areas. As the blurb on its back cover trills, as well as the goals and the glory, the DVD promises 'the brushes with the law, the burglaries and the pigeons!' To the casual observer, it is Ferguson's life summed-up.

When Griffiths asked him to appear on it, Ferguson did not refuse point-blank. "'Leave it to me, leave it to me," he told me,' says Griffths. "'I will do it for you, not anyone else." But in the end he did not even do it for me.'

There is, though, an interview included, one rescued from the archives, from shortly after he joined Everton in 1994. The clip causes the viewer to jolt; so *that's* what he sounds like.

Ferguson has managed to remain unknowable. In an era of 24-hour sports news channels, this is quite a feat, something I reflect upon while approaching the seven-storey hotel, where a throng is already gathering. It is not only me who appears desperate for some interaction with the headline act.

The Adelphi is an institution in Liverpool, yet I can't help but feel the event is a little low rent, even given the genuine star quality of the special guest. Perhaps the reason for this is the hotel itself. It was once a jewel in the city's crown. These days were long ago, however; the term 'faded grandeur' could have been invented for it.

As with many such places, there are redeeming features, including, in the Adelphi's case, a cavernous lounge which doubled as the interior of an ocean liner in the television series *Brideshead Revisited*. While you can still sense a certain air of opulence, these days – rather than be remembered for its past association with the likes of Charles Dickens, who regularly stayed here on his visits to Liverpool – it has become more synonymous with the rather lower brow 1990s fly-on-the-wall documentary series *Hotel*, chronicling all the kitchen calamities and front-desk fall-outs at the Adelphi. It made a star of the then general manager, Eileen Downey, with her bleeped-out rants, and also coined a catchphrase: 'Just cook, will yer?'

The Grade II listed building still looks imperious, though. It stands at a crossroads, between Liverpool's cultural quarter and

China Town, between the Empire Theatre and the Philharmonic Hall. But there is a sadness that clings to it.

At the bottom of Brownlow Hill, outside the Vines pub, a floral tribute has been tied to a lamp post in memory of a young man. The cause of his death is not clear, but it presents a sobering contrast to the Fergie-mania that is building inside the hotel. They know how to mourn on Merseyside, it is said. But they also know how to canonise, how to treat an outsider as one of their own, let him into their Liverpool homes. Ferguson had managed to assimilate himself rather well into life in the area. As Tony Hibbert, the long-serving Everton full-back, once said: 'Dunc's more Scouse than the rest of us.'

Now, as I enter the hotel, I realise that I haven't really got as far as making a game plan for introducing myself to Ferguson; I can't quite bring myself to believe that he will actually be here – and I suspect I am not alone. But I know that he knows about the book. It has been endorsed, in so far as I have not suffered Steffen Freund's fate and been throttled by him. Yet.

When Ferguson sees a journalist, he appears to think instinctively of another J – jail. This Pavlovian association could be bad news for me, as I attempt to discover whether the two years he's spent in the Majorcan sun have helped melt away his old prejudice.

Just after 7 p.m., Duncan Ferguson bounds down the stairs of Cromptons, the small bar/French restaurant that, tonight, doubles as the VIP room. Not only has he shown up, he is early. He orders a pint of water at the bar and, for a few minutes, looks ill at ease. And, if this is possible in a room where everyone wants to be his friend, almost lonely.

I am told later that he is in the company of a couple of Merseyside heavies, although he is hardly in need of protection. No one in their right mind would take liberties with Ferguson, especially on such a night. Indeed, you get the feeling that there are people here tonight who would die for him.

The Mediterranean lifestyle is clearly suiting him. He appears in almost better shape than when he played. A slightly goofish grin stretches across his tanned face, but he is undeniably handsome – and tall, of course. It's just as well that, according to the pamphlets that are dotted around the foyer, 'high ceilings' are one of the hotel's selling points.

'He looks like a film star,' says one female next to me. And it's true. What a contrast to when I first set eyes on Ferguson playing up front for Dundee United in the early 1990s; lanky, angular, almost geeky. But there is one constant, one thing linking him to the footballer then glimpsed at the start of the journey to this love-in in Liverpool. He is still chewing gum.

Alan Myers, from Sky Sports, manages to catch a few words with him.

'You're looking well, Duncan,' he tells him.

'Aye, it's the sunshine,' he replies.

Later Myers says, 'Even in conversation, he was a man of few words. I always got the impression that he could not be doing with the bother of stupid conversation.'

Ferguson is still drinking what looks like water; indeed, he is downing glass after glass. Being a legend is clearly thirsty work. And legend is what Ferguson is to the blue half of a city where they love an anti-hero. Such is the fervour whipped up by his return that they are prepared to forget the bad times, the injuries and the lack of interaction. They overlook the apparent fact that, despite apparently having a season ticket, Ferguson has not been inside Goodison Park since that final appearance. But he is at the Adelphi now. Everything is all right. Everyone can 'drink a drink a drink' to Duncan Ferguson, as the terrace song goes.

He is well turned out, wearing what is a footballer's idea of being well turned out. He has chosen to step out in a sleek grey suit, which someone describes as being the kind of thing a mobster might wear. It marks him out as even more conspicuous, if that's possible. Beneath this he sports a dark shirt and a dark tie. A ring on his finger denotes over a decade of marriage to Janine, with whom he now has three children, Evie, Cameron and Ross.

Someone at Bluenose Promotions, the organisation behind the dinner, has a sense of mischief, clearly, since Ferguson is seated next to Tony Kay at top table. Kay has also been voted into the Hall of Fame but can be compared with Ferguson for a number reasons. In 1962, when Everton paid £60,000 to Sheffield Wednesday for the left wing-half's services, he too knew what it was like to be the costliest footballer in the land. What you could say Ferguson and Kay also have in common is the need to fend off criticism that neither made enough of their careers. But their principal association is one that is hard to ignore – even amid the burble of excited chatter that engulfs the room. They both share the ignominy of having been detained at Her Majesty's Pleasure when in their playing heyday. You imagine that they can both still taste the bitterness, as they contemplate the bowls of soups that have been set down in front of them.

Earlier, in the VIP room, someone mentioned Kay's name. It caused Ferguson to pause. It was now his turn to feel star-struck. 'Is that Tony Kay?' he asked.

Kay's story, according to his friend Becky Tallentire, is 'one of the saddest in football'. But you don't have to have been close to him to reach that conclusion. Kay's career came to an abrupt and sensational end the season after he helped Everton win the First Division title in 1962–63, after being implicated in a betting scandal. This pre-dated his move to Goodison Park and actually occurred during his spell with Sheffield Wednesday, his hometown club.

Along with teammates Peter Swan and David Layne, Kay placed a bet that Wednesday would lose a game against Ipswich Town. This they duly did, although in the *Sunday People*, the paper that later broke the story, it was reported that Kay actually received the 'man of the match' award that day. He had clearly not tried very hard to lose.

Kay was fined £150, banned from playing professional football for life and sentenced to four months in prison. Kay served 11 weeks in an open prison near Leeds and though the life ban was later lifted, his last senior game remained the one he played with Everton when only in his mid-20s. One popular theory, proposed by Evertonians mostly, is that, had Kay never made this unwise foray, gambling on his team to lose, or had he never been found out, then Nobby Stiles would not now be famous for his jig around Wembley after England's 1966 World Cup win. Kay would have been in the team instead of him.

Kay's life, however, took a rather different course. He mingled with the Kray twins and became mixed up in another criminal case, this time connected to a forged diamond he had sold. Kay lay low in both Spain and London before, in 2002, being invited back to Goodison Park to celebrate the club's 100th season in top-flight football. It was the first time he'd been back in nearly 40 years.

'This is how it is with Everton – they always come back eventually,' says Tallentire.

Kay has now returned to the area full-time, to Southport, the small seaside resort north of Liverpool, which has always been a popular place of residence for footballers. 'I think I am living in another world after so many years away,' he says, above the din of cheers after being called up to receive his Hall of Fame plaque. 'Long live Everton!' As he sits back down next to Ferguson, the Scot turns to shake his hand. It is possible to interpret it as a reach of empathy.

'That was the first time he had ever met Duncan,' says Tallentire. 'Tony said he was a gentleman and genuinely worried about the kids. He was just so desperate to be back in Majorca with his kids.'

Though Kay and Ferguson have much to talk about, this is neither the time nor the place. The MC for the night, the local radio personality Billy Butler, is fighting a losing battle as he appeals for calm. The atmosphere is getting more fervent as Ferguson's coronation nears. Rather than fine wine, heavy boxes of Budweiser have been slammed down on tables. Food is clearly an afterthought. Ferguson continues to sip water, barely touching the main course that has been slopped onto the plate in front of him by cheery waiters and waitresses who spend the night shimmying between the tightly packed tables.

The Gwladys Street Hall of Fame dinner might as well have been in said end at Goodison Park. And this is true even before the singing starts. To the tune of 'Go West' by the Village People, the room shakes to: '*Dun-caaaan, Duncan Ferguson, Dun-caaaan, Duncan Ferguson, Dun-caaaan, Duncan Ferguson!*'

As the alcohol continues to get drained, things become freer and looser. Inhibitions are lost. Liberties are taken. Diners begin to mill around Ferguson. Some ask him to sign items, including, in one instance, a plate. This all occurs under the watchful eye of the two security men, who stand guard throughout, though they seem redundant. Not only is this a love-in, but Ferguson looks more than capable of looking after himself should there be anyone left on Merseyside still foolish enough to invade his personal space.

Ferguson does not refuse any request, even after Butler has made an appeal for everyone to leave the diners on the top table alone during the actual meal. Someone even taps him on the shoulder and asks him to speak to a friend on a mobile phone that is thrust into Ferguson's hand. He has clearly steeled himself for a long night of indulging the whims of those he must also accept have helped fund the lifestyle he can now enjoy in Spain. One more night of this, then back to Majorca. Back to the kids, back to anonymity.

Yet who would not wish to be the subject of so much adoration? Who would not wish to be reminded of the rush that comes from scoring a goal, and the bliss of seeing so much joy on a sea of faces tightly packed into the 'Street End'? One more phone is pushed into his hand and from it emerges a voice he can at least recognise, even if the tone is hushed. It is Mark Ward, his old compadre from nights out on the town in Liverpool and another former Everton player with experience of prison. The difference is that he, at the time of the dinner, is still in one.

Ferguson, who never actually played with Ward, had gone to visit him in Buckley Hall prison in Rochdale. The support had been appreciated by someone who was happy to relate his experiences of being in jail in the well-received memoir *Right Wing to B Wing*. Ward, who made just short of 100 appearances for Everton in the early '90s, was sentenced to eight years in prison for possession of cocaine with intent to supply. Ferguson had accompanied Howard Kendall on the trip to see Ward, who the former Everton manager had signed on two occasions, for £1 million each time. Ward gained great succour from hearing Ferguson's own tales from Barlinnie – 'We had a good laugh, he told me about dishing out food in the hospital ward,' he recalled – and so was determined to play a part in the Scot's special evening in Liverpool, even if circumstances prevented him from being in attendance himself.

'This is how much I love the man,' Ward says later. 'I was still in prison and you are not supposed to use a mobile phone, but I had arranged to phone Tommy Griff [a mutual friend, who was at the dinner] that night.

'I'd love to have gone to the dinner, but obviously I couldn't,' he adds. 'I couldn't even get home leave. Griff said to me: "Phone my mobile and I will get him on the phone." So I rang his mobile and you can imagine the scene. Griff said: "He is surrounded by so many people, ring me back in five minutes. So I did and got him on the phone. Through the bedlam, I could just make out: "Wee man, wee man . . . how are you?"

'I told him I was sorry I couldn't be there, but I was thinking about him. He said: "I will catch up with you soon, when you get out . . .'"

The evening is hotting up, though a slight downer is provided by the news that David Moyes won't be present. He has been an enthusiastic supporter of the event in the past and has sent his apologies for his non-attendance on this occasion, which more than one person tells me is significant.

The manager's continued presence at Goodison Park is floated as one reason why Ferguson has not been seen back at the club. But Everton are scheduled to be playing at Portsmouth on Saturday, now fewer than 48 hours away. Moyes's appearance must surely have been in doubt in any case. The official line is that he is attending to 'club business'.

Bill Kenwright, the club chairman, passes on his manager's best wishes when he stands to address the throng. The flamboyant Kenwright was made for this kind of occasion. Although he has had his own run-ins with fans, his undoubted love for the club means that many of his perceived sins can be readily forgiven, as his own inclusion in the Hall of Fame testifies. Peter Johnson is afforded no such grace. Mention of his name by Kenwright is greeted with a wall of boos.

Kenwright knows how to play to an audience and he isn't planning on sparing Ferguson as he continues with his emotional tribute.

'You should have seen it in the VIP room earlier, Jack Rodwell and Dan Gosling [then two younger members of the Everton first-team squad] looked up to him like he was a god,' continues Kenwright.

Others, too, use their own spot in the sun to salute Ferguson. Graham Stuart is a popular recipient of Hall of Fame recognition and speaks eloquently about his feelings for the club. He praises Kenwright for the letter he sent to his home after he left the club, thanking him for his efforts over the years. It is now framed in his living room. And then he turns his attention to Ferguson, offering something rather profound and which, given the drunken delirium present all around, does not perhaps receive the measure of recognition it deserves.

'I know exactly what he means to all of you,' says Stuart. 'But he was a great talisman for us as a team. I think Duncan Ferguson needed Everton, and Everton needed Duncan Ferguson.

'It was a match made in heaven.'

The moment is approaching. Ferguson should be introduced soon. The man handed the responsibility of preparing the way for Ferguson is Kendall, who first made him captain at Everton. Unlike Ferguson, Kendall has not been sticking to water. He begins with a yarn dating back to his second spell as manager at Everton after a run of poor form saw him called into the boardroom.

'We are not happy about Rideout,' Kendall is informed.

'I am sure he'll come good; it was only £500,000,' Kendall replies.

'No, Howard,' it is re-emphasised, 'we are not too happy about Rideout.'

'But you gentlemen around this table at the last board meeting told me to go and get Rideout,' points out Kendall.

'No, Howard, we told you to get *dried* out . . . '

Kendall clearly thinks he had been hired as the main speaker. Experienced and talented after-dinner performer though he is, he has lapsed into default mode here. The organisers are beginning to look uneasy. Though loved by all, patience is wearing thin as Kendall delves into his back catalogue of well-rehearsed anecdotes. The punters want Duncan, not this. What is now unfolding before them is a slapstick routine involving Kendall and another Everton star from the past, Ernie Hunt, resplendent in an absurd wig.

The former inside-forward, who only stayed for six months at Everton, approaches Kendall from his seat a few paces away and attempts to steal the microphone. 'Is this a hint?' asks Kendall, as Hunt grapples with him. 'Don't blame me, I didn't sign him,' he adds.

Kendall is not distracted enough to forget entirely why he is here. He re-positions his spectacles and returns to his notes. 'I named him captain on one particular occasion and he scored a hat-trick,' he recalls. 'I knew he did not like publicity, I knew he did not like talking to the press. But I got him to do Clubcall one particular day and it was a club record. I got him to speak for one and a half minutes. The club received £3,500 and no one could understand a fucking word he said!

'He invited me to one of his children's christenings,' continues Kendall. 'I was the last to leave. We were going across his lawn and he grappled me and took me to the deck. "You all right, boss?" he said. I looked up and thought: "Thank fuck I am not a burglar."'

Ferguson, perhaps surprisingly for those who recall his brooding demeanour on the pitch, is displaying an ability to laugh at himself and is chuckling along with everyone else to these stories. But it is also possible to detect some nervousness as he fidgets at the table. Notably, he has eschewed the crutch of alcohol. Water is his chosen method of keeping his mouth moist ahead of an assignment most top footballers have grown used to undertaking after many years of blanket coverage of the game. Ferguson, however, is not most footballers. Standing up to speak in public is as much of a novelty for him as it is for most of those in attendance.

His moment finally arrives. Kendall, in his own inimitable style, invites the star turn up to the microphone. 'Here's the man, absolutely fantastic!' he exclaims, before Butler adds: 'Ladies and gentlemen, welcome to the Hall of Fame . . . Duncan Ferguson!'

Hell's bells. The reception he is granted as he unfolds himself from his seat behind the table, extending his full 6 ft 4 in. frame, simply confirms who this night is all about, even though the phrase 'Hall of Fame' implies a gallery of names. Those others who join Ferguson in this pantheon are deserving-enough entrants, but perhaps only Kay can begin to match the Ferguson package, one that includes an element of roguishness and mystery.

For many here, the 90 or so seconds of platitudes mumbled down a phone line on the club's old information service is the extent of their exposure to Ferguson away from the football pitch. Those quaint days of Clubcall seem long ago now.

Digital cameras are held aloft to capture images of a radiant Ferguson, who waits for the bedlam to die down. With the microphone in his right hand, he prepares to begin his most comprehensive burst of public interaction with the fans in ten years, during two different spells, at Everton. And he elects to do so without notes, as well as without alcohol.

'Thank you very much, Howard – I thought you'd forgotten about me,' he smiles. 'You kept me waiting . . .

His thoughts quickly turn to the fans, to those seated in front of him, or at least who *were* seated in front of him. Many are now standing on their seats in order to get a better view, as Ferguson speaks about the 'fantastic' relationship he shared with the supporters. 'I have been at other clubs, relatively big clubs with good supporters, but nothing, *nothing*, compares to you,' he says. 'I mean that. I am not just saying that.'

Ferguson talks about the other greats in the Hall of Fame and is sure to include a tribute to Kendall, who 'saw things in me other people never saw'. While recalling his last game for Everton and the emotional lap of honour with his family, he's interrupted by a good-natured heckler: 'You'll get a game on Saturday, no fucking problem!'

'Thanks very much,' Ferguson replies. 'I look well, like?'

'It's very emotional,' he continues, as he recalls what it felt like to represent Everton, to go out 'with that blue jersey on'. He stresses how special it was to be captain under three different managers. Ferguson's deep affection for the club, for the people hanging on his every word, appears genuine. He describes the fans as being 'unbelievable' to him for ten years.

'They were the best years of my career,' he adds. 'In fact, it's the only club I actually ever played for. That's what happens when you play for Everton.'

He pauses for a moment, then adds: 'You forget the rest. The rest are *nothing*. I miss youse, I love youse. God bless.'

Ferguson sits down, wipes away what seems to be another tear. A struggle though it might have been for him, he had made it a worthwhile evening for those who had paid £40 a head to attend.

However, he was not prepared to give *everyone* what they had dared hope for.

Earlier, in the VIP lounge, having already watched as one intrepid young radio reporter's request for a few words is blanked by Ferguson, I approach him, intending to raise the subject of this book: a biography of him, of Duncan Ferguson. But foolishly, I confess to being a sports reporter in my opening line. Possibly I even let slip that I am a journalist – that dreaded 'J' word again. I also stretch out a hand, by way of introduction.

Instantly, I sense a drawbridge being hauled back up. Ferguson has planned on giving only so much of himself away.

'I don't speak to you,' he says, and walks away. In what had been the space between us, my hand remains; ignored, spurned, just as David Moyes's hand had been. Ferguson has gone, again.

CHAPTER 22

Building Bridges

Steve Jones, editor of Everton fans website Blue Kipper, remembers it well. The camera panned down the line. One by one, the figures standing at the side of a Liverpool v. Everton Under-21 fixture came into view. 'It can't be,' he recalls thinking. 'It can't be. It is. It's the big man.' Joe Parkinson, the former Everton midfielder, was in shot too, as was Alan Stubbs. But that was definitely Duncan Ferguson, he concluded, and he was wearing an Everton tracksuit. The big man was back – but why?

This is the sort of exclusive bulletin of news you can pick up if you find yourself watching a reserve clash on the Liverpool FC channel, as Jones, he admits slightly shame-facedly, was doing one evening. There were other sightings, too. Back in Britain this time – rather than in Majorca or lurking in the background of glitzy celebrity wedding photographs in a high-class Italian coastal resort.

He was spotted by the side of a pitch in Thorp Arch, Yorkshire. Ferguson, the *Daily Mail* reported, was watching an exit trial, where players who have recently been released from club academies up and down the country try to take one last chance to fulfil their dreams of becoming professional footballers in front of dozens of gathered scouts.

His presence there has got internet sites buzzing. 'I read in a newspaper he is thinking about setting up an academy in Spain,' someone has posted on an Everton fans website.

'For football or bull-fighting?' someone else wonders.

Like Jones, I too had received a jolt to the system. It came at the once-popular Scottish holiday resort of Largs, after a Scottish Cup draw held at the national sports training centre. Coincidentally, Alan Stubbs was one of the guests invited to make the draw. Later, as I am writing my report in the on-site café, Ray McKinnon, by now a coach with the Scottish Football Association, wanders in and we begin to chat, the former Dundee United player having been a helpful contributor to the book.

'The big man will be here later this summer, of course,' he says. The big man?

'Big Dunc. His name's down to do his coaching badges.'

This piece of information contained enough punch to floor anyone with even passing knowledge of Duncan Ferguson. First of all, no one I had spoken to expected that he would ever return to football. Second, he was supposed to have an aversion to coaching. He wasn't one for listening. David Prentice, of the *Liverpool Echo*, recounts a story about Joe Royle sitting Ferguson down to show him a brief clip of some intelligent movement in the box from the Italian striker Pierluigi Casiraghi. He puts the video in, sits down and then turns round to see Ferguson almost immediately switch off. 'Nah, just forget it, Duncan,' says Royle, aware he has already lost the battle for his concentration.

But the most outlandish part of this revelation is that he has opted to begin his coaching development under the auspices of the SFA, the governing body he viewed with such bitterness, having blamed them, to a large degree, for the time he spent in Barlinnie and for leaving him, he felt, with no option but to turn his back on the Scotland national team.

The startling news makes for another story: 'Ferguson ends feud by joining SFA coaching course' runs the headline. I could barely get the facts down quick enough. They tripped off the tongue, rattled off the keyboard. After being immersed in his life for so long, they were hard-wired in my head; Anstruther, McStay, jail, international exile. It seemed scarcely credible.

'That's Dunc, for you,' more than one of his ex-teammates told me, when I sought their reaction. Ever the enigma. So, having gone in search of Duncan Ferguson, he was now coming back to Scotland, into my orbit. His mission? To learn the craft of those whose patience he had once tested to the extreme, at the knee of a governing body he once bitterly accused of feeding him to the wolves. Not only was he liaising with the enemy, he was paying for the opportunity to study on one of their courses.

I noted that a player worth a combined total of nearly £20 million in his career had forked out the initial £975 enrolment fee, which covered the provision of such items as an official ring-binder folder, with the SFA's crest on it. I was reminded of Michael O'Neill's anecdote about Ferguson's inability to comprehend why he had a box full of books and pens on his arrival at Dundee United all those years ago, and his still deeper puzzlement when O'Neill explained they were to aid his efforts to gain a university degree. Yet here now was Ferguson, the eager student coach.

As well as stumping up for the starter fee, Ferguson had to clear nine consecutive days from his schedule to attend the course. Being based outwith Scotland, he was also expected to provide a 'letter of support' and two 'relevant references'. One of them, reportedly – and surprisingly – was obtained from David Moyes.

I, of course, headed down to Ayrshire to watch as Ferguson embarked upon a new career path. 'Largs. 4/6/11' is written in my notes. 'It's the first time I have had the boots on for five years,' I overheard him say.

It was a windy afternoon on the Ayrshire coast; an international hockey tournament was being staged next door to the grass football pitches where an assortment of budding coaches were being put through their paces. On the way in, I noticed a banner strung between two tree trunks. 'OMG Dunc is 50,' it read. Someone was marking a major milestone in their life on the day their namesake was also taking a significant step. This is an inclusive course, open not only to ex-professionals. Ferguson and other former and current professional footballers, such as one-time Hearts and Celtic midfielder Paul Hartley, and Scott Wilson, formerly of Rangers and Dunfermline, were mixed in with passionate amateurs. It was genuinely a case of all shapes and sizes.

Still a long way from turning 50, Ferguson looked in fine enough fettle to be leading the line at Everton. However, he did sit out the full-sided game they played. Injured, I was told.

Later, I handed a letter to Ray McKinnon, for Ferguson. As expected, perhaps, there was no reply. And yet there was one surprise; the Ferguson story hadn't ended in mystery, behind the gate and high walls of a Majorcan villa, where Ferguson had decamped with his family and even his pigeons. It had taken a new, completely unanticipated course.

'You could have knocked me over with a feather,' Jim McLean said in the *Daily Record*, after he heard the news of Ferguson's coaching ambitions. 'I'm the last person he would consider picking up the phone and asking for advice on his new career, although he knows the number,' his old manager added. Given that he did not even own a mobile phone for a spell in Majorca, it was hard to believe that Ferguson has kept a note of McLean's contact details after nearly 20 years of non-contact. McLean knew he was unlikely to hear from him.

Others, too, were taken aback, including David Moyes, He was contacted by Ferguson five years after the player had walked out of his office, having so pointedly snubbed the offer of a handshake. Ferguson wasn't looking for advice, at least not initially. Instead, he was in search of forgiveness.

Just a fortnight before he attended the first day of the UEFA B Licence course, Ferguson had made another rare but well-publicised return to Meryseyside for yet another awards dinner, one where he was again trailed as the star attraction. He was being inducted as an Everton Giant, an officially endorsed title to add to his status as a Gwladys Street Hall of Famer.

Ferguson, it seemed, was edging back towards a re-acceptance by established football society. Some cynics also interpreted this invitation to be a sign that the club were fretting about unsold seats in the conference hall of the cavernous Liverpool Echo Arena.

Just as at the Adelphi Hotel two years earlier, Ferguson had those in attendance eating out of his hand as he made another short but well-pitched speech, again without the aid of notes. 'This club has been a big part of my life and this city has been a big part of my life,' he told the assembled audience, which numbered nearly 800 guests. 'I met my wife here and my three kids were born here.'

There then followed some gentle questions lobbed at him by broadcaster Ray Stubbs, the compere for the night.

'Does this count as an interview, Duncan?' Stubbs asked cheekily at the end.

It was on this visit home that he took the first steps to building bridges with Moyes, asking to see his former manager in his office at Finch Farm, the club's new training facility. There he apologised for walking out of his office the way that he did, for leaving the manager's hand dangling in mid-air. 'I thought about it every day in Majorca,' he told Moyes. 'I have regretted it every day.' He told him he missed 'the smell of football – the adrenaline, the goals, the training, the craic and banter with the boys'. And then he did what he knew he should have done nearly five years earlier.

He shook Moyes's hand.

The upshot of this was Ferguson's return to the Everton fold, where, initially unsalaried, he worked with the age-group teams at the Everton academy. 'He is there from dusk until dark,' says Alan Irvine, the academy manager. 'He brings the milk bottles in and turns the lights off when he leaves.'

I ask Irvine about the charge directed at Ferguson that he simply didn't love the game enough, the old Jim McLean accusation that reverberates throughout this book. 'Maybe it was true one time,' says Irvine, who had first-hand experience of McLean's ways during a couple of years at United at the end of his career, when Ferguson was just starting out at Tannadice.

And what of McLean, the man who inspired such fear in many of his players, but who admits he found a match in Ferguson? Now in his mid-70s, his health is failing. He gave over 30 years of his life to Dundee United and yet it was only in 2011, before a game against Inverness Caledonian Thistle, that the club named a stand after him – a decade after the punch he landed on a reporter that meant his official association with the club was swiftly terminated.

Unfortunately, in what would have been an irony of ironies, the stand is not the one paid for by Ferguson's transfer all those years ago. After he has been bestowed his honour, McLean entered the press room at Tannadice – or at least the pantry that doubles for a press room at the time – expecting to be interviewed by reporters. 'Does anyone want to speak to Jim McLean?' the press officer asked. I recall barely anyone moving a muscle, preferring to wait instead for whoever had been judged to have done something of merit that afternoon and so was expected to make the headlines the following day. It meant I was therefore able to conduct an 'exclusive' interview with the legendary manager in the corner of the room, amid plates of half-eaten sandwiches and discarded pies.

It struck me as remarkable that no one else felt he was worth speaking to, although one also has to remember that McLean had issued bans on several of those present in the room at varying stages in the last few decades, usually due to some minor or perceived offence – perhaps this was their payback, a chance to take some control? The fans, though, had been more generous, as was expected.

When they applauded McLean onto the pitch that afternoon, it wasn't hard to reflect on what might have happened if the 'new breed' had remained at the club; if the new money hadn't flowed into the game, if agents hadn't started to make their presence felt to the extent that nearly 500 now operate in England. Even in a pool as small as Scotland, over 70 are currently licensed.

What might have happened if Ferguson had stayed longer and remained less restless at United? What would have happened if those digs in Dundee had proved more to his taste? That was never likely, of course – the bed, the town, the club itself were too small for him in the end.

Alex Cleland recalls speaking with Ferguson about their time together at United when they were reunited again at Everton. 'He used to always talk about the days at Dundee United,' recalls Cleland. 'I thought it was a great grounding. But Fergie thought of it completely differently. He thought he was picked on.'

They used to talk about driving up to Tannadice together in a limousine. 'We wanted to pull up outside and talk to Wee Jim about the old days,' says Cleland. 'That's what we spoke about. We wanted to say: "Look, this is what we have achieved." While I was grateful for the chance I was given at United, Fergie seemed a bit more motivated by bitterness when he talked about returning.'

If his love of the game began to be sucked out of him at Dundee United, it didn't necessarily return elsewhere. He wasn't a great watcher of football when he was a player, which is why Steve Jones did a double take when he spotted Ferguson at the side of the Under-21 game of all things. More than one Everton insider had informed me that it was a struggle to persuade Ferguson to attend a first-team fixture if he wasn't playing in it.

Jones recalls an awards night in Croxteth, the area of Liverpool where Wayne Rooney grew up. It was at the end of the 2003–04 season, when Ferguson had performed decently enough when fit, scoring five times in twenty league appearances, although he had just blotted his copybook somewhat, getting sent off against Leicester

City in the infamous strangling incident with Steffen Freund. Nevertheless, Blue Kipper, the website that organised the do, still wanted Ferguson to attend and came up with a spurious award to hand him.

'I think it was True Evertonian, or something like that,' says Jones, who arrived at the bar of the function suite and noticed Ferguson standing with his back to the television screen, on which was being shown a match between Newcastle United, his former club, and Southampton. '"So, who do you fancy, Duncan?" I asked him,' recalls Jones. 'He just shrugged, without looking up at the TV, and said: "I don't really care."'

Did he reply to the letters I sent? No, he didn't. Did he agree to the interview requests made via the club, via David Weir and also outlined in a letter to his parents, my first port of call?

No, he didn't. Not that I expected him to. The deeper I delved into the project, the less it seemed to matter, strangely. In any case, I got some feedback from Gordon Parks, who has been a helpful contributor to the book. In early 2013, he secured an interview with Ferguson, a reunion between the pair who once played together as strikers for Dundee United in a Youth Cup final.

Now a sports writer with the *Daily Record*, Parks was astounded when he received word that Ferguson would welcome a call from him. They hadn't spoken for over 20 years, not since falling out in 1995, after Ferguson accused him of selling a story to the papers about his time in Barlinnie. Then, at the start of 2013, Ray McKinnon gave Parks Ferguson's phone number. 'Give the big man a call,' he urged.

Ferguson was intent on building bridges, it seemed. When he and Parks met, in the canteen in the Everton academy, their rift went unmentioned. Instead, Ferguson opened up about his Scotland career and insisted that had it not been for the SFA, he would have had a hundred caps and, presumably, at least one goal.

As for this book, Ferguson told Parks that he knew someone had been trying to speak to him. 'And I am not interested,' he said. 'I honestly don't see the point. But I don't have a problem with it, it doesn't bother me.'

These comments reminded me of a conversation I'd had with Osmo Tapio Raihala when I'd travelled to Helsinki to interview the composer. He had gone outside for a cigarette and I joined him beneath the canopy of the bar in the rain-splattered street. I wanted to ask him a question that had long intrigued me. Had he ever been given any indication that Ferguson had heard the orchestral work that had been written about him, or even knew of its existence? He said he imagined Ferguson must have known, via the internet. 'I mean, I don't know one single person who has an article about themselves on Wikipedia who hasn't looked at themselves; everyone is googling themselves all the time,' he told me.

But, in the case of Ferguson, I wasn't so sure. After all, in a blog on the Scottish Football Association website – Duncan Ferguson blogging for the SFA, a once doubly unthinkable scenario – he admitted that he was far from technologically gifted: 'The guys are here with their iPads and laptops, but I'm old-fashioned: I am still a pen and paper guy,' he said, with reference to his first PowerPoint presentation in front of his fellow coaches.

So, whether he has navigated the internet to search out more information on *Barlinnie Nine*, or even stumbled upon it while seeking out what people have written about him, is debatable.

And what about this book? Does he feel any curiosity whatsoever about it? During their time chatting at Everton's training base, Parks suggested to Ferguson that he should be flattered that someone wished to make him the subject of a biography.

'I don't see what he can have to write about because the people who know me wouldn't have spoken to a journalist,' he replied. 'Unless he is doing all the writing in it, what can he have to write about?'

He was wrong about people refusing to speak. Perhaps they felt emboldened, realising that he was out of the country. The fact was, I heard very few uncharitable words uttered about Ferguson by former teammates. Only one, an Everton colleague from his first spell at the club, was reluctant to go on the record about Ferguson, explaining: 'I can't help you – I have only negative things to say about him.' Knowing this particular player's strictly professional outlook, I would have been surprised to learn they had got on. Even Jim McLean had mellowed to the point where he hinted for Ferguson to give him a phone if ever he needed advice about coaching.

And then there was the un-publicised charity work. I contacted Alder Hey, a children's healthcare hospital in Liverpool. A member of their charity arm, Melanie Fletcher, told me Ferguson was a 'freestyler' on trips to the hospital. When he was involved, the planned itinerary for the player's visit was thrown away, since he was forever darting in and out of wards to see stricken children, many of whom he remained in touch with even after he left for Majorca.

I spoke to a former Everton groundsman, who regaled me with the story of Ferguson taking out the staff from the training ground for a farewell meal at the Sir Thomas Hotel in central Liverpool. Included in the group were gatemen, groundstaff, cleaners and secretaries. The evening ended with cigars and 'very expensive' brandy. They were invited by Ferguson to order whatever they wanted all night.

There was, however, no farewell party for the player himself, not that this is unusual in football's forever changing environment, where even those who have given long service to a club can disappear without acclaim, the old culture of testimonials having been rendered redundant due to soaring salaries.

'When a player leaves, he just leaves,' says Kevin Kilbane, his former Everton teammate. 'There is no special announcement in the dressing-room; there is no special recognition from anyone.

'When Duncan left the club, he just left, and that was it. I don't remember anything particularly special being said at the time, considering what a true Everton legend he had become over the years.'

Ferguson was undeniably different. Of course, there is that pigeon obsession; something that always hinted at a softer side, even if the rigidly working-class sport can be an archly competitive, big money concern. 'Although they might never be mentioned in the same sentence, there is an oddness that both Mike Tyson and Duncan had this interest – there's a beauty in the "doos" world, courting rituals and things like that,' says Stuart Cosgrove, who once regularly lampooned Ferguson on his BBC Radio Scotland show, *Off the Ball*.

'Whenever I heard of Duncan and his pigeons, I always thought of this rather camp environment, where they would get birds and put pink dye on them,' he says. 'It's almost like making them up . . . camp, in a way. But they were nearly always hard men, too.'

'I remember on *Off the Ball* we used to do these sketches which were predicated on being inside his cell,' he adds. 'We had a thing where it was him and his cellmate, and it was all cod-tacky jokes. But this idea that you could imagine him in this prison cell, there was something quite bizarre about it. I don't know what the cell physically looked like, but it was this idea of him being in exile, as it were.

'But that was the thing with Duncan, you never felt he was properly of Scottish society, although he had so many of the traits which you would attribute to it, what with the drinking and the laddishness.

'He seemed to exist outside of that, almost as a loner.'

Ferguson was far from the brooding, menacing figure of popular media portrayal, although he could play that part if he wanted to, clearly. Gary Neville remembers it being part of Manchester United's game plan to try to avoid making Ferguson angry by steering clear of anything he might react to. 'You'd ask what he'd had for his dinner, something like that,' he recalled just after Ferguson had given an unexpected interview to Sky Sports' Geoff Shreeves before an Everton v. Manchester United clash in 2012. In the footage, shot in a studio, Ferguson appears almost comfortable, although there are times when he narrows his eyes slightly, as if he is really trying to concentrate on what the interviewer is saying and remind himself where he is. When Shreeves asks about his previously strict media exclusion policy, a big grin breaks out across Ferguson's face.

'I'm just shy, like.'

EPILOGUE

The Smell of Football

Carrington, 16 November 2013

The young man who stood impassively on the sidelines chewing gum while his teammates went through their warm down; the player who argued with his coaches and quarrelled with his disciplinarian managers; the man who could never quite fulfil his potential, or squeeze enough from his talent, because he didn't love football enough, now stands on the sidelines of a pitch at Carrington, Manchester United's training ground, putting his Everton Under-18s through their paces.

He indulges himself first, performing 50 keepy-uppies and ending the routine with a flourish: headers, shoulders and a back heel. Then his attention turns to his young charges. The man once dubbed 'Duncan Disorderly' carefully arranges the plastic markers on the pitch, pacing out the distance between each one. The players gather round the 41-year-old Ferguson, slightly balding now but bronzed, exuding a healthy glow and as lean as ever, as he barks out instructions.

About a hundred people look on, parents and obsessives, but the sound that rings around the ground is Ferguson's voice: a guttural, broad Scottish accent that is not unfamiliar in these parts, with portraits of Sir Matt Busby and the recently retired Sir Alex Ferguson hanging in the nearby building, and, of course, the recent arrival of David Moyes, though he has not been spotted so far.

It is an autumnal morning of vivid reds and oranges, but the green of the pitch is most vivid of all. There is a glorious scent in the air, a mixture of freshly cut grass, whitewashed lines, the faint scent of embrocation. This is what has drawn Big Dunc back: 'the smell of football'.

Ironically for a man who, for some, embodied the largesse (and profligate waste) of the Premiership era, this is football stripped of its excesses and glamour: Reds vs Blues, and visceral in its intensity; strapping 17- and 18-year-old boys urging their team on with coarse language and crunching into slightly built, more skilful players who yell as they collapse to the turf. By a strange coincidence, most of these boys were born the same year their coach, Ferguson, was serving time in prison: 1995. They'll be too young to remember, which for Ferguson may add to the appeal of a posting on the lowest rung of the coaching ladder: assistant to the Under-18s. He has been where they have been, but they haven't been to the places he has seen.

Ferguson had emerged early, ahead of the 11 a.m. kick-off; boots on, stopwatch hanging around his neck. The regulation uniform of the coach, seen on the side of pitches throughout the land, but not a look you ever imagined being sported by Duncan Ferguson. Yet he appears to be in his element. After his ball-juggling, he gathers the players together, then stands over them, encouraging and cajoling as the ball is fired like a pinball along the grass, in the little square marked out, in what appears to be a well-practised drill.

'Quick passes! Good pass, good pass. Into feet! Into feet! Take that pass, take that pass!'

They don't all have his chewing-gum feet; they don't all have his talent. The drill wraps up as their opponents emerge from the changing rooms, while the Everton boys peel off their training tops by the side of the pitch, then pull on club shirts. The impression is of the home club as a well-oiled, more corporate machine, even at this level.

Before kick-off, Ferguson searches out the referee to shake his hand. The match gets underway and, on the sidelines, he is, at first, surprisingly passive; just the odd shout: 'Narrow, narrow. Get the ball, get the ball!'

He doesn't bawl when mistakes are made. He seems relaxed, the only sign of anxiety his fidgeting hands and arms, alternately folded in front of him or buried deep in the pockets of his tracksuit trousers. Early on, Everton's number six introduces himself with a crunching tackle on the United danger man, the number ten, which further underlines the contrast between the two teams that sit first and second in the table. A disciplined, meticulous United side, with a sprinkling of continental-sounding names, are slick and polished, while Everton are raw, gnarly and physical, scrapping for the ball as United spray passes around, maintaining possession with ease, to Ferguson's mounting frustration.

As the match picks up pace, Ferguson becomes increasingly more involved, and then, with Everton pressing for an equaliser, he can be seen contorting on the sidelines, on the balls of his feet, heading an imaginary ball as the real one flies back and forth inside the Manchester United six-yard box. Again, his voice is the one that can be heard above all others.

'Win a header, lads! C'mon, c'mon – do you want it? Do you want it?'

It could almost be Jim McLean's anguished scream to a young Ferguson: 'You don't love it enough, do you? You don't want it enough.'

But here Ferguson is the one posing the question, the one prowling along the touch-line, the one who stands here, proven after all. He is the one who thumps his fist into his hand as Everton concede a penalty to go 1–0 down in the first half. And it is he who kicks the air in frustration when Everton let in another goal, the game's winner, with just minutes to go, after they had only just managed to get back into the game with a penalty.

'That's Everton out of jail,' says one spectator to his friend when they score their short-lived equaliser.

Later, although they lose 2–1, Ferguson emerges from the dressing-room looking satisfied, content. He is last out. What has he been doing? Clearing up the dressing-room, picking the discarded stocking tape up off the floor? Perhaps that's what's in the huge holdall he is carrying in his hand.

'Look, it's Big Dunc!' says one middle-aged parent, still waiting at the reception area to pick up his son, as the tall, tanned Ferguson emerges, then strides across the car park and steps into the waiting bus.

The door hisses shut, the bus moves off and the security barrier preventing unauthorised access into Carrington rises into the air.

This isn't a limousine sweeping him out of the gates of a prison. It is a team bus. And Ferguson isn't folded up in the back seat, head bowed. He is looking out of a window in a seat at the front as the bus turns slowly right down the narrow, tree-lined lane. I follow on behind until we come to a fork in the road; I turn my steering wheel one way, while the bus – and Ferguson – go the other.

On the long way home, I stop for a break and thumb through the pages of my notebook while sipping a cup of coffee, re-tracing the steps of another journey, one that began several years ago. My eyes are drawn towards something Ian Ross told me when he was still employed as director of communications by Everton. I hadn't thought much of it at the time. Indeed, when it came to writing this book, I had not even thought to include the episode where he remembered speaking with Ferguson during pre-season in the summer of 2004, so fanciful did the player's comments seem.

This was the period that was described to me as Ferguson's 'paranoid' phase, something that being left behind on Merseyside while his then teammates headed away on tour can't have helped. (Ferguson needed a special permit for entry to the United States due to his criminal conviction and Everton had left it too late to acquire one; in the end, it was decided that the player should just remain at home.)

At the time, Ross, who, like Ferguson, is a man comfortably over 6 ft in height, was letting a work experience girl shadow him. She asked what he describes as the 'inevitable' question, the one people tended to ask when they were on Everton property: 'Is Duncan around?'

They went up to the training ground. 'There were just a couple of coaches, the canteen staff and Duncan Ferguson,' Ross recalled. Later, with no one else around to talk to, Ferguson sat down at the table where Ross was sitting. He started peppering Ross with questions.

Keith Wyness had just taken over as CEO at the club and

Ferguson asked, 'What's the new chief executive like, then? What's my future? Who's my best strike partner?'

'All these questions,' recalled Ross, who eventually got to ask one of his own. 'So, what are you going to do when you finish up, Duncan?'

There was a pause.

'It was like he had spent the last eight years sussing me up and now, finally, he was going to entrust me with some information.' When the reply came, Ross was again startled.

'I am going to go away and then come back one day and manage this football club,' said Ferguson. Ross wasn't sure whether he had heard correctly.

Ferguson removed any doubt.

'I am going to go away and get the badges,' he continued. 'I am going to surprise everyone and come back and manage this football club.

'That's what I want to do.

'That's what I am going to do.'

And with that, Ferguson got up from the table.

'See you around, big man,' he said, and walked away.

Select Bibliography

Auclair, Philippe *Cantona: The Rebel Who Would be King* (Macmillan, 2010)

Berman, Jon and Malcolm Dome *Everton Greats* (Mainstream Publishing, 2003)

Bower, Tom *Broken Dreams – Vanity, Greed and the Souring of British Football* (Pocket Books, 2007)

Cassidy, Denis Newcastle United – *The Day the Promises Had to Stop* (Amberley Publishing, 2012)

Cosgrove, Stuart *Hampden Babylon – Sex and Scandal in Scottish Football* (Canongate Books Ltd, 2002)

Durrant, Ian *Blue and White Dynamite: The Ian Durrant Story* (First Press Publishing, 1998)

Ferrier, Bob and Robert McElroy *Rangers: The Complete Record* (Breedon Books, 2005)

Grant, Michael and Rob Robertson *The Management: Scotland's Great Football Bosses* (Birlinn Ltd, 2011)

Henrik, Hairdryers and the Hand of God – Extraordinary Tales from the Press-Box (BackPage Press Ltd, 2012)

Jeffrey, Robert *The Barlinnie Story – Riots, Death, Retribution and Redemption in Scotland's Infamous Prison* (Black & White Publishing, 2011)

Johnson, Steve *Everton: The Official Complete Record* (DeCoubertin Books, 2010)

Lovejoy, Joe *Glory, Goals & Greed – Twenty Years of the Premier League* (Mainstream Publishing, 2011)

MacDonald, Kenny *Scottish Football Quotations 3* (Black & White Publishing, 2009)

McLaren, Andy with Mark Guidi, *Tormented: The Andy McLaren Story* (Mainstream Publishing, 2007)

McLean, Jim with Ken Gallacher *Jousting with Giants – The Jim McLean Story* (Mainstream Publishing, 1987)

Mumford, Jonathan and David Cregeen *Tales from the Gwladys Street* (Sportsbooks Ltd, 2012)

Onslow, Tony *The Scottish Footballers of Everton* (Countryvise Ltd, 2012)

Rathbone, Mick *The Smell of Football* (Vision Sports Publishing, 2011)

Rooney, Wayne *Wayne Rooney – My Story So Far* (HarperSport, 2006)

Royle, Joe *Joe Royle: The Autobiography* (BBC Books, 2005)

Rundo, Peter and Mike Watson *Dundee United: The Official Centenary History* (Birlinn Ltd, 2009)

Sharp, Graeme *Sharpy: My Story* (Mainstream Publishing, 2007)

Southall, Neville *Neville Southall: The Binman Chronicles* (DeCoubertin Books, 2012)

Stubbs, Alan *How Football Saved my Life* (Simon & Schuster, 2013)

Sweeney, John *Wayne Rooney: Boots of Gold* (Biteback Publishing, 2012)

Tallentire, Becky *Talking Blue – A Collection of Candid Interviews with Everton Legends* (Breedon Books, 2004)

Tallentire, Becky *Still Talking Blue – A Collection of Interviews with Everton Heroes* (Mainstream Sport, 2012)

Watson, Mike with Mathew Watson *The Tannadice Encyclopedia: An A to Z of Dundee United* (Mainstream Publishing, 1997)

Weir, David *Extra Time: My Autobiography* (Hodder & Stoughton, 2012)